T0164550

The Valediction

Resurrection

Paul Fitzgerald
Elizabeth Gould

VALEDICTION – RESURRECTION

This is a memoir; it is sourced from memories and recollections. Dialogue is reconstructed, and some names and identifying features have been changed to provide anonymity. The underlying story is based on actual happenings and historical personages.

Backcover photo credit: Laurel Denison

Published by:
Trine Day LLC
PO Box 577
Walterville, OR 97489
1-800-556-2012
www.TrineDay.com
trineday@icloud.com

Library of Congress Control Number: 2022937989

Fitzgerald, Paul & Gould, Elizabeth,
VALEDICTION—1st ed.
p. cm.
Epub (ISBN-13) 978-1-63424-407-7
Trade Paper (ISBN-13) 978-1-63424-406-0
Cloth: (ISBN-13) 978-1-63424-408-4
1. Memoir -- Fitzgerald, Paul -- 1951- . 2. Memoir -- Gould, Elizabeth -- 1948.
3. Afghan Wars. 4. Irish History. . 5. World politics. 6. Fitzgerald family history.
I. Title

FIRST EDITION
10 9 8 7 6 5 4 3 2 1

Printed in the USA
Distribution to the Trade by:
Independent Publishers Group (IPG)
814 North Franklin Street
Chicago, Illinois 60610
312.337.0747
www.ipgbook.com

Publisher's Foreword

Hickory Dickory Dock
The mouse ran up the clock
The clock struck one
And down he run
Hickory Dickory Dock
– *Tommy Thumb's Pretty Song Book*, 1744

To every thing there is a season,
And a time to every purpose under the heaven:
A time to be born, and a time to die;
A time to plant, and a time to pluck up that which is planted;
A time to kill, and a time to heal;
A time to break down, and a time to build up;
A time to weep, and a time to laugh;
A time to mourn, and a time to dance;
A time to cast away stones, and a time to gather stones together;
A time to embrace, and a time to refrain from embracing;
A time to get, and a time to lose;
A time to keep, and a time to cast away;
A time to rend, and a time to sew;
A time to keep silence, and a time to speak;
A time to love, and a time to hate;
A time of war, and a time of peace.
– Ecclesiastes 3:1-8, KJV

Ah, yes, where does the time go? It seems like only yesterday – but then again it has been a long arduous journey with much travail and tribulations. My generation had our political leaders violently murdered, been prevaricated at, and have been subjected to horrific psychological warfare abuse and manipulation. William J. Casey, CIA Director in 1981 said, "We'll know our disinformation program is complete when everything the American public believes is false."

Kudos to Paul Fitzgerald and Liz Gould in combating our shared malaise brought on by the covert conscious actions of establishment players.

The Valediction: Resurrection continues the stunning revelations from *The Valediction: Three Nights of Desmond* adding the historical mystic adventures of the Fitzgerald family.

Should we care?

Where does our future come from? Where does our past go? Will we survive? What will our children do? These are timely questions.

Paul and Liz's explorations both in this world and other realms help us to understand where we are and what needs to be done. I have great faith in humanity, which has been bolstered by reading their edifying odyssey.

Recently I watched an interview with actress and playwright Anna Deavere Smith on the PBS show *Tell Me More With Kelly Corrigan.* In the interview Ms. Smith was asked, "What is the difference between hope and optimism?"

> So that is Cornel West. I went to talk to him when I was redrafting my play *Twilight* to make a version of it that was going to go on the road.
>
> And he differentiates between hope and optimism by basically saying optimism says, "Huh. Looks pretty good out there. Things are gonna be better. You know, we can go sailing today, or whatever, but hope looks at the evidence and says, 'It doesn't look good at all. Doesn't look good at all.'
>
> "I'm going to make a leap of faith, go beyond the evidence to attempt to create new possibilities based on visions to allow people to engage in heroic actions, always against odds, no guarantee whatsoever." ...
>
> And in America, especially in the theater, people say – you know, my plays about catastrophes, all the time say, "Is there any hope?"
>
> They don't really mean hope. They want something at the end of the show that lets them think everything's going to be all right, but that's different than hope.
>
> Hope is a lot more work.
>
> Hope is a real act of imagination.

The Valediction brings vision and heroic actions. I am very hopeful.

Onward to the Utmosts of Futures,
Peace,
R.A. "Kris" Millegan
Publisher
TrineDay
May 4, 2021

To Alissa and Devon, This one is for both of you!

Epilogue from: *The Valediction – Three Nights of Desmond*

I'd plunged myself into the Afghan enigma thinking I'd get the answer and a career to go with it, but instead I found myself on the other side of the mirror.

Trapping the Soviet Union in Afghanistan freed America from its Vietnam guilt trip and bought the U.S. military time to recover its reputation. But instead of healing a wounded nation, it merely authenticated the fictional narrative that ideologues like Zbigniew Brzezinski and Richard Pipes were using to push their globalist agenda. There was obviously a deeper political story being covered up and so began our shift from news to the telling of that story by writing screenplays.

Hemingway had done it and so had Fitzgerald. It couldn't be duller than writing stories for the evening news with Dan Rather, so I gave it a try.

The move away from journalism was a welcome relief. That was until we realized bringing our experience to the big screen came with even bigger problems. The L.A. scene wasn't just about glamor and money. L.A. was about framing a reality for the masses and that's where some very strange things began to happen. In late 1987 we'd tagged along with some Hollywood types on a trip to the Soviet Union and saw with our own eyes what the Soviets had been trying to achieve all along. The Soviet bureaucracy had been desperate to get out of the Cold War for decades but Hollywood could have cared less. Our Soviet guide was astonished by the American naiveté and told us in no uncertain terms.

"People come here from all over the world," she said, shaking her head in disbelief after a few days of pointless conversations. "They come from capitalist countries and communist countries and tell us what life is like where they come from. Only the Americans brag to us about how free they are. But as far as I can see Americans are the most conformist and narrow minded people I've ever met."

I wasn't surprised by what the woman said and I often thought of the comment over the next few years as we struck out time after time in our effort to circumnavigate the Hollywood narrative-creation machine.

Our 1988 screenplay on the Soviet Union's coming collapse was rejected because it was viewed as "unimaginable." Our 1989 screenplay about the emerging dangers of genetic engineering was greeted as out of touch with where the human race was headed. And our 1990 screenplay about the use of Vietnam Veterans as test subjects for developing a "brave pill" was first received enthusiastically but then rejected once Hollywood embraced the drumbeat for war in the Persian Gulf. Hollywood appeared to be a deader-end than the news business dominated by fossilized World War II archons who were blind to what we'd come face to face with in Afghanistan. As the new decade progressed we realized we had nowhere else to turn but the personal and as we dug into the Fitzgerald family history we stumbled upon a hidden link to the assassination of John Fitzgerald Kennedy in the 12th century politics of the Norman invasion of Ireland. In the nearly 30 years since the assassination, no one had ever considered the cause might lie outside the intrigues of 20th century American politics. But as we followed the trail of revenge and retribution down through the centuries we realized a more ancient vengeance may have played a role. We titled our discovery *The Voice* in honor of its calling to us from the past and that's when the voice began speak to us in ways we could never have imagined.

Authors Foreword

July 6, 2021.
Bagram airfield, Afghanistan – 15 miles north of Kabul. Midnight.

U.S. soldiers steal past a row of Russian Mi-8 helicopters parked in front of a utility bunker at the center of the fortified compound, then without a sound, unlock its heavy reinforced steel doors. Generators hum and pumps whir inside the concrete building as the soldiers swing open the metal doors of the control panel and one by one switch off the breakers. It's time to say goodbye. When all is done they stare at each other and shake their heads, then move quickly outside. The base is dark now – silent with a bright moon overhead. "What's the frequency Dan?" One soldier jokes.

In 1979 Dan Rather and Zbigniew Brzezinski wanted to turn Afghanistan into Russia's Vietnam and free Washington from its Vietnam syndrome. In the end, what they delivered was a second American Vietnam. But they were blind to that at the time.

The silence at the airfield doesn't last long. Nobody told the Afghan National Army the U.S. was sneaking out in the middle of the night so there is no one to stop the looters when they show up.

It's been happening in other parts of the country for years. Mine resistant Mraps, Humvees and new American weapons, piled high in warehouses just waiting for the Taliban to liberate them. Ah, the Taliban, in Arabic – the "seekers of knowledge." In American, "a wholly owned subsidiary of Pakistan's Inter-Services Intelligence Directorate, the ISI." That's what Chuck Cogan, the CIA's Near East, South Asia Chief called them and he should 'a known.

Nothing about Afghanistan was on the level – not the Soviet invasion, not 9/11and most all not America's twenty year war there and leaving the Taliban with billions in new weapons just confirmed what everybody already knew.

The evidence was there from the beginning when the U.S. let them flee back to Pakistan after the invasion. Rumors had been spreading for years the U.S. and the Taliban were working the secret heroin ratline together as journalist Seymour Hersh called it. Heroin funded the CIA's black operations in Indo China during Vietnam and paid for the war against the Soviet Union. But as the American Empire surrenders Afghanistan to Chinese and Russian influence, the reason why the place is known as the graveyard of empires may finally break over the Washington elite.

Prologue

By 1990 we had given up on Afghanistan. The Soviet departure on February 15, 1989 ended the international crisis begun by their "invasion" in December 1979 once and for all. The destruction of the Berlin Wall only nine months later signaled that the post-World War II era was rapidly coming to a close. There was really nothing left for us to contribute as Afghanistan reverted to what the British had once described as the Great Game for Central Asia.

An August 31, 1987 New York Times article titled CHEMICAL WARFARE; Declassified Cables Add to Doubts about U.S. disclosures on 'yellow rain' finally dared to approach the truth. The article revealed that evidence used by the Reagan administration in 1981 and 1982 to support charges "that Soviet-backed forces had waged toxin warfare against resistance fighters... collapsed under scrutiny." But despite the growing list of "negative findings" to support years of damning charges against the Soviet Union, a chemical warfare expert at the State Department announced "We feel there is no basis to change our conclusion." Major Karen McKay had been right. The U.S. government didn't need proof to get the results it wanted. The Russians were guilty whether they did it or not.

We'd kept our hand in the Afghan fire for as long as we could and got an inside view of the operation. As intended by the planners, the outcome was bad for the Soviets but meant atomization to Afghanistan's society.

In a less foreseeable but predictable way, the Mujahideen "victory" spelled doom for the U.S. too, but at the time nobody saw it that way. Afghanistan had opened the highest levels of the American government to an old-world fascist cabal. They'd sold their story to the American public and it had found a home. Their perceived victory at winning the Cold War assured them a permanent seat at the table and their appetite for ever more victories over the Soviet Union would become insatiable.

I fully realized now that our efforts at changing the narrative never had a chance. Since the assassination of JFK anyone departing from the official narrative faced an invisible wall. The CIA had even made up the term *conspiracy theorist* to blackball those who could see through the subterfuge.

But after all this time, why was seeing the truth about JFK so dangerous? And why would they apply the same standard to Afghanistan? The wall between reality and fiction was imaginary. The mainstream news media crossed it every day without a hint of skepticism. President Jimmy Carter and Zbigniew Brzezinski had got together with the Chinese and a host of Saudi extremists to give the Soviet military a case of its own Vietnam insanity. That much was simple but the reasons were not. Underneath the surface of the geopolitics was a boiling cauldron of racial and religious hatreds built up over a millennia but nobody let on. As a Knight of Malta, Reagan's CIA director William Casey saw no difference in the extremities of Saudi Wahhabism and his own mystical right–wing Catholic dogma espoused by Opus Dei. Together the two presented an explosive political combination. But I came to suspect the reality behind their merger was more profound than just geopolitics.

I'd begun by approaching the subject as a simple case of fact versus fiction but I had come to think that mythology might be more important. I should have known the establishment would turn our first-hand evidence to their advantage. Instead of helping the Soviets end their occupation, Democratic Congressman Charlie Wilson had transformed the Islamic insurgency into a cause celebre for worldwide holy war and Washington had cheered it on. The booming heroin industry had freed the world's intelligence services from government oversight and most of Congress wanted to claim credit for defeating the Soviet Union. "We've got Communism on the run just about everywhere and it's all because of Afghanistan," a supposedly anti-war congressman–friend of Charlie Wilson boasted to me. What point was there in risking my life for seven minutes of prime time television news that amounted to nothing? There was none. So why had I done it?

I asked myself that question a lot. What voice drove me to pursue such pyrrhic victories? Who was I to dare think I could actually make a difference? Where could I go to get an answer to that? As it turned out I didn't have far to look.

Chapter 1

December 1990, St. Anselm Abbey Church – Goffstown New Hampshire

Weddings and funerals were a big part of growing up in a large Irish Catholic family but I always found the funerals more interesting. The wake was an old tradition with the Irish. In the old country you were waked in the same house you lived in and were probably born in. After you died a window would be opened to let your spirit leave the room and closed two hours later to prevent its return.

In the interim, friends and family were called to ensure that no evil spirits approached lest they attempt to steal your soul and for the next 24 hours they stood guard as a guarantee your journey to the next world was a safe one.

Growing up, wakes and funerals came under the auspice of the Roman Catholic Church and never more so than at my uncle Ray's Funeral. The true nature of the death ritual hadn't struck me before now but as I watched the Benedictine monks form a wall around his coffin – led by Ray's brother Father Michael – I was struck by my own sense of cold-detachment. This family is what I had been born into. But as I first realized at my father's death, I felt no emotional connection to them at all and I didn't know why.

Uncle Ray was my godfather, pillar of the Darien Connecticut community and unquestioning servant of the One, Holy, Catholic and Apostolic church. He'd married my father's sister just out of the Navy after World War II and risen in the corporate ranks to controller of a large, iconic American electronics company in New York City. Arrived at work before sunrise and went home after dark. New blue Cadillac Coupe DeVille every two years – smoked his cigarettes through a stylish, black holder and dedicated his life to three things: God, the company and his family. That was until he realized what his blind loyalty to the company had bought him as a Catholic and re-ordered his priorities to God, his family and the company. But by then, he admitted to me, it was too late.

Ray was as unlike my father as any man I'd ever met. Or so I thought. He epitomized the kind of suitor my father's mother wanted her five daughters to marry and everything my father rejected as one of her four sons. By marrying my mother, he'd broken the lease on the family contract and we'd all grown up knowing he had not been forgiven for it.

After putting himself through pharmacy school my father had joined the big drug company in 1935 and was working his way up too. But when he found himself on the front lines staffing the pharmacy at the 173rd military hospital in Nancy France during the Battle of the Bulge, something happened.

As a drug salesman he was just a cog in a huge machine, but as a medicine man he was now healing the wounded and that's where he found his calling. The war in France had brought my father face to face with his purpose and when he got back to the U.S. he chucked the sales route for the corner drug store.

For the next twenty years he'd dedicated his life to his Cambridge neighborhood and become its anchor. But as the neighborhood declined so did he. I'd spent my teenage years watching his health deteriorate along with the family finances and the experience had hardened me. But it wasn't until I found him that Saturday morning on the living room floor, gasping for breath, that I realized a part of my heart was dying with him.

My uncle may have reordered his priorities about his company but it was clear that Ray had been saving himself for God and now I understood, so had my father. I had severed myself from his humanness at the moment of his death, but now at forty I needed it back. I was a father myself now, with two children. Alissa had come first and Devon followed two years later. And so I decided to reach out to my father's brother Joe for advice.

"We should really get together while you're here," I said as we stood side by side at the reception following the burial. "I hardly know my father's family at all. We never get to see you."

"Too much trouble," he said turning away abruptly. "It's not something I want to get involved with."

And with that one disconnect, was summed up my relationship to my father's family.

"I can't breathe here, let's go." I said to Liz as she approached.

"What's wrong?"

"My family. Whatever my father did, Joe obviously holds me responsible for it."

"Well, that's wrong. But if you don't follow this thing through you're going to wind up like him. Besides, you need to talk to your Uncle Harold about our research. I told him about the Cambrensis book and the prophecies and he wanted to hear all about it."

***

Unlike Ray, Harold had already worked his way up in the system before marrying my father's youngest sister. The "system" in this case was the State Department. But Harold's real passion was for genealogy and after marrying my aunt had focused his research on the Fitzgeralds.

"Liz has been telling me about the Cambrensis book. It's all beginning to fit together." He said, musing over the idea.

I was mystified. "Fit together?"

"Who exactly the Fitzgeralds were. It's really something of a mystery." Harold said, shaking his head.

"I assumed the name was French."

"Well it is." He answered. "Norman/French, and they certainly were by the time they got to Ireland. But there are branches of the family all over Europe, from southern Italy to Germany not to mention England and Wales."

"Wales plays a big part in the story," I said. "Geraldus Cambrensis is Latin for Gerald of Wales."

"Yes. I've heard of him – Gerald de Barry." Harold said approvingly. "Your great grandmother was a Barry."

"I hadn't made that connection before. Any way, he placed a great deal of faith in Merlin and his prophecies."

"Why do you think?" Harold asked.

"Because he thought they pertained to the Fitzgerald family. He intended to expand on them in a separate book called The Prophetic History of Ireland."

"And what stopped him?"

"The editors speculate it's because the rational scholar in him triumphed."

Harold laughed. "Five hundred years before rationalism. I love academics. But you don't believe that."

"I believe he wanted to link his family's role in fulfilling Britain's destiny to Merlin."

Harold seemed impressed. "Instead of the Angevins' role."

I had to agree. "Cambrensis had been working directly for Henry II. He knew the Angevins were sensitive about the Welsh. He recalls an event when Henry even called Merlin a liar because he believed something he'd written eight hundred years before challenged his authority."

"That's pretty sensitive." Harold said, smiling. "But what do these prophecies say?"

"Here's one I memorized. 'A new martyr will be revealed by a new kind of miracle. In western lands, and in the age when the world is drawing to its end, he will, by his own peculiar power, restore to the maimed and wretched, limbs that have been wrenched out or cut off."

Harold was taken aback. "That's pretty strong stuff."

"I think he's talking about the Resurrection." I responded.

"That would be something to be careful about, wouldn't it?"

"Especially if you think this miracle worker is a member of your family and not Henry's."

Harold grew more serious as I continued. "And you believe that's the case."

"The modern editors believed that Merlin's spirit hung over the whole book. Cambrensis scoured the Welsh countryside to find an original copy of Merlin's manuscript so he wouldn't make any mistakes in the translation. It haunted him."

Harold contemplated the idea for a moment. "As if he was being guided by the Merlin himself?"

"That seems to be what the editors are implying."

At that moment an old friend of Ray's joined us and spoke in a low voice. "Father Michael is about to give a benediction. We want everyone to gather at the front."

Harold took a moment to think before speaking. "I hadn't thought about this before now but I'm sure you know that Wales is also the source of the Grail legends. I've got lots of stuff that might fit with what you're looking at. I'll send it to you as soon as I get back to D.C."

***

We'd made the car ride home from Bedford on many occasions, but today was different.

"I give Ray a lot of credit for accepting that his devotion to the company had hurt his family. But it didn't stop him from putting God first." I said to Liz.

"And you think that was the mistake your father made as well?"

"I don't think these men could think any other way. It was a code of honor."

"And what about your uncle Joe? Was that his code of honor you encountered or yours?"

Liz always went for the sore spot. "What do you mean?"

"I want you to consider this. You don't even know Joe and he doesn't know you. The experience you just had is about you and your father, not him."

I could feel the old anger creeping back. "I always admired my father for what he was doing. I thought I knew what it was costing him but I felt he had a right to do it."

Liz was on it. "But he crossed a line with you when you were seventeen."

I didn't want to go there. "It was the first time I ever argued with him about my mother. We never argued. And then just that once I called on him to stand up for me." I said.

"And then he dropped dead the next morning." Liz whispered.

I took a deep breath. "I didn't understand how weak he was."

This was the look of the woman in Paul's dream with the multi-sided crown. Nikolai Bruni's Saint Grand Duchess Olga – 1901 St. Olga, also called Helga or Saint Olga of Kiev, (born c. 890-died 969, Kiev; feast day July 11), princess who was the first recorded female ruler in Russia and the first member of the ruling family of Kiev to adopt Christianity. She was canonized as the first Russian saint of the Orthodox Church and is the patron saint of widows and converts. (From the *Encyclopedia Britannica*)

Chapter 2

At home near Boston

Ray's funeral reopened doors I'd kept locked for years. The problem was the doors opened only to fragmented memories housed in boxes of yellowed photographs. My grandmother had died before I was born, my grandfather when I was eight and my father when I was just beginning to know him. My aunts and uncles were strangers. Not just to me but to each other. It was a Fitzgerald thing that cold detachment. All the sisters had married-up and after the war the boys stayed as far away as possible. Eddie in Oregon managing a lumber business, George in Miami Beach managing a hotel and Joe as a chief mechanic at O'Hare airport in Chicago. It struck me Joe would have been happier in the priesthood but when he found himself on Tinian Island in July 1945 refitting a B-29 – for something called an atomic bomb – his career as an airplane mechanic was sealed.

After the war, the girls had roped him in to compensate for my father's departure and therein lay the foundation of his resentment.

As I pondered which way to turn I kept recalling a life-altering turning point I'd had in the winter of 1975. At the time, I was living alone in New York City and for the first time in my life growing desperate for work. I had been shown the red carpet to Broadway but suddenly that red carpet was gone. Should I stay the course and struggle to make a go at theater or should I commit myself to becoming a writer and journalist. The answer arrived in a vivid dream when I became aware of a woman in a long white medieval-style dress, standing in the clouds, her long blond hair tucked under an eight sided pillbox crown. She wasn't just real. She was surreal, calm and serene as she held back three rearing black horses in her right hand. I thought I was seeing a vision of my death and that she'd come to take me away as she slowly raised her left hand. But instead of beckoning she turned her palm toward me revealing a blood-red downward pointing triangle. I watched as the horses strained against their reins, eyes bulging, hooves batting the dark sky – but the woman didn't budge. Then like a shot the triangle flew at me before it stopped and danced before my eyes. Close up it looked alive, veined like a pulsing heart ready to burst. Whatever I thought it was at that moment I knew I must retrieve it from the dream when suddenly I was awake in my room with it still there, suspended before my eyes. I had never had anything happen like this before, a dream image materializing before me. But as I reached out to embrace it, it disappeared; dissolving into a thousand grains of red sand that ran through my fingers like dried blood and I was left alone in my dark and empty room.

***

I was only twenty four when I arrived at that moment in my life. Seven years after the sudden death of my father and five years after I'd ignored my faculty advisor's invitation at Boston University to "work for my government." I thought I'd found a better way to move my life forward; an escape route from the humdrum, parochial life of a student athlete. I'd met the girl of my dreams in Liz, found a modicum of fame as a singer and set out to conquer the future. I'd travelled the world and learned a lot about the way it worked in a short time. Five years later I felt that world had come to an abrupt end in a cold apartment overlooking the Hudson River. The midnight visit from the lady, her three horses and the triangle had shaken me into a stark awareness. I was supposed to be doing something with my life I wasn't doing. I needed to move on and I did.

I left New York, married Liz, began a family and started over. But by the early 1990s I was at another crossroads. The dream with the woman and the red triangle had haunted me for years – long before Afghanistan. It had catapulted me out of my old life, but what did it mean to me now? The dream had echoes of my father's death – the way my relationship to him ended like grains of sand running through an hour glass. But after my decade-long experience with Afghanistan, I realized there was much more to decipher.

Liz shared my fascination with the symbolism and was more determined than ever to crack the code.

"It was right in front of us all the time," she said breathlessly as she laid a large book on ancient symbols out on the kitchen table. "There's a lot more meaning to the symbolism in that dream than I ever imagined; the horses, the triangle, the octagonal crown? It's a language."

"That says what?" I asked.

Liz paused as she thought about it. "The first Christian churches built in Syria and Palestine were octagonal like the crown on the lady's head.

The octagonal represents what they call the 'Fourth Quadrant mentality' a mathematical symbol of transition."

"From pagan to Christian?"

"From three dimensional thinking to fourth and beyond – from material to spiritual."

I was mystified. "Then what about the triangle," I asked.

"It's not just a triangle. You said it had depth."

Liz squinted to read more closely. "That is the Mystic Tetrahedron," she said reading. "A three dimensional triangular figure of ten points in four rows that represents the fourth triangular number where all four combine. That's sacred architecture."

I couldn't help but stare. "Ok, go on." I said.

"The first four numbers symbolize the musica universalis."

"Which is?"

"The Music of the Spheres – the harmony of the planets." She said reading. "'The prayer of the Pythagoreans refers to it as the Mystic Tetrad, the mystical nature of the Kosmos. Monad, Dyad, Triad, Tetrad – the mystery of life itself embodied in the tetrahedron, the three combined in the four. I think the Pythagorean prayer sums it up."

Liz continued, growing deeply serious. "Bless us, divine number, thou who generated gods and men. O holy, holy Tetrad, thou that containest the root and source of the eternally flowing creation! For the divine number begins with profound, pure unity until it comes to the holy four; then it begets the mother of all, the all comprising, all-bounding first born, the never swerving, never-tiring holy ten, the key holder of all."

I had to admit I was staggered. "The divine number who generated gods and men?"

"The holy Tetrad is the womb of creation that begets life itself. All life. And that's where the downward pointing triangle comes in. The Tetrad sent the triangle into your life and helped you make the changes you needed to make. I'd call that divine intervention."

"Divine intervention or Liz intervention. At the time I actually thought of it as you, offering me your heart."

"And you took it," she said as she pretended to tear up.

"And it's taken all these years to discover where you were helping me go."

"Desmond FitzMaurice gave you a clue." She said. "You've got to figure out your family's part in this – and because of Cambrensis you can start."

***

What had started out as a phone call from a friend to meet a couple of political legends in Hyannis back in the summer of 1979 had by 1990 taken me halfway around the world and then found its way into my family.

"Thanks to Harold I think we've hit the motherlode of convergence between fact and myth, including the Grail." Liz said smiling.

"I didn't know the Grail was connected to Wales, but I'm stunned by what I've been reading about Gerald de Barry. Listen to what this contemporary historian says about him." I said as I read from the book.

> Cambrensis is a man who has to be dealt with when it comes to Irish History. He wanted to recount an epic. He was also a notable figure in the context of the 12th century renaissance of classical letters and framed his family's adventure with a sense of historical perspective in the tradition of the great epic, the Aeneid.

Liz shook her head in disbelief. "The Aeneid? Cambrensis compared the invasion of Ireland to the adventures of Aeneas? Why would he do that?"

"To make it seem more important? I don't know. Maybe it's a clue." I said.

Liz smiled. "That sounds mysterious. Aeneas was a Trojan wasn't he?"

"I think. Escaped from Troy and became the ancestor of the Romans, as the story goes. Twelfth century writers reveled in the classics. They'd actually brought them back to life after the dark ages."

"But this book is all about the Normans." Liz said scrunching up her brow. "The editor says it right here, 'their identities, their mentalities and their prejudices. And without it we would be largely in the dark about their coming to Ireland.'"

"So, we've got Wales, Normandy and Troy before the Fitzgeralds even get to Ireland." I said scanning the pages of Cambrensis' *Expugnatio Hibernica*. "By 1169 the Anglo-Normans living in Wales were considered English. But the English weren't really English. They were Norman French."

Liz was curious. "So, after 1066 the language of the English royalty was French and not English?"

"Yea. But in 1066 English wasn't exactly English either. It was more like German. But everything was written in Latin." I said, reading down the list of "Adventurers."

"I don't believe this. The whole family is here backing up Strongbow. Maurice Fitz-Gerald, Reimund Fitz-Gerald, Griffith Fitz-Gerald. Seven of them. There's even one with my father's name William Fitz-Gerald. That's my great grandfather and great, great grandfather's name too."

"We'll have to copy this and send it to Harold. He's gonna' love it." Liz said staring down at the page. "De Cogan, de Bigarz, de Barry? Didn't Harold tell you your great grandmother was a Barry?"

"Yeah. It's all in the family. A family of mercenaries fighting for a Norman warlord named Strongbow." I added.

APPENDIX II.

A LIST OF THE MOST PROMINENT PERSONS CONCERNED IN THE CONQUEST OF IRELAND UNDER HENRY II.

A. Adventurers.

Richard de Clare, Earl of Pembroke or Strigul ["*Strongbow*"].
Maurice Fitz-Gerald.
Reimund Fitz-Gerald
Griffith Fitz-Gerald.
William Fitz-Gerald.
Gerald Fitz-Gerald.
Alexander Fitz-Gerald.
Milo Fitz-Gerald, of St. David's.
Hervey de Montmaurice.
Robert de Barri.
Philip de Barri.
Robert de Barri, junior.
Milo de Cogan [*Cogham*].
Richard de Cogan.
Robert Fitz-Stephen.
Ralph Fitz-Stephen.
Meredith Fitz-Stephen.
Meiler Fitz-Henry.
Robert Fitz-Henry.
Henry Fitz-Henry.
Reimund de Kantitune.
Reimund Fitz-Hugh.
Walter de Ridenesford.
Maurice de Prendergast.
William Mascarel.
Philip of Wales [*Gualensis*].
Richard Fitz-Godobert.
Alice de [A]berveny.
Robert de Quency.

Richard de Clare (Strongbow) depicted in Gerald of Wales' *Expugnatio Hibernica*, c. 1189.

Chapter 3

"Tell me how the Normans got to Normandy?" Liz asked.

I smiled politely. "The Vikings were called Norsemen by the French. The men who came down from the North. Rollo the Viking conquered Paris in the 9th century. The French King gave him lands in Northern France to buy him off and that became Normandy. Strongbow is a Norman north-man descended from Rollo."

"Didn't your aunt Mary tell you that you were related to Strongbow too?"

"The family that slays together stays together." I said, smiling again. "The Vikings had been trading all over Europe, Russia and the Near East since the 790s A.D. They hired out as mercenaries to anyone willing to pay – occupied southern Italy and Sicily. By 1066 they were challenging to rule England and established a Norman Kingdom at the battle of Hastings."

"So how do all these Fitzgeralds fit in?"

"The guys in this book are all the sons and grandsons of Gerald of Windsor."

"As in Windsor Castle?" Liz asked.

"Gerald was the constable. He was in charge of it, guarded it. He may have even built it."

Liz's mouth dropped. "The ancestor of the Fitzgeralds *built* Windsor Castle?"

"Probably with his father Walter fitz Otho. They were hereditary castellans. Sort of Medieval governors."

"And how did they get to be that?"

"Harold said it was a mystery but there are a few theories. Walter's father was a man named either Oter, Otho or Other. Depends on who you read."

"Of course, fitz Otho – son of Otho. And who is Otho?" Liz asked.

"That's the mystery. One story has him as Otho Geraldino landing on the beaches with William the Conqueror as one of his chief commanders. Another has him as a descendent of the dukes of Tuscany who moved from Florence to Normandy and then England a decade before the Conquest. And a third variation skips Otho completely and cuts right to three brothers of the Florentine Gherardini family, Gherardo, Maurizio and Tommaso a hundred years later joining their Geraldine cousins in the invasion of Ireland."

"Poor Otho."

"Poor historians. They hate that story but even the Geraldines and the Gherardini claimed it was true. And that was in the 15th century."

"And who are the Gherardini?"

"One of the Medieval ruling families of Italy. The Gherardini fought on the side of the emperor in the Guelph and Ghibelline wars – 12th century."

"Oh, *those* Gherardini," Liz added sarcastically. "And you think that's where Otho came from."

"It's definitely Italian. There was a 1st century Roman emperor named Otho."

"So it's a real mystery," Liz said.

"But Gerald's father Walter fitz Otho isn't. He and Gerald are all over the record books working their way up the Norman ladder. After 1066 William the Conqueror's son William Rufus continued the conquest into Wales and employed Gerald to do the job. Rufus made a deal to smooth the way and married Gerald off to the Welsh princess Nesta – according to legend, a descendent of King Arthur."

Liz's curiosity was peaked. "Arthur? And when was he king?"

"After the fall of Rome. Somewhere between 410 and 595 A.D. Nobody knows for sure. That's why he's a legend."

"I had no idea that was why JFK's presidency was called Camelot!" Liz said. "I didn't know any of this was real."

"Neither did I. But apparently Gerald got the original Grail princess. That's why eight hundred years later the heir apparent to the British throne is called the Prince of Wales. But the current royal family isn't even close to William the Conqueror. At the outbreak of World War I they went out looking for a new name. Saxe-Coburg and Gotha was a bit too German with Gotha bombers leveling London."

Revelation struck. "So Windsor is a taken name?" Liz added.

"Today they call it rebranding. They say Fitzgerald was one of the names they considered because it went back to the beginning."

"Ahh. So the Fitzgerald family is more directly connected to the original Norman King of England than the Windsors and they even built and protected the castle he lived in. I get it."

I *had* spiraled down into the distant past and as I read more of the *Expugnatio* I found myself feeling uncomfortably familiar with it.

"Addicted to dreams and visions," is how this editor described Cambrensis' accounts of the invasion. Educated in the finest schools in Europe, private tutor to Prince John, in line for the Bishopric of St. David's in Wales. Lectured on French law in Paris. Gerald de Barry is in the thick of it.

Liz detached the extensive genealogical tables from the back of the book. "De Barry is a cousin to the Fitzgeralds and a grandson of Nesta and Gerald. He must have got an earful working at the court of Henry II. They ran an empire back then. Small by today's standards but still – England, Normandy, Aquitaine, Brittany, Maine, Anjou and Tourmaine. That's a lot of real estate to manage."

"And a lot of rents to collect." I added.

Liz chimed in. "Not to mention prophecies to fulfill."

"May I see that?" I asked.

"'Geraldus gave considerable credence to the supposed prophecies of Merlin Silvester of Celidon.' It says. 'He cites them ten times in the *Expugnatio*. He eventually found a copy of the prophecies in Welsh at Nefyn, in the province of Lleyn, on Caernarvon bay in North Wales.'"

Liz was suspicious. "How could they be 'suppose-ED' if he found a copy of them?"

I laughed. "This historian wants to discount Cambrensis. To him Merlin is a myth, not history."

"So what is history anyway? Historians we've met had no problem believing Afghan drug dealers were Freedom Fighters. What's the problem with Merlin?" Liz asked.

I read on. "'The character of the *Expugnatio* was influenced by the Merlin prophecies, which were made to chime in with Geraldus' belief in the predestined importance of the Normans and the Geraldines in particular, for Irish history.' This guy is biased against Cambrensis because he's writing about his own family, the Geraldines. But it doesn't mean it's inaccurate."

"The Geraldines?" Liz asked.

"All the families that descend from Nesta. The FitzHenrys were her children by Henry I, the FitzStephens by Stephen – Constable of Cardigan and the FitzGeralds her children by Gerald."

Liz gave me a look. "And he's the only one she married?"

"Married or not the genealogical tables are labeled the Children of Nesta. Need I say more?"

I scanned through the pages of the Cambrensis book and a chill ran down my spine.

"I mentioned this to Harold but I thought you'd want to hear it. 'From the time Giraldus penned the opening lines of the first preface of the *Expugnatio*, a troublesome spirit stood looking over his shoulder, waiting to take possession of the book. The shadow of the disturbing presence of Merlin of Celidon can be seen at several points in the work, and is again strongly evident when Giraldus was writing the very last paragraph of the book.'"

Liz was astonished. "This editor sounds like he believes the Merlin's presence is real."

"All right. So let's look at the last paragraph of the book."

I waited as Liz tore through the pages.

> The Britons relate the story, and the ancient historians tell us. But enough of this. The publication of the third book and the new interpretation of the prophecies must wait until the right time has arrived. For it is better that the truth should be suppressed and concealed for a time than that it should burst forth prematurely and perilously into the light of day, thereby offending those in power.

"Sounds like he's more concerned with Henry than the ghost of Merlin." She said.

"Yea but what's the truth he wants to suppress?" I asked Liz as she read on.

"I'm getting to it. 'On the other hand Giraldus does not elsewhere indulge in mythological pedigrees to quite such a degree as here, where the ancestry of the Norman-Welsh invaders is traced back through Brutus to *'Dardanus the sonne of Jupiter."*

Liz was as stunned as I was. "Jupiter?" she said squinting in the morning sun. "What does he mean by that?"

"Zeus. Jupiter was the Roman name for the Greek god Zeus." I said, finally realizing what Cambrensis was afraid to reveal. Cambrensis was tracing his Welsh ancestors back to the gods."

"No wonder he's concerned about offending those in power." Liz said, laughing.

My classical history was a little rusty so I grabbed a book on Greek mythology off the shelf.

"Dardanus, in Greek legend, the son of Zeus and the Pleiad Electra, mythical founder of Dardania and ancestor of the Romans and the Britons through Aeneas who'd fled from Troy. Why, there's Aeneas again. From Troy."

Liz continued to scan the footnotes of the Expugnatio for clues. "It all goes back to the Trojan wars. Cambrensis says it here. 'Giraldus traces the original inhabitants of Wales back to Camber, son of Brutus, descended from the Trojans through his grandfather, Ascanius and his father Silius. Brutus led the remnant of the Trojans, who had remained in Greece, to the British Isles, and before his death divided that kingdom into three parts. And from him descend all the kings of Britain.'"

"So what about Henry II? Where does he fit into this?" Liz asked.

"He doesn't. And that's what Cambrensis is making clear. He doesn't want to rock the boat."

Giraldus Cambrensis was born c.1146, the youngest son of William de Barri of Manorbier, and Angharad, daughter of Gerald de Windsor, by his wife Nest. Giraldus, therefore, was the son of an Anglo-Norman knight, the great-grandson of a king of Deheubarth, a nephew of Prince Rhys ap Gruffudd (The Lord Rhys) and of Bishop David Fitzgerald of St David's, a kinsman of the Geraldine invaders of Ireland and of the Flemish lords of Haverford, and of most of the Welsh princely families.

CHAPTER 4

It took more digging to locate the source of the Jupiter quote from our copy of the *Expugnatio* but even that offered more questions than answers.

"The editor of the *Expugnatio* states that this is from the Hooker translation and that it might not be Cambrensis' words at all, but his own." Liz said studying the text.

"That doesn't make sense," I added, taking the book and reading down the page. "He claims Hooker is known to be a close translator and says his translation is a fine one. So what are the chances he's making it up?"

"He also says that Hooker edited out Cambrensis' mention of Thomas Becket because Becket was 'a froward and obstinate traitor against his master.' So if he's willing to edit out Thomas Becket you can imagine what else he's willing to do."

***

Finding the Hooker translation of Giraldus Cambrensis' *Expugnatio* was easy. Accepting what he had to say about the Fitzgerald family was not.

"Hooker's translation is part of Holinshed's *Chronicles of England, Scotland, and Ireland*. The translation was published in 1586 and dedicated to Sir Walter Raleigh – Knight," Liz said reading down the page, "and it's not just about Cambrensis. It's a four hundred year history of Ireland from Henry II through Queen Elizabeth I."

"1586? That's just after the Desmond wars."

"That's for sure. And boy does he not like your branch of the family."

I scanned the pages and read out loud. *"I began to consider the too great and wonderful workes of God, both his severe judgement against traitors, rebels and disobedient; and of his mercie and loving kindness upon the obedient and dutiful."*

"Uh oh." I said, fearing what was coming. *"'But of all others, none to be compared to this tragicall discourse of Ireland, and the most unnatural wars of the Desmonds against hir sacred majestie.'* Her Sacred majesty?"

"It gets better," Liz said as she pointed to a paragraph toward the end of the page. *"'Whose disobedience the Lord hath in justice so severely punished and revenged, as the like hath not in our age beene seene nor knowne.'"*

"This thing is creepier than I expected." I said contemplating the rabbit hole we'd just gone down. "Can I see that?" I asked, taking the book in hand. *"'The Earle of Desmond, named Girald Fitzgerald, was descended of a younger house of the Giraldines of Kildare, and both of them descended from one and the same ancestor Girald of Windsor, a noble gentleman of Normandie; who after his arrival into England, travelled into Wales, and there married the ladie Nesta daughter to the great Roesines prince of South Wales, and by others had issue Moris Fitzgirald, ancestor of the aforesaid Giraldines. And for their truth and fidelitie were advanced to honor."*

Liz was shocked. "Hooker is certainly making it clear that the Fitzgeralds were originally revered by the royals," she said, shaking her head. "They must have really crossed a red line."

"Oh did they ever," I said, continuing on.

"And in the beginning of king Edward the third's reigne, in the yeare one thousand three hundred and twentie and seven, Moris Fitzthomas a younger brother of that house was created earle of Desmond; and from thense as before, they continued [as] faithful subjects, for the course of sundrie hundreds of yeares: until this brainesicke and breakdanse Girald of Desmond, and his brethren, alies, and complices, forgetting the honour of his house and forsaking their faith, did break into treasons, and shewed themselves open enemies, traitors and rebels, using all maner of hostilities and outrages to the impeach of hir most sacred majestie, and the destruction of the commonwealth."

"Oh, wait a minute." Liz said. "Hooker is saying they had no problem with the Fitzgerald family until the last earl of Desmond came along? That doesn't figure. Cambrensis was concerned about their relations to the royal family back in the 12th century."

"You're looking at Elizabethan claptrap." I said. "Or better yet how you justify a genocide against one of your own. And this is the payoff right here. *"'the price whereof in the end he paied with his and their own bloods, to the utter destruction of themselves and that whole familie. For first the earle himself, the cheefe of his familie, after his long repast in his traitorous follies, was driven in the end to all extremities and penuries, and at the last taken in an old cottage, and his head was cut off and sent to London, and there set upon London bridge, and his lands and inheritance confiscated and discontinued from his house and name for ever. A notable and a rare example of Gods just judgement and severe punishment, upon all such as doo resist and rebell against the higher powers of his anointed: And the Lord shall root him from out of the face of the earth that shall blaspheme his gods, and curseth the prince of the people."*

"I think your take on Theodore Eliot was right on the money." Liz said, grimacing. "His attack on you *was* about being one of *those* Fitzgeralds as if you were the ghost of JFK. I understand it now."

I shook my head in disbelief. "For Hooker, Raleigh wasn't committing genocide. He was fulfilling a commitment to God. Elizabeth I and the Fitzgeralds are all descended from Nest's father, Rys ap Tewdwr, the king of Deheubarth in Wales. They're cousins and they can challenge her claim to the throne.... But if you spill Fitzgerald blood in a sacred cause...." I thought about it as the idea sank in.

"You don't just get rid of the competition, you sanctify her rule as queen by making a blood sacrifice." Liz said as she saw the logic.

"Yes, sacred murder. Walter Raleigh is in league with a London's secret societies. John Dee, Walter Raleigh, Phillip Sydney and Edmund Spenser were up to their waist coats in black magick. He knows the ancient rules of the game. And Hooker knows what Raleigh knows. Empire requires an offering to the gods."

"So your aunt Mary was right." Liz added. "The British Empire began with the murder of Gerald, the last earl of Desmond. And that is why Herr Hooker emphasized Reimund Fitzgerald's 's speech." She said proudly. "As proof of the Tudor family's divine lineage."

We both quickly traced through Hooker's translation of the Cambrensis claim until we hit page 153.

"Here it is. *The Conquest of Ireland*. The Oration of Reimund." I said as Liz prepared to read.

"And who is Reimund again?" She asked.

"He's listed in the back – one of the Geraldine 'Adventurers' – grandson of Nesta, like Cambrensis. *'Let it appeere vnto them as it is knowen vnto vs, of whạt race we came, and from whom we descended. Camber (as it is well knowen) the first particular king of Cambria our natiue countrie, was our ancestor, and he the sonne of that noble Brutus, the first and sole monarch of all England, whose ancestor was Tros the founder of the most famous citie of Troie, and he descended from Dardanus the sonne of Jupiter, from whom is deriued vnto vs not onlie the stemme of ancient nobilitie, but also a certeine naturall inclination of valiant minds, & couragious stomachs, bent to follow all exploits in prowesse and chiualrie, and wherein all our ancestors haue béene verie skilfull and expert. [who] when in 'times past all the princes of Greece kept warres for ten yeares & od moneths continuallie against our ancestors in the famous citie of Troie, and could not preuaile against them, vntill they vsed treasons and practised treacheries, which bred vnto them a more infamous victorie than a glorious triumph?"*

Liz's jaw dropped. "He's talking about the Trojan horse as if it were family history. I've never heard anyone do that."

She continued. *"Shall the honor of our ancestors be withered by our sluggishness, and the glorie of their prowess be buried in our cowardness? Shall we be afraid of a few, and unarmed, when they withstood infinit multitudes of the most worthiest and valiantest personages then in all the world?"*

Liz shook her head in disbelief. "I see why Cambrensis withheld the prophecies. If Henry II knew your family would marry the land of Ireland and become more Irish than the Irish he would have killed them all."

"And four hundred years later Elizabeth and Walter Raleigh almost did." I said.

***

Geraldus Cambrensis had backed off on interpreting the prophecies of Merlin to spare his family retribution but in the end they'd been subjected to the *"utter destruction of themselves and that whole familie."* Was that where that deep sense of nihilism in me had come from – the utter destruction of my own family? That was the feeling I'd picked up from my uncle Joe. Without intending, I found myself connecting to the past and getting answers to something I felt very close to.

"The physics of the JFK synchronicities are beginning to make sense." I said to Liz as she continued to scan the pages of Holinsheds chronicles. "Engaging Afghanistan put me on a path from Dealey Plaza to the invasion of Ireland in 1169. But what do I do with that? Tell the world that JFK's assassination was caused by a sacred vendetta for something done six hundred years before?"

"No." Liz said, putting Holinshed's book down on the table. "I think it goes back to Troy. Let's see what old Jupiter was up to and maybe we'll get an answer we can work with."

Chapter 5

May 1991. A suburb near Boston

I'd abandoned the news business for Hollywood and after years of trying to crack the code as a screenwriter, it had gone to my head. I felt the pressure to make something happen, and I was having vivid dreams. It was early in the morning. I was half awake and found myself watching a black caped figure pacing around a circular catwalk that encases a glowing orb. The orb was protected by rings of dark energy. The caped figure was testing the energy field with a sword, hacking it here and there to determine its strength. I understood the caped figure wanted to access the orb's power because I knew him. He was me – or at least an aspect of me. I even knew his name; the Black Knight. I could feel his presence in my heart – like the pain of a spiritual wound that would not heal.

"Do not define yourself by the face of your enemy." He said, in a voice that sounded like a boot stepping on crushed glass.

"What was that?" Liz asked as I woke up with a start.

"You heard that?"

"I heard you. That voice you sometimes use. The really gruff one."

I was awake now too. "The black knight. I saw him, finally."

I'd known the black knight for years as an intolerant personality with a gravelly voice that sometimes made it difficult to sing. I'd left the stage because of him. He'd shown up in the middle of an audition for Gower Champion and I figured further resistance was useless. He'd come in handy on the football field and high school fistfights and he was my go-to personality in Afghanistan. I'd sensed his presence all my life, but when he barked "I will not be interfered with" in the hospital recovery room after surgery on my ruined vocal chords, I knew he'd be back.

"Did I just say that?" I asked the attending nurse as I emerged from the drug induced sleep.

"Oh, everybody talks like that when they come out of the sodium pentothal. I'm used to it." She said. The nurse had heard it before. But I hadn't. Now he was here in my room.

Since Afghanistan ended we'd had numerous meetings in L.A. and discovered an esoteric side to screenwriting that only the initiated knew about. Not that they'd tell you straight out. There was the number of pages of course. Numbers translate to time – time translates to money. One page equaled a minute. Sixty minutes an hour. Two hours made a movie. Money, money, money.

But why was the spacing of the words on the page and the way the page looked just as important? As we sat in on numerous meetings with studio producers who scanned our scripts line by line without reading them, I guessed at an answer. Screenplays were more than just words on a page that told a story. Screenplays were numerical codes that secretly conveyed one of "The Seven Origin" stories. Man against man, man against nature, man against himself, man against woman, man against society, man caught in the middle and man against God. Yes there were only seven official stories and every movie in Hollywood got shoehorned into being one of them.

The first ten pages set the tone. What followed was conveyed in a triangle of plot points that delivered a dream – the perfect location for a story to unfold and you weren't just making it up. Screenwriting was about divination and prophecy – about revelation and if you bothered to listen to the voice it talked to you. You argued with it – reasoned with it – tried to understand it. Yes, there were only seven stories. But the most important one – the one that involved me and my family was *man against God*. And that was where the story began to transform into something very personal.

***

Hooker's translation of the Expugnatio obsessed me. *"Let it appeere vnto them as it is knowen vnto vs, of what race we came, and from whom we descended. Camber (as it is well knowen) the first particular king of Cambria our natiue countrie, was our ancestor, and he the sonne of that noble Brutus, the first monarch of all England, whose ancestor was the founder of the most famous citie of Troie, and he descended from Dardanus the sonne of Jupiter."*

I was muttering now. "As it is well knowen? Well knowen to whom? Official court historians knew this history in the 12th century. They still believed it in the 16th century." I said to myself with growing frustration. "How come we don't know about it in the 20th century?"

"We do know about it," my precocious nine year old Alissa said as she quietly joined me at the kitchen table. "But not as history – as legend."

"Legend?" Alissa took me by surprise. "Yes of course, legend." I admitted, trying to be fatherly. "But they must have had some basis in fact. The people in this book were a thousand years closer to the original documents than we are. They kept oral histories. Do you think they were just legends to them?"

"Well they're real to me."

"All right. Here's the problem. The guy in this book, Reimund Fitzgerald claims he descended from Jupiter through the Trojan race."

"Maybe he did." She said confidently.

I followed up, half-kidding. "Well if his name is Fitzgerald and he's descended from Jupiter, you must be descended from Jupiter too."

Alissa scrunched up her nose and thought about it as she poured the milk over her cereal. "That would make sense," she said confidently. "When I was little I thought I was a mermaid. I dreamed about it."

"And what does being a being a mermaid have to do with descending from Jupiter?" I asked politely.

"The wives of all the gods came from the ocean. Tethys and Oceanus gave birth to the Oceanids. Zeus's first wife Metis was an Oceanid. There were thousands of them."

"I didn't know that," I admitted.

"You gave me the book about it for Christmas. *D'Aulaires' Book of Greek Myths*. Didn't you read it?" She harrumphed. "*Everything* goes back to the Greek gods and the war of the Titans – the old gods against the new ones, the Olympians." She said, trying to get me to understand. "Never mind I'll get it."

Alissa was in love with Greek mythology. She had also inherited what I suspected were some of my mother's unusual powers of perception. But this new discovery was making me think I might have underestimated my father's role in this.

"It's right here," she said returning with the book. "Oceanus and Tethys were Titans. Zeus was king of the gods of Mount Olympus but he hated humans."

"Jealous?"

"Too much bother. Prometheus was a Titan. He supported Zeus in the war of the gods but he took pity on humans."

"So he gave them fire."

"He stole the fire and Zeus was very angry."

"So he punished Prometheus."

"He wanted to, but when the humans offered up delicious steaks and chops in thanks, the other gods loved it."

"The gods got steaks and chops?"

"They got the *smell* of steaks and chops. Burnt offerings, ya'know? The gods didn't need to eat the steaks and chops."

"But the humans did."

"Yea. And that really upset Prometheus who saw all this good food going to waste. So he played a trick on Zeus."

"Prometheus tricked Zeus?"

"Yea. It was really good. He told the humans to butcher up an ox and separate it into two piles with all the chops and steaks in one pile and all the guts and stuff in the other."

"And then what did he do?"

"Then he ordered them to cover up all the good stuff with bones and sinew and cover the guts with snow-white fat to make it look really delicious."

"And when Zeus found out..."

"He got really angry because not only had he stolen the sacred fire, but he'd taught the humans how to cheat the gods."

"And humans have been paying for it ever since."

Our son Devon joined us at the table, rubbing the sleep from his eyes.

"Morning Dad." He said knowing he was interrupting Alissa – one of his favorite activities.

"Good morning Devon." I said.

Alissa began to pack up her book, annoyed by Devon's presence.

"Can I see that?" I asked, trying to break the tone. "You did tell me I should read it."

Alissa smiled. "Sure dad, but I want it back."

"Would I steal a book from a descendent of Zeus?"

At that moment Liz entered the kitchen. "O.K. boys and girls the bus is coming. Mt. Olympus will have to wait."

I'd found Alissa's book on Greek Myths totally by chance at one of my favorite bookstores and it turned out to be a classic. Now as I scanned the pages I realized it rhymed with what I was reading in the *Expugnatio* and what I'd experienced in Afghanistan.

"You know, the Greeks brought their gods and goddesses to Afghanistan and combined them with Buddhism." I said to Liz as she cleaned up. "Gandharan Buddhism they call it. That temple I visited near Jalalabad – the Hadda Temple. The place where they swept for land mines?"

"What about it?"

"The ancients only put temples in sacred places. The temple might have been in ruins but you could still feel it."

"Feel what?"

"A presence. At the time I didn't realize the place was dedicated to the Greek gods."

"You had a lot on your mind at that moment."

"I had a lot on my mind the whole time, but that one place got my attention. I had to go back and re-edit that part of the documentary, because I'd called it a Hindu Temple. I had to fix it and research it. But now I wonder."

"Wonder what?"

I tried to shake off the feeling of Déjà vu. "That I got the gods' attention at Hadda and they are coming back at me through Alissa."

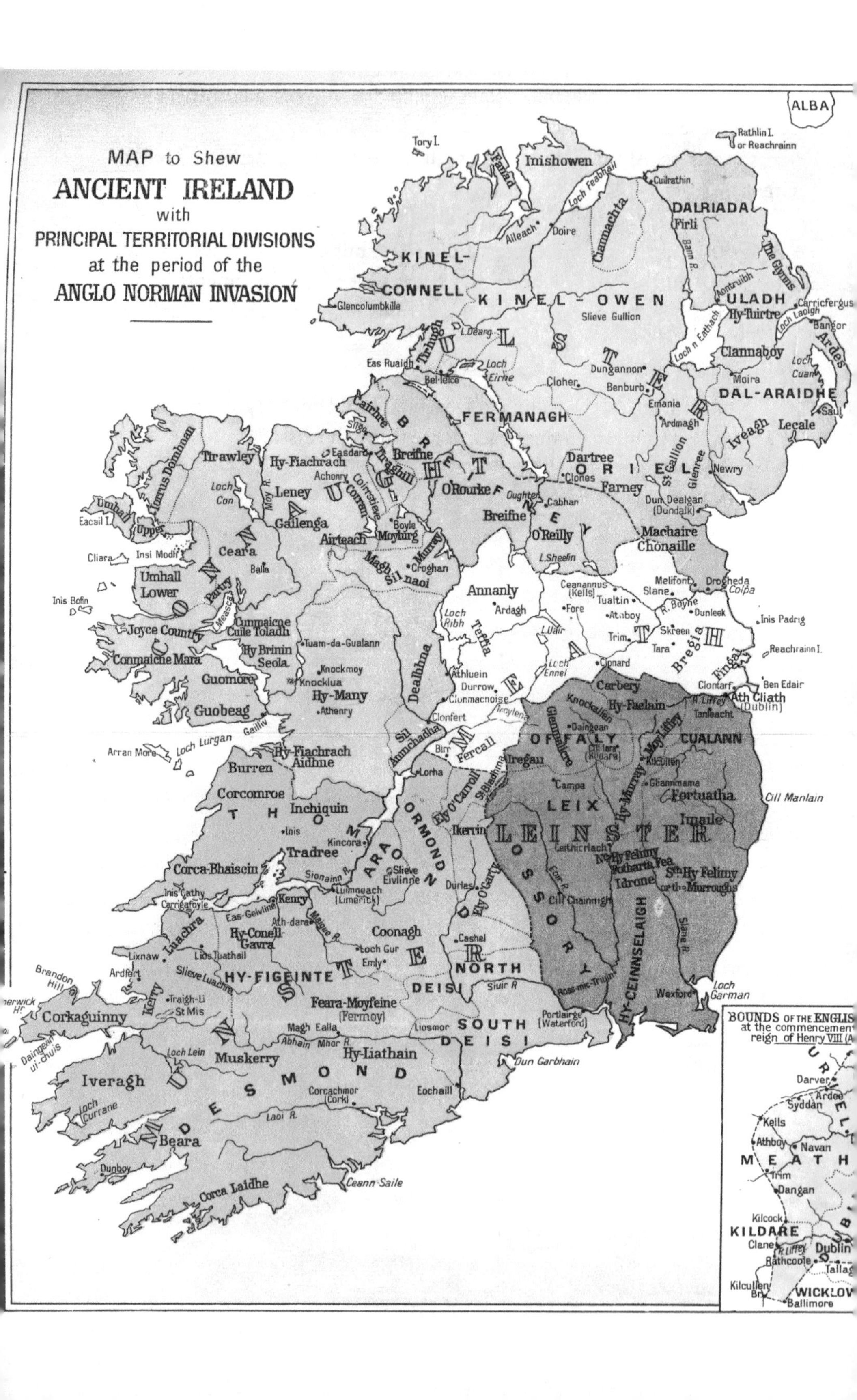

MAP to Shew
ANCIENT IRELAND
with
PRINCIPAL TERRITORIAL DIVISIONS
at the period of the
ANGLO NORMAN INVASION
ALBA
Rathlin I. or Reachrainn
Tory I.
Inishowen
KINEL-CONNELL
KINEL-OWEN
ULSTER
DALRIADA
ULADH
Clannaboy
DAL-ARAIDHE
FERMANAGH
ORIEL
BREIFNE
CONNAUGHT
MEATH
LEINSTER
OFFALY
LEIX
OSSORY
HY-CEINNSELAIGH
CUALANN
THOMOND
ORMOND
DESMOND
NORTH DEISI
SOUTH DEISI
HY-FIGEINTE
Corkaguinny
Iveragh
Muskerry
Beara
Corca Laidhe
Ath Cliath (Dublin)
Luimneach (Limerick)
Corcachmor (Cork)
Portlairge (Waterford)
Wexford
BOUNDS OF THE ENGLISH at the commencement reign of Henry VIII
MEATH
KILDARE
WICKLOW

Chapter 6

The realization had come to me on my first trip to Ireland back in 1971. I'd gone searching for the intangible – kicked open an old rusty gate into a green pasture and found myself staring into a land that time forgot. Until that moment I hadn't realized you could do something like that – but when I did, I was in – and my experience in Afghanistan had only drawn me deeper.

The world hadn't caught up to Ireland back then. Cows still grazed the green pastures among ancient stone circles – memorializing long forgotten battles between long forgotten heroes. New Ford automobiles were bought from dealers' catalogues on Grafton Street in Dublin – not showrooms – and if you listened carefully you could hear the natural rhythms of ancient life that the 20th century had long since left behind.

My friend Dick Reed had actually driven through the town before I realized where we'd been.

"I think that was it." He said as he slowed his Ford Capri on the outskirts of Abbeyfeale, the tiny market-town my grandfather Mike had deserted for America in 1898 as a young man.

"*What* was it?" I asked, straining my neck to look back at the small cluster of stone and masonry buildings by the side of the road.

"Where you come from." He said, struggling to point the nose of the car 180 degrees in the opposite direction. "We've almost reached the crossroads of Limerick and Cork." Dick had been a voice coach, mentor and friend and while on sabbatical had grown a beard that rendered him the spitting image of Captain Ahab. He'd been studying for his doctorate in Irish history for a year at Trinity and probably knew this place as well as the locals. He'd also done a fair share of his research on the Desmond branch of the Fitzgeralds and cued me in to what he'd called their "complicated" relationship with each other and to London.

"This is the place," he said as he dropped me off at the door of an unassuming storefront with a sign reading the Pallas Inn Pub, swinging overhead. "It has to be."

"Where are you headed next?" I asked as a backseat passenger shifted up to my empty seat.

"Down to the Ring of Kerry and Dingle. We'll be back through in a couple of days so we'll pick you up on Sunday afternoon." He said, revving the engine before speeding off.

Abbeyfeale was the village my father never got to see and I had returned to find out what he'd missed. Cousin Greta and her husband Willy received me with a welcome befitting a king and my backpack was soon quartered in the upstairs guestroom. But there was no time to sleep now. It was Friday and this was Ireland, and a local festival was about to begin.

"It didn't take long to figure out where my father's easy going manner had come from as I joined in the partying and the music. These strangers were like old family members coming back for Christmas and as the pints of Guinness flowed and the talk turned to American politics, the time sped by.

"Come escort me to the dance," a pretty young girl said after an hour or so as she wrapped her arm in mine, unexpectedly. "Pretend you're my new beau from America and make all the local boys jealous."

It turned out the dance was boring and she soon slipped away with a wink and a local boy, but by the end of the evening I'd found myself at home.

The next morning Greta and Willy took me up the hill to Meenahalla to meet my cousin Pat and his father, great uncle Ned. My grandfather Mike had turned the farm over to Ned when he left for America and deeded it over in 1957 after my father made it clear he wanted nothing to do with it.

But I wondered. Meenahalla was in the heart of Desmond. Four hundred staggeringly beautiful acres in the foothills of the Mullaghareirk Mountains overlooking the valley of the river Feale. Was severing his 5 daughters and four sons from this place the origin of the bitterness in Mike's children – to be cut off from the source of their existence before they'd had a chance to be a part of it?

I felt strangely out of place with a sick feeling in my solar plexus. I was fulfilling a ritual my father should have completed as Mike's eldest son, only to have to sit at the feet of his replacement as the new patriarch of the family. It had taken too many miles and too many years to get here. Ned was ninety by the time I met him and nearly blind from his days toiling under the sun and as we greeted each other for the first time, he seemed burdened.

"Move closer." He said in a gruff voice, squinting to get a better look at me. "I want to see Billy's boy."

Ned didn't need to say much more and he didn't. It was a homecoming by the turf fire on a very typical, gloomy Irish afternoon in June. My mission as a family ambassador from America had been accomplished and we both knew it.

The rest of the day was spent with Cousin Pat and his wife Nancy touring the local sites, including the old Desmond fort by the river.

"There's really not much left of it," I offered as we wandered through the ruins.

"You can thank Pelham for that." Pat said in an Irish brogue so thick it made me squint.

"Who?" I asked.

"Pelham. Sir William Pelham. And there wasn't much left of the Desmond Fitzgeralds either after Pelham came through here."

"And what year was that?" I asked, bending an ear in Pat's direction as he gazed thoughtfully at the overgrown stonework.

"1580. Purt Castle, it was called. The Castle of the Three Enemies. The old Abbey was sacked as well because it was Catholic."

"The Abbey by the river Feale." I found myself muttering – Abbeyfeale.

I tried to imagine what the place looked like before Pelham and his army got hold of it and a feeling of doom set in. "How did this happen?"

"It all started after the Normans invaded." Pat said. "The Fitzgeralds found themselves at home with the Irish and married into their families. The English were against that sort of thing and made laws against it. The Statutes of Kilkenny they called them, but no one paid them any mind until the Earls got too powerful to ignore. So they were accused of treason and breeding a race of their own. It all came down at the end with the rebellion against Elizabeth. Gerald the last earl wrote to her – from right here – asking for a truce. He signed it April 15th 1583, Garrot Desmond, Abbeyfeale. But as you can see, it was already too late by then."

That last night was spent with Willie and Greta's family and their friends. At the end of the evening we all wound up in the kitchen after closing hours singing songs – but HAIR was not among their favorites.

"Surely you must know Bing Crosby and Pat Boone." They said as I tried to explain that Bing and Pat were part of another era, but they'd have none of it.

My friend Dick arrived the next day on schedule. I introduced him to Greta and Willy and we were soon gone – back to Dublin with my heart in my throat.

"How was that?" Dick asked glaring at me suspiciously from the corner of his eye.

"I'm not really sure," I said, feeling that fight or flight feeling creeping back into my solar plexus. "There's something about this place. Everyone seems happy, but there's something missing."

"You've been called, Paul." Dick said with a look that crossed somewhere between panic and jubilation. "You've been hearing the voice of this place all your life and you've answered it."

I tried not to smile. "What are you talking about?"

"Your family came here nearly nine hundred years ago for a reason. Gerald, the very first Gerald of Windsor was sent here as an ambassador to the provincial king of Munster, Muirchertach Ua Briain in 1102 almost seventy years before the Norman invasion. By 1169 the relationship between South Wales and Desmond was already well established. They were just going through the motions as a pretext to fool Henry the II. Muirchertach was the grandson of Brian Boru, the legendary Irish king. They wanted to unite the Kingdoms of Wales and Ireland to roll back the conquest of Britain and Gerald was helping them do it."

I was confused. "So Gerald was forging a political alliance with the Welsh and Irish natives against the King of England. That must have been pretty risky. But what is this voice you're talking about."

Dick grew quite. "The old Irish claimed descent from the mother of the Irish gods, Aine, Dana, Danu – an ancient line that hadn't lost its connection to the otherworld. After a couple of whiskies you can get the old professors at Trinity to talk about them. Evans-Wentz did a study back at the turn of the century and wrote a book about it – *The Fairy Faith in Celtic Countries.* It was much easier to hear back then – without the cars and the TV's. But when you come down here, you understand why the Normans wanted to be the kings of Ireland – because the kings of Ireland have a straight line to the gods."

CHAPTER 7

I hadn't fully appreciated what Dick Reed revealed to me back in 1971. But now that I understood the context of the Fitzgeralds in Ireland through the Elizabethan writers like Hooker – I couldn't stop thinking about what he'd said.

"Dick was totally taken by the Geraldine embrace of the Celtic otherworld and its embrace of them." I told Liz as she shuttled around the kitchen getting dinner ready. "He really believed in what they'd set out to do in 1102."

"And he really believed you were fulfilling it." Liz said.

"I don't know what he really believed but I know we made a stop in Wexford at the tomb of Strongbow on the way down to Abbeyfeale."

"I thought Strongbow was buried in Dublin at Christ Church."

"I did too but he insisted that Christ Church was just a memorial and that Wexford was the real place. He said he'd brought me there to see the grave of my ancestor."

Liz shook her head in disbelief. "You know, a lot of people claim to be descended from the rich and famous. But how many can trace themselves back to the mother of the gods?"

"I don't know about that." I said, trying to dampen her enthusiasm. "Some ancient myth about bringing fertility to the land by impregnating a local sun goddess by the banks of a river sounds a little fishy don't you think?"

"But that *is* the mythology, isn't it? You said he filled you in on it on the ride back to Dublin."

"Yea, he spent the whole ride talking about it. Gerald's son Maurice found Aine, the mother of the Irish gods bathing on the banks of the river Camogue. He seized her cloak and took her for his own."

"Took her?" Liz said raising an eyebrow. "Really?"

"The Irish are very demure when it comes to sex. Anyway, the product of the union was Geroid Iarla – Gerald the Earl which gives all their descendants otherworld powers."

"That certainly explains Alissa." Liz said as she rattled through the cabinet for plates. "I remember when you went off on that trip to Europe. They called you from New York to come for Superstar. You missed getting your picture on the cover of Time Magazine. Was it worth it?"

"I wanted Superstar but I needed that trip more. It was my own little Aeneid. Dublin to Paris, driving to Rome, Greece and Turkey – the beaches in Crete, the bazaar in Istanbul – Santa Sophia?"

"I'm surprised you didn't get to Troy."

"We got as far as the Bosporus but the bridge wasn't completed. Then the VW camper broke down. We were lucky to get back at all."

"And you were rescued by those three French kids in a '57 Peugeot."

"I've had a soft spot in my heart for the French ever since."

"It all seems to go back to France, doesn't it?" Liz said with a glint in here eye. "Did you ever ask your mother about the time your father spent there in World War II?"

"She never talked much about it. She has some old photographs and a book about Carcassonne he brought her."

"You should talk to her about it this weekend when you take Alissa for her sleepover. I'd like to see that book on Carcassonne."

***

"Tell me about Dad's time in France." I asked my mother as Alissa settled in, in front of the TV.

"He was gone for almost two years," she said, shaking her head as she hauled out the ever present box of photographs. "He really shouldn't have been drafted at thirty five with a wife and three children. But he didn't complain. They sent him to Longview Texas for training and then Nancy France to staff the pharmacy at a military hospital. It had been a French Cavalry school before the war – Caserne Thiry. That's where he met J.Y. the Circus Doctor."

"He probably took it as a vacation." I replied reaching in to pull out a handful of old dog-eared black and white photographs.

"He probably did." She said. "Men like wars you know. He'd been working full time since he was eight years old. I don't think he knew anything else *but* work."

I shuffled through the pile reciting as I went. "Dad standing at the gate of the 173rd General Hospital, in his lab with German POW's, receiving an ambulance with the wounded, standing where Hitler stood in front of the Eiffel Tower, dad on the steps of Notre Dame, dad in the chaplain's jeep with J.Y. Henderson. Dad at the Arc de Triomphe, dad standing in the snow with the pharmacy gang, January 9, 1945." It was almost too much to think about. "I never realized he'd arrived in Nancy right in the middle of the Battle of the Bulge." I said.

"It's amazing he survived. He caught pneumonia twice in England and was nearly put on a ship that was sunk on its way to France."

I hadn't heard that before. "Nearly?"

"Actually he *was* put on the ship but they took his unit off because they needed engineers more than pharmacists."

"Imagine being sunk in the English Channel by a German submarine in January." I said, grimacing. "Makes you wonder."

"Wonder what?"

"Why some people live and others die."

"Maybe because it's an experiment." My mother said staring back at me with a peculiar look. "I do wonder about that sometimes – whether all of this isn't all made-up – that we're just being tested to see how much we can take."

"Sounds like the *Twilight Zone*." I said. "But who's doing the experimenting?"

"The gods," Alissa pronounced – her eyes still glued to the TV set. "The war of the Titans never ended. It just changed."

My mother smiled and averted her eyes. But I knew she agreed with Alissa.

"It could be," she said, quietly staring at the back of Alissa's head. "I've come to think it has to be something like that."

My daughter and my mother were two peas in a pod. They were both gifted with second sight and they both knew it. My mother, Theresa was prone to insights – mystical and sometimes quite scary. She was haunted by the dead and deeply superstitious. When I was young her favorite pastime was to roam the graveyards of Dover New Hampshire looking for relatives who hadn't found their way home.

She could take one look at someone and sum them up in a second and her judgements were usually final, whether right or wrong. My older siblings didn't like my mother's old Irish ways but over the years I'd gotten used to them and even come to appreciate them. But this one about life being an experiment was new.

"Do you still have the book on Carcassonne that Dad brought back from France," I asked as I came upon a handful of miniature postcards marked La Cité de Carcassonne on the back.

"Here." She said reaching over to a table by the window. "The war in Europe ended in May and the boys had nothing to do. The army didn't care that they had wives at home. They just wanted to send them all to the Pacific to fight Japan. But after they dropped the bomb they let them go off sightseeing."

"Did he ever say anything to you about this place?" I said, taking the book from her hands.

"He never talked about France much, but he did say he felt as if he'd already been to Carcassonne the first time he walked through the gates. It wasn't like him to say something like that either so it must have meant something."

***

"Here it is," I said, handing Liz the old book. *The City Of Carcassonne, An Historical, Archaeological and descriptive Handbook*"

"Judging by the inscription your father must have given it to your mother as a present that Christmas Eve he got home." She said, inspecting the inside cover. "There's a post card in here too that you sent to her – July, 1971from Chartres Cathedral. Did you ever get to Carcassonne?"

"No, but I remember driving by it on the way to Cannes. It's very big – if you didn't know better you'd think it was a theme park."

"The mystery of the remote origin of Carcassonne is unfathomable." Liz said reading from the Introduction. "'In the Middle Ages, the true scholars of the time were fond of ascribing the foundation of the town to Aeneas, the son of Anchises.' Unfathomable alright – we're back to the Trojans."

"So if we're back to the Trojans we're back to the Greek gods." I said, thinking back to what Alissa had said. "May I see it?"

Liz handed me the book and I read from the inscription. "'To Theresa from Bill September 17- 1945. From the city of Carcassonne France. Missed you very much darling.' Darling? I don't remember him ever calling my mother darling. That's a shock."

"Why should it be a shock?"

"By the time I got there they had left the darling phase of their relationship. I came six years after *darling*. Six years after the war. Carcassonne must have got to him, the way the Hadda Temple in Afghanistan got to me. My mother told me he felt as if he'd been there before."

"So he had a déjà vu? What could have caused that." Liz was thinking now. "He left as a drug salesman and came back a healer. That's a pretty big change." She acknowledged. "And that change opened the door for you to deliver the answer he was looking for."

"And what was he looking for?"

"He was looking for the road home. We know the Fitzgeralds were English before they were Irish and French before they were English. Carcassonne narrowed it down to one place in France for your father." She said.

"I think they call that Déjà visité." I said. "That sense of having been in a place you've never been before."

"Well maybe we'd better find out what Carcassonne is all about."

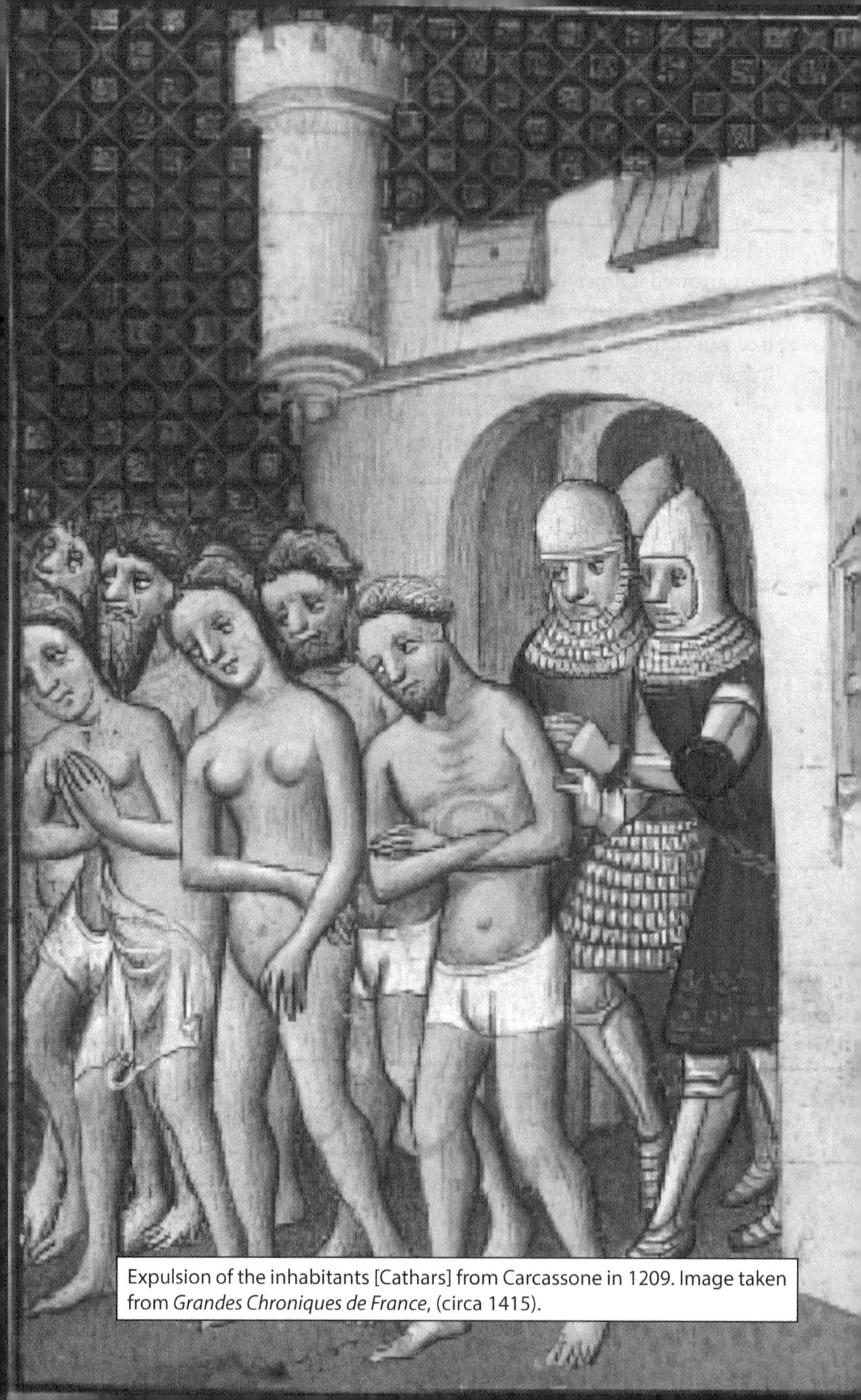

Expulsion of the inhabitants [Cathars] from Carcassone in 1209. Image taken from *Grandes Chroniques de France*, (circa 1415).

Chapter 8

What was so special about the medieval French town of Carcassonne that it triggered my father's memory? Had it been the architecture, a day in the French countryside – a glass of cognac? Or was it some profound experience that lay buried in his psyche? It didn't take more than a minute to find out about the medieval village on the top of the hill in the Languedoc and it left me dumbstruck. For a start Carcassonne and the nearby city of Albi were the focus of the Albigensian Crusade, the beginning of the Inquisition and the total liquidation of a heretical Christian cult known as the Cathars. Like the Zoroastrians and the Manichean's before them, the Cathars believed in absolute dualism between good and evil, spirit and flesh, light and darkness, God and Satan. To a Cathar the human body was the repository of evil and the objective of life was to leave it behind. The idea that God would descend into a human body was unthinkable. So why then would Carcassonne also be known for the legend that Mary Magdalene settled there following the crucifixion of her husband Jesus of Nazareth? And how could it be that their child would continue the house of David as the foundation of a royal French dynasty that would come to claim its inheritance at the end of time?

The Nazi defeat in May of 1945 gave my father the opportunity to visit the epicenter of a heretical movement that had plagued the Catholic Church from its inception. And in 1982 it suddenly resurfaced to claim its earthly inheritance as the clock ticked down to the end of the millennium.

A trio of author/researchers named Michael Baigent, Richard Leigh and Henry Lincoln grabbed onto the radical legend about Jesus of Nazareth, Mary Magdalene and the origin of the Merovingian Kingdom of France and by 1990 had transformed it into a burgeoning industry with a global cult following.

"So far no one has presented proof that Jesus of Nazareth even existed let alone married Mary Magdalene and had a child by her." Liz said. "But we know for a fact that there are rabbis today that can trace marriage records back at least 2500 years. Even today, certain orthodox groups deny marriage if you can't prove your lineage. Any rabbi living in Palestine coming from a royal Jewish household, would have been married off to an equally powerful household and had children. That's common sense."

"If that's the common sense then why hasn't anyone produced the proof?" I asked.

"Because this story fits someone's political agenda." Liz answered. "This thing called the Priory of Sion has been pushing this story since the 1960s. What if this group were tied into the New World Order agenda?"

Liz's idea hit home. "It sort of fits. We already know that Himmler and Albert Speer wanted to restore Europe's monarchy after Germany won World War II. That was the plan. Northcote Parkinson thought Speer had it right. Bring back the old feudal nobility ruled from Berlin and establish a new Holy Roman Empire. According to Baigent and Lee, Himmler set up the spiritual headquarters at an old castle near Paderborn in West Germany at a town called Wewelsburg to revive the Teutonic knighthood of King Friedrich Barbarosa, the Crusader."

"But they didn't win." Liz responded.

"But they didn't go away either. The Bilderberg meetings started in 1954 initiated by Prince Bernhard of the Netherlands. Before the war started the Prince was a member of the Nazi party and an elite unit known as the Reitler-SS. He switched sides after the Germans invaded Holland and fled to England. But that didn't stop him from leading the CIA's effort to reinvent Europe after the war."

"So he didn't exactly protest the Nazis coming back." Liz said.

"I remember hearing some ex-Nazi general claiming NATO was actually Himmler's plan for the SS – a transnational military elite backing up a fascist European economic challenge to Soviet communism."

"So how does the Priory of Sion fit in with the Nazi agenda? The Nazis couldn't possibly be happy with the House of David running the world." Liz added.

"The Germans weren't running it, the Americans were, and the Americans were being run by you know who."

"The British."

"And who were the British before they were British?"

"French. I get it." Liz realized.

"The Germans, the French, the British and the Romans all traced their lineage back to one place."

"Troy. And the Trojans all traced themselves to the Greek gods."

"Whoever the Greek gods were." I added. "So maybe Alissa is on to something. We're talking about a very special group of people and I think Carcassonne is a signpost to who they were and where they came from."

***

Baigent, Lee and Lincoln had got me thinking. If someone could claim a lineage back two thousand years to the House of David without showing proof, what about an Irish family from Desmond tracing its proven lineage through historical documents to medieval France or a Welsh family from Dyfed tracing its roots back to Troy. Voices call to us all the time but who wants to believe they're real? Then all of a sudden a lightning bolt strikes and you start paying attention.

"So there's got to be competition between all these families." Liz said. "We're not just talking about control of the narrative; we're talking about control of everything in between heaven and earth."

"I found a picture of the Wewelsburg castle that Baigent and Lee mentioned. Himmler was preparing it for ritual ceremonies as a sort of Nordic Vatican. It reminded me of that dream in the crypt with the smoke and the Nazi banner where I couldn't breathe." I added.

Liz seemed disturbed. "Did your father ever get there?"

"If he did he never mentioned it. But my grandfather did after he retired. He sent a postcard from the Hoffbräuhaus in Munich in 1954. '"This is the place where Hitler got started. I was here last night.' He wrote. 'Returning by Basel Switzerland and Amsterdam, then on to London and Ireland.' I suppose he could have passed through there on his way to Holland. But that's not much to go on."

"So where does this all connect?" Liz asked.

"I've been thinking about it and the one place that links, Wewelsburg, Carcassonne, Ireland, England and the Fitzgeralds is the 12th century and what led up to it. So I think we'd better start there."

***

"By the year 1086 the Fitzgeralds had firmly established themselves in the Norman hierarchy. Gerald's father Walter Fitz Otho is recorded in the Domesday survey with extensive holdings up and down the Thames River Valley. By 1096 Gerald is married to Nest, the Princess of Dyfed."

Liz was thinking. "So all this was happening in the reign of William Rufus. And you already told me Rufus must have arranged for Gerald's marriage."

"But then something happened to Rufus at the turn of the millennium that changed everything. He was assassinated while hunting in the New Forest on August 2, 1100 in the company of Roger and Gilbert de Clare – Strongbow's great uncle and grandfather. And not just that. Gilbert's daughter was married to the assassin – Walter Tirel."

"That sounds convenient. Tirel? Where have I heard that name before?" Liz asked?

"In the list of Royal Officers at the back of *Strongbow's Conquest of Ireland*," I said, moving to the bookshelf.

"Hugh Tyrrel – Walter Tirel's grandson accompanied Strongbow on his invasion of Ireland seventy years later in 1170. Here, take a look." I said pointing. "'The Earl's intrinsicke friend.' It says. They were cousins."

"So the grandson of King William Rufus's killer is a cousin to the Earl of Pembroke, Richard de Clare? You're very own Strongbow?"

"The family that slays together stays together."

"I thought you were kidding." Liz said.

"No kidding here. All these families are familiars of the king – Familia Regis – special insider status. Not courtiers. They're the ruling elite – soldiers, diplomats, ambassadors. Some think the practice started under the Norman king of Italy and spread to France and England. Over time it evolved into the Privy Council."

"So what happened to Walter Tirel?"

"Nothing. No one held him accountable. No one even chased him. He caught the first fishing boat to France and that was it. Rufus's brother Henry galloped off to Winchester where they kept the treasury and declared himself king Henry I."

"And that's when the Fitzgeralds began their challenge to the crown?"

"Whatever relationship Gerald had with Rufus, two years later Gerald traveled from Wales to Desmond as an ambassador to King Muirchertach, the grandson of Brian Boru in a bid to unite Wales and Ireland."

"At whose bidding?"

"Arnulf de Montgomery – another Norman – his older brother was raising a rebellion against the new king Henry I."

"So was Gerald caught up in the rebellion?" Liz asked.

"I don't know. But I do know that Rufus's death brought the Fitzgeralds directly into the royal power struggle. Nest's family had strong ties to the Irish in Desmond. I'm sure sending Gerald off to make an alliance didn't go unnoticed by Henry I."

Liz was staggered. "So the death of Rufus provided the impetus to make a move with the Irish – which culminated in the invasion of Ireland 70 years later."

"And the same families that were in the hunting party with Rufus were involved in the invasion of Ireland." I said.

"I can see now why Hooker was so clear about the hatred for the Desmond Fitzgeralds." Liz said, staring into space. "Do you realize how unique this story is? Your family was making blood connections to the most ancient British royalty from the very beginning. But by the 16th century London realized the Desmonds were dedicated to the Irish people and not the crown."

"And that's where we enter the motives behind JFK's death and the rarified realm of the sacred sacrifice."

William the Red (William Rufus) was "accidentally" and fatally shot with an arrow in the forest. Artwork by Joseph Martin Kronheim, from *Pictures of English History: From the Earliest Times to the Present Period* (1868).

CHAPTER 9

"Historians are puzzled by the numerous stories surrounding what happened to William Rufus, the second Norman King of England that August 2, 1100." I said, picking through a pile of old history books.

"The only thing certain is that he was shot by one of his companions with an arrow, broke the arrow off where it projected from his chest which hastened his death and was left alone to die. In every version the arrow is loosed by someone he knows and in all but one that person is Walter Tirel. Rufus was then transported to Winchester Cathedral in a cart by some Anglo/Saxon peasants who'd stumbled onto his body – his blood dripping to the ground all the way."

Liz raised her eyebrows. "It sounds like a ritual."

"William of Malmesbury wrote about it in 1128. He said it all began the night before when Rufus was given six arrows but gave two of them to his best archer Walter Tirel, saying "Bon archer, bonnes fleches" ("To the good archer, the good arrows.") leaving Rufus with four. And that's the first clue of the ritual."

"And why is four a clue?"

"It's the hallmark of the heresies. It's the Tetraktys again. Four represents the transition from the metaphysical to the physical, the transfer of god-like power to the king. The divine word made flesh. That night William dreamt he went to hell and met the devil who told him, "I can't wait for tomorrow when we can finally meet in person."

"So William Rufus is consorting with the devil." Liz said.

"No, Rufus *is* the devil and the grandson of Robert the Devil Duke of Normandy."

Liz's curiosity was peaked. "I don't understand."

"It's the old witch religion. I found a two volume Oxford history of Rufus at the library. This Victorian author – Edward Freeman, 1882 – is suspicious of the *Chronicles*. He thinks the whole story was concocted for public consumption. Let me read it to you. 'In the crowd of conflicting tales with which we are now dealing, we must not insist on any one as a trustworthy statement of undoubted facts. Of the events of the next day we may say this much with certainty; 'Thereafter on the morrow after Lammas day was the King William in hunting from his own men with an arrow offshot, and then to Winchester brought in the bishopric buried.'"

"That doesn't say anything." Liz observed.

"Exactly. It says everything." I said. "Freeman writes – 'These words of our own Chronicler state the fact of the King's death and its manner; they suggest treason, but they do not directly assert it; they name no one man as the doer. Nearly all other writers agree in naming Walter Tirel as the man who drew the bow; but they agree also in making his act chance-medley and not willful murder. Yet it is clear that there were other tales afloat of which we hear merely the echoes.'"

"Chance Medley? How lyrical. So what do you think?" Liz asked.

"I think Freeman knows the Chroniclers are covering up. But he doesn't know who or what they're covering up for. They don't even seem to care that the king is dead. They focus on who gets blamed, then they tell you it doesn't matter. Listen. 'William may have died by accident by the hand of Walter Tirel or of any other. He may have died by treason by the hand of Walter Tirel or by any other. In this last case there were many reasons why no inquiries should have been made, many reasons why the received tale should be invented or adopted. It was just such a story as was wanted in such a case. It satisfied curiosity by naming a particular actor, while it named an actor who was out of reach, and did not charge him with any real guilt.'"

Liz looked at me suspiciously. "You said something about 'the morrow after Lammas day' at the beginning. What is Lammas day?"

"That's the biggest clue of all. It's the first day of the harvest. 'Rufus was killed on the morrow of the Lammas' (2nd August). Thomas Becket on the fourth day before the kalends of January (29th December). The Divine Sacrifice took place on one of these festivals, apparently every seventh year.'"

"So they harvested the king with his fresh blood fertilizing the ground?" Liz said half-joking.

"It would appear so." I said seriously.

"What are we dealing with here, Paul?" She asked, now staring at me.

"Something the proper Victorians didn't want to talk about. The ritual killing of a sacred king. The evidence is written all over it – just like JFK."

The idea stopped Liz in her tracks. "And that's why the investigations never get anywhere?"

"It's easy to get distracted by the palace intrigue." I said. "Was King William Rufus shot accidentally or intentionally? Was it the mafia or the CIA? He was said to be a nihilist, a gnostic, and a known anti-Christian. The "people" have no say in whether the king lives or dies. Their fate is in the hands of the nature gods. They must be appeased for them to survive. If Rufus needs to be sacrificed, so be it."

Liz was thinking. "So nobody on the inside wanted the real answer revealed. Everyone at court is a part of the secret – probably at different levels – but they don't want anyone outside the court knowing about it."

"And the secret remains hidden," I said pulling a thin dog-eared book from the pile. "But there is definitely a secret. I found this one in my search at the library. *The Arrow and The Sword: An essay in Detection* by Hugh Ross Williamson. It was written just after the war in 1947 and it fits that idea to a T. He thinks that both William Rufus's death in 1100 and Thomas Becket's death in 1170 are evidence of cult murders."

"Cults? What kind of cults?"

"Pagan fertility cults. 'The king embodies the *psychic whole* of the community and the divine source of all life.' He writes. 'Therefore he must die so that, in his resurrection, both God and man may live.' He even sites Freeman. He believes he was on to something but that Freeman didn't understand it."

Liz was growing intrigued. "May I see that?" She said, beginning to read from the page. 'That the year 1100 was looked upon as an exceptional year there can be no doubt.' He writes. 'Freeman, the Victorian historian of the reign of William Rufus, unsuspicious of such factors as we have been considering, is made aware of this by the mere objective reporting of the old chroniclers. 'At least within the range of the Red King's influence, that year seems to have been marked by that vague kind of feeling of a coming something… Coming events do cast their shadows before them in that first half of the year 1100. In that age the feeling that weighed on men's minds naturally took the form of portent and prophecy, of strange sights seen and strange sounds listened to. There is not the slightest ground for thinking that all these tales were mere inventions after the fact…. Man's minds were charged with expectation; every sight, every sound became an omen.'"

Liz scanned the pages of the Preface. "How strange. The Preface is written by the Reverend V.A. Demant, canon of St. Paul's. Williamson thanks his friend T.S. Eliot in the Foreword for his work in critiquing his thesis. These are some very serious people taking this very seriously." Liz said holding the copy closer to the light.

"I'd say deadly serious given where it leads to with JFK. He connects the two killings, William Rufus and Thomas Beckett seventy years apart and then suggests that Thomas Becket was a secret Cathar."

"As in Carcassonne and Albi Cathar? How does he know that?"

"Because of the numerology. Becket's Catharness is a dead giveaway and the Chroniclers are trying their best to hide it. Read the bottom of page 130."

I sat back and listened as Liz began. "*The Omissions of John of Salisbury.* One of the most curious discrepancies is that, of the fifteen authorities, all except two either omit the date, 1170, or give it incorrectly as 1171. 'The full explanation of these errors' says Abbot, 'must be left to chronological experts.' The chronological explanation is that at least two systems of reckoning dates were in use – one beginning the year at the feast of the Annunciation (25 March), the other at Christmas (25 December). Certainly to contemporaries 29 December 1170 would immediately indicate the possible nature of the killing. Another circumstance of the same kind is that one of the eyewitnesses took pains to record that Becket ascended *four* steps and that a later writer specifically mentioned that it was *seven* – which makes Abbot ask in surprise: Are we to suppose that Fitzstephen was so keen an observer that he noted the exact number of steps to be "four" and thought it worth recording, simply as a statistical fact, and that Herbert, who was not present, knew Fitzstephen's tradition and thought it worth contradicting?' If 'symbolical' is read for statistical then 'Seven' could be and had been 'Christianized', 'Four' could not."

Liz handed the book back to me. "So the evidence would seem to indicate that the later Chronicler was changing the eyewitness accounts to cover up any hint of the deep Cathar connection that everyone was a part of."

"Williamson followed up by writing that 'one of the men who was with Becket in the cathedral at the time of the murder – John of Salisbury – one of his closest friends who was in a position to know exactly what had passed was careful to omit both the date and the number of steps.'"

"So then we have it," Liz said gazing off into the distance. "As part of the Familia Regis the Fitzgerald family is intimately involved in seventy years of court intrigue from King Rufus to the events surrounding Becket's murder. The Fitzgeralds are the king's family. Gerald's wife even had a child by William the Conqueror's son Henry whom Gerald raised as his own son. They were probably riding with Rufus in the hunt. Their rise to fame falls exactly into the same time period. The marriage of Gerald to

Nest in 1097 – the death of Rufus in 1100 – Gerald's trip to Munster in 1102, Becket's murder in 1170 and the invasion of Ireland that same year are all connected to the same thing – the most important secret of the Roman Church."

(Top) A marble relief, 0.53 m tall, of Mithras in the act of killing the astral bull, the Tauroctony was as central to Mithraism as the Crucifixion is to Christianity. On it Mithras is accompanied b two small figures of the torch-bearing celestial twins of Light and Darkness, Cautes and Cautop within the cosmic annual wheel of the zodiac. At the top left, outside the wheel, Sol–Helios asc the heavens in his biga; at top right Luna descends in her chariot. The heads of two wind-g Boreas and Zephyros, are in the bottom corners

(Bottom) The temple site was uncovered in September 1954 during excavation work, the ruin wa mantled and moved 100 metres to Temple Court, Queen Victoria Street, where in 1962 the founda were reassembled at street level for an open-air public display. In 2007 plans were drawn up to retur Mithraeum to its original location. In May 2010 the Mithraeum remained in situ at Temple Court, th in the same month there was talk of reviving the Walbrook Square project.

The Walbrook Square project was purchased by the Bloomberg company in 2010, which decided t store the Mithraeum to its original site as part of their new European headquarters. The new site is 7 tres (23 ft) below the modern street level, as part of an exhibition space beneath the Bloomberg buil

Chapter 10

I almost didn't want to believe the premise of the book I'd uncovered but as I read more deeply into it, I could tell that the historian and playwright Hugh Ross Williamson and I were hearing the same voices. The core belief system of the early Roman church was rooted in ancient Gnostic practices – including human sacrifice.

"The more one studies Rufus, the more impressive do the clues become." Williamson wrote. "Why 'the Red King"? Red – the color of blood – is and always has been all over the world pre-eminently the witch color. At least from the days of the Pharaohs, when the salute to the Incarnate Sun was: 'Life! Blood! Health! Pharaoh! Pharaoh! Pharaoh!' it had been specifically associated with the Sun cult. 'The Red King' would bear this inference to thousands of his subjects. It was even clearer than Rufus' grandfather's surname 'the Devil.' As his dead body was taken from the New Forest to Winchester, followed by the peasantry, the blood dripped to the earth during the whole journey. This is still the folk-legend in those parts today [and] is consistent with the belief that the blood of the Divine Victim must fall on the ground to fertilize it."

"What has that ritual got to do with the French Cathars that Rome destroyed over a hundred years later?" Liz asked taking the book.

"Gnosticism. Williamson names three eleventh century movements that Rome eventually came to define as heresies and 'they're all derived from Gnosticism.' Inside the church it was the Manichaean sects – mostly the Cathars. Outside the church were the inheritors of Persian Mithraism, a soldiers religion left over from the Roman occupation. The Cathars expressed their beliefs through the poetry of the Troubadours and the spirit of Chivalry – the Mithraists through the Grail Romances."

"And the Third?" Liz asked.

"The Third was just plain old witchcraft – the old pagan fertility-worship – the popular religion of the people."

"And that's what we have with Rufus."

"Rufus was an outspoken pagan. His willingness to embrace death was intended to ensure the Norman's legitimacy as divine kings. But he brought something more – something very Cathar. Williamson says this: 'Rufus was a portent of a new age. He was the incarnation of the spirit of 'chivalry'. It might be going too far to say that William Rufus was the first gentleman … but he was certainly the first man in any prominent place by whom the whole set of words, thoughts and feelings which belongs to the titles of knight and gentleman were habitually thrust forward.'"

"And how does being a knight and a gentleman make him a Cathar?" Liz asked.

"Because knights and gentlemen symbolize the very virtues of what it means to be a Cathar. Williamson traces it back to the Sacred Band of Thebes. 'Its uniqueness as a fighting force lay in the fact that it was composed of pairs of lovers and a band cemented together by friendship founded upon love is never broken, and invincible; since the lovers, ashamed to be base in the sight of their beloved, and the beloved before their lovers, willingly rush into danger for the relief of one another.'"

Liz tried to contain her shock. "Are you saying what I think you're saying?"

"Williamson goes on. 'The principle of the Theban band survived to become the basis of feudal *chivalry*. It is conventionally assumed – as part of the conspiracy of silence – that the key to chivalry was the extravagant worship of Woman. The Knight fighting for his *Lady Fair* is almost the stock synonym for romantic love between the sexes. But the truth is almost the exact opposite.'"

"Conspiracy of silence?" Liz asked.

"That chivalry was really about men loving men – not about men loving women and Rufus was the first great representative of 'chivalry'. He says it on page 42. It was the same with the Mithraists – the religion of soldiers dying with each other for each other and without women. The Ritual becomes the Romance and the Romance is pure Platonic love." I said finishing up.

"So the men go looking for the female in the male and the women go wanting." Liz said shaking her head.

"The Orphic Mysteries were so obviously homosexual that Orpheus met his death at the hands of infuriated women who considered him the embodiment of perversion." I added.

"I'm getting the feeling," Liz said, pursing her lips suspiciously. "That Tirel got away with killing Rufus because he was his lover and everybody knew it."

"Apparently Williamson thinks so too. 'Of the king's behavior,' he writes, 'nothing is known, though Tirel is spoken of as his 'familiar' and it is impossible that he should be excluded from the general assumption.' He says that Rufus's court was openly homosexual and crowded with 'effeminati' – long hair, extravagant manners and luxurious dress. He says the ecclesiastical chroniclers particularly deplored the courtier's habit of shaving so that their beards should not chafe their friends when they kissed.' So you can see why they had to keep all this a secret. Rufus was notoriously celibate towards women and procreation was anathema to a Cathar. The Christian priesthood adopted the practice and so did the Knights Templar who were founded just a few years later. But the celibacy derived from a Gnosticism that preceded Christianity and the Church never accepted the Grail-cult proper because they wanted to keep it hidden. The Grail idea was finally accepted when they managed to transform the secret into the Chalice for the Eucharist. To a Templar though, the Holy Grail was never a cup – or the bride of Jesus or the Ark of the Covenant. The Holy Grail was the lady in the man – Sophia – Wisdom and pursuing it was the initiation rite of the Mithraic ritual. Williamson writes on page 54, 'J. L. Weston has established that the original stories which developed into the Arthurian romance – those of *Perceval* and *Gawain* – had their rise in precisely those regions where Mithraic remains are known to exist. She has identified the original author, Bleheris, with Bledri, the son of that Cadavor who entertained William the Conqueror on his visit to Wales and who died in the year that William Rufus ascended to the throne.' Gerald of Wales even makes reference to him."

"So Bledri was known to the Fitzgeralds." Liz said.

"And this Bleheris-Bledri is keeping the Mithraic Mysteries alive at the court at Dyfed." I said. 'The earliest version of the Grail story, represented by our Bleheris form, relates to the visit of a wandering knight to one of these hidden temples, his successful passing of the test into the lower grade of Life initiation; and his failure to attain the highest degree.'"

"So Dyfed is the origin of the Arthurian Grail legend before it spreads to France and Germany and the Cathars get hold of it. And Nest is a Princess of Dyfed married to Gerald, the father of the Fitzgerald family." Liz said, gasping.

"And all during the same moment in time. According to Jesse Weston the Grail 'legend' isn't some Romantic fairy tale either. It's a record 'of an ancient ritual, having for its ultimate object the initiation into the secret sources of Life, physical and spiritual.... In its esoteric 'Mystery' form it was freely utilized for the imparting of high spiritual teaching concerning the relation of Man to the divine Source of his being and the possibility of a sensible union between Man and God.'"

"A sensible union between Man and God?" Liz said. "No wonder the Elizabethans became so upset. Rufus had given the father of the Fitzgerald family access to the secrets that gave the royals divine authority."

"And by the time the Tudors realized it the Fitzgeralds had become a force to reckon with." I countered.

"Do you suppose Gerald was acting as an earthly surrogate for Rufus?" Liz said, giving the idea some thought.

Now *I* was curious. "How do you mean?"

"Rufus was the son of a bastard – William the Conqueror – and the grandson of Duke Robert the Devil and an open homosexual. Somehow I don't think conventional morality is an issue with these people – but power is and you can't retain royal power unless you make a sacred sacrifice." She said. "And Rufus knows he must die."

"It goes with the job." I replied. "Williamson says it right here. 'Rufus was killed on the morrow of Lammas' (2nd August); Becket on the fourth day of the kalends of January' (29th December) – dates with a definite pagan significance. The Divine Sacrifice took place on one of these festivals every seventh year.'"

"So you think Rufus was sending Gerald on a quest?"

"Rufus dreamed of expanding the kingdom into an empire. 'He compared himself to Alexander the Great.' Williamson says so. But you can't do that unless you fulfill the ritual and the ritual according to Jessie Weston is Mithraism."

"And Gerald is positioned to bring his family in line with that quest."

"It's eleven hundred A.D. The first Crusade was in 1099. Things are happening – Europeans are traipsing back and forth from Jerusalem – cultures are on the move – the twelfth century renaissance is growing – Gerald of Wales is a major player and records the Fitzgerald family's adventures in Ireland."

"So we have somewhere to look."

CHAPTER 11

"By 1170, the Roman Church had made it clear and the numerology confirmed it. Three was in – four was out. The church was replacing the Pythagorean mystic Tetrad with the holy trinity. The Old religion with its blood sacrifice, the Cathars and their 'Church of Love' and the Mithraic allusions to the Zodiac were impossible to Christianize – the numerology too revealing to reconcile."

"You're saying the Pythagorean Tetrakis was too powerful a metaphor?" Liz asked.

"I don't think the Tetrakis was a metaphor. I think it provided a blood connection that we've lost touch with. Remember that reference to the Afghan's mystical communications network from that Senate Select Committee on Narcotics? The U.S. government recognized the mystical power of the Afghans. Why not us? Pythagoreans were about sacred numbers and each individual's connection to their own creation. Birthdates – death-dates – ascending to heaven through the planetary alignments."

"So the numbers connected you directly to the Zodiac from your personal address – your birthdate – not as superstition but as fact." Liz observed.

"The Church was about faith and the priesthood. Four carried formulas that made talking to God a direct personal experience and the rising priestly class of bureaucrats, irrelevant."

"So the Gnostics had to be gotten rid of." Liz added.

"But the Gnosticism was embedded deeply in the Church. No matter what the Christian Church said, the old gods had to be appeased and by 1170 they had come roaring back to life. Williamson talks about it here on page 121. 'In the seventy years between the deaths, [of Rufus and Becket] Catharism, with the Troubadours, had spread over Christendom like a flame. In particular it was associated with the Angevin house which now ruled England. When Henry II came to be crowned in 1154 he brought with him Bernart of Ventadorn, the greatest of the Troubadours.... Nor was the Angevin house alone in devotion to Catharism. In that age – the eve of its greatest flowering – no less than thirteen of the reigning princes of Europe were of the Brethren.'"

Liz was impressed. "So the Cathars were really threatening to expose the Manichean core of Roman Christianity."

"And that's where the murder of Thomas Becket comes in." I said, trying to put it into perspective. "Becket's murder is portrayed as a classic struggle between church and state. But the 12th century state was nothing more than dozens of self-anointed royal families fighting with each other and over Rome's authority. According to Williamson, that struggle had nothing to do with Becket's death; it was the king's divinity that mattered. And the only way to get it was through a blood sacrifice. He believes Henry II and Rufus faced the same issue and that his archbishop's death is further proof of a recurring Gnostic agenda that he saw resurfacing back in 1947."

"But why was Becket sacrificed and Henry II allowed to live?" Liz asked.

"Williamson believes Rufus did have the option to choose Anselm – his archbishop but chose not to. Apparently the custom from Saxon times onward was that *either* the king or his Archbishop could stand in for the 'Devil'. In 1163, the ninth seven-year cycle after Rufus, Becket fled the country. But in 1170 he returned to England and reconciled with Henry, 'just in time for the death which he, like Rufus, anticipated.'"

"So the idea of using a sacred surrogate was already in the system." Liz said.

"It was a mathematical formula. The old religion was very clear about the divine sacrifice being either the king or his chief priest and it was all determined by the numbers."

Liz could see the picture forming. "Alright – the troubadours are connected to the French Cathars through the Welsh Grail legends but the Grail legends come from the ancient Persian religion that worshipped Mithra and was brought to Wales by the Roman legion. Mithra is a Manichaean Indo-European sun-god so similar to Christ he could be Christ or at least Christ's dark side. The Romans worshiped Mithra as Sol Invictus, the conquering son. Mithra, the warrior god anticipates the rise of Christianity completely. The Apostle Paul was a Mithraist before his conversion to Christianity but brought Mithra's 'armor of light' and a number of other Gnostic elements into his new religion to give it some punch. How am I doing?"

"Sounds good – continue." I said.

"Gerald's grandfather arrived in Wales with William the Conqueror and got caught up in the Mithraic rituals. As time went on the sons of Gerald became initiated into the cult of Mithraic black knights and by

1170 were about to conquer a country of their own." Liz said exploring the Williamson book.

"So all those Fitzgeralds listed as 'Adventurers' at the back of *Strongbow's Conquest of Ireland* are already Grail knights on the path to some higher order."

"They're physically connected to the mythology. They originated from the same castle in Dyfed as Bledri and their matriarch was a Princess from a royal line connected to King Arthur. What more proof do you need?" Liz asked.

"An explanation for my black knight dreams about the Nazis in World War II." I answered, growing frustrated. "Being related to black knights in the court of William Rufus and Henry II eight hundred ago years is one thing. Vivid dreams about being in a German Castle with Nazis and shouting out 'I renounce you' is something else."

Liz had already thought it out. "How's this?" She said, picking up a thin black book from the growing pile. "I read in this book *The Nazis and the Occult,"* that Himmler was trying to initiate his SS soldiers into the pagan Grail rituals. That's why he bought the castle at Wewelsburg so he could do it in secret."

"And the Fitzgeralds are directly connected to the pagan Grail rituals." I said.

Liz continued. "The book claims the SS officers were successful in 'their deep research into family genealogies'. They even sacrificed their own SS men to commune with the dead. Listen to this. 'For a week once a year, Himmler and his twelve Knights of the Round Table, in an atmosphere of secret confinement, gave themselves over completely to mental and spiritual exercises of visualization. The cult of ancestors, which Himmler fostered to give his men a feeling of being part of a great continuum, also took in the Germanic forebears of the Middle Ages while SS members delved into occult mysteries of the Grail legends.'"

"So the SS were invoking Mithraic initiation rites which are still out there in this great continuum?" I asked.

"And Mithraic initiation rites included a renunciation – like in your dream." Liz said, half grinning. "Look at Williamson page 55."

I picked up the book and read from the pages.

"'In the Mithraic ritual proper there were seven grades. These, in ascending order of importance were the Soldier, the Raven, the Persian, the Lion, the Hidden One, the Sun and the Father. After the initiate had passed various trials of fortitude, subdued his passions and made an act of renunciation, he was given the 'Crown of Mithra' ('Mithra is my Crown') and sealed on the forehead as a 'tried soldier of Mithra.'"

"So you dreamt of becoming a soldier of Mithra. You achieved eternal life." Liz said handing me the copy of the *Nazi's and the Occult*. "And here you are."

"And all because of Heinrich Himmler."

"That does explain your dream. The author even titled this Chapter *The Black Knights*."

"Okay, but why me?"

Liz looked at me strangely. "The Black Knights were delving into medieval rituals your family had been a part of. They went looking for their ancestors through these genealogical studies and found you."

I felt that sick feeling in my solar plexus again – facing something that felt oddly familiar but that my conscious mind believed impossible.

"My family had nothing to do with Germany." I said.

"But they *were* Catholic. Himmler was known as the Black Jesuit. He was steeped in ritual mind control. It says here, 'he copied the Jesuit mental disciplines but replaced the Catholic catechism with his own series of questions and answers. Didn't you spend eight years with the nuns learning the catechism?"

"Yes." I said realizing the connection. "And that's why they were in my dream. So you're saying he went looking for the Grail quest in medieval German families but couldn't find it so he went looking for it in families where he could."

"You did say that Cambrensis spoke of the twelfth century German emperor Frederick Barbarosa and we know the Fitzgeralds were identified with the mythology surrounding him." Liz said.

"Hitler did invoke his power by naming the invasion of the Soviet Union Operation Barbarossa." I added, thinking about it. "And Gerald of Wales wrote about a visit to Henry II by Barbarossa in the 1190s when he came looking for support for a third Crusade."

Liz was rolling now. "Then we've hit the motherlode. The secret rituals conducted at Wewelsburg had to be Mithraic. The Templar and Hospitaller knighthoods of the Middle Ages and the Jesuits were all initiated Grail knights and Himmler's SS resurrected their mission."

"So is the secret they're all looking for?" I said, accepting the proposition. "Resurrection?"

"Maybe that's what the sons and grandsons of Gerald went looking for when they went to Ireland. You can tell that Williamson sensed something was coming when he wrote the *Arrow and the Sword* and pulled in the Rector of St. Paul's and T.S. Eliot to confirm it. World War II and the rise of Nazism had shaken the Anglican hierarchy to the core. Himmler had reached out through time and pulled you into his vortex."

"That's a disturbing concept."

"No it's encouraging. It means the process is ongoing and real and you have completed its course. You went to Afghanistan on your own to get the truth about the Soviet invasion but you got something deeper. You went to where the Mithraic rituals began. The final degree in the Mithraic ritual is the Father. Your father only got as far as Carcassonne but never got to Ireland. You completed his journey for him in 1971. Now I think you're free to complete it for yourself. "

President Ronald Reagan presents Paul Nitze with the Presidential Medal of Freedom. The East Room of the White House, Washington, D.C., November 1985.

CHAPTER 12

September 1991

So if I was free to complete my journey why did I feel that something was missing – a connection I hadn't made. It grated on me.

"There's got to be something else." I said to Liz as I stared at the growing stack of research.

"We've covered MK Ultra, JFK, Vietnam, Daniel Ellsberg and the *Pentagon Papers* – Walter Bowart and *Operation Mind Control,* The CIA and the *Control of Candy Jones…*"

"I talked to her." Liz said. "Remember?"

"I do. I also remember Fred Kaplan and the *Wizards of Armageddon,* Marchetti and Marks and *The CIA and the Cult of Intelligence* and that the OSS director William Donovan referred to his agents as Knights Templar. We've bought so many books, Barnes and Noble will be putting us on their board of directors. But how does it work? All that political stuff we did. All that Cold War, Afghanistan and the Soviet Union. Afghanistan's over. The Berlin Wall has come down. What's it all got to do with this Grail business? Where does it connect to what's happening now?"

"The library called and said they'd found another book you'd be interested in. *Lancelot and Guenevere.* I told them you'd be down to pick it up."

"Great. Just what we need. Another romance about the Holy Grail."

"Do you want it or not?"

"Of course I want it. I need to get out anyway."

The 1970 edition of *Lancelot and Guenevere: A Study on the Origins of Courtly Love* came with two strange coincidences. Not only did the 12th century Grail Romances – made so popular by Chrétien de Troyes and favored by the Troubadours – originate in Ireland "centuries earlier." But, one of its authors possessed a surname that embodied the Cold War, Team B and perpetual hostility toward the Soviet Union – William Albert Nitze.

"Nitze's an unusual name I said to Liz thumbing through the diminutive book. You don't suppose this guy and Paul Nitze are related, do you?"

"Wouldn't that be unusual." Liz said as she picked up the phone and called back to the library.

"William Nitze is Paul Nitze's father." She said listening to the librarian. "And if you didn't notice. Paul Nitze's father, your father and my father all share the same name. You're doppelgangers."

So what if Nitze's father and mine shared the same name? Big deal, but four synchronicities together left me wondering. Paul Nitze was all over the Cold war and even before. He'd testified to Congress prior to World War II that if he had to choose between Nazi Germany and Great Britain as allies, he'd choose the Germans. He'd joined together with John Kenneth Galbraith and George Ball on the Strategic Bombing survey in 1945. He'd drafted the blueprint for the National Security State with National Security Directive 68, and been behind the post-Sputnik run up of the Cold War in 1957 with a special panel of outside experts called the Gaither Committee. He'd campaigned for higher defense spending through a pro-war business group called the Committee on the Present Danger and been the driving force behind Team B. Paul Nitze was the singularly most important man in the U.S. for over-hyping the Soviet threat and here he was the son of an influential Medieval scholar focused on the origins of the Grail rituals and their Irish roots.

"Where did this guy come from?" I asked Liz.

"You don't want me to call the library again, do you?" She said frowning.

"No. I'll call them myself."

My inquiry produced a recent book on Nitze by Strobe Talbott called *Master of the Game*. I'd had a personal experience with Talbott following the first trip to Afghanistan in 1981 when *TIME* magazine published an interview he'd done with Afghan President Babrak Karmal. *TIME* claimed Talbott's interview was the first granted to an American journalist. But when I challenged it they'd put the blame on the Afghans for lying and then onto the fact that I "appear to have done so independently" and not as an "American news/journalist." The fact that I was an American journalist not working for *TIME* and had appeared on CBS News interviewing Karmal seven months before Talbott even got there apparently didn't qualify as being the first.

Talbott's *Master of Game* was a mostly predictable and bloodless account of Nitze's career on Wall Street and at various high level U.S. government posts from Roosevelt to Truman to Kennedy to Johnson. Nitze was a high roller. But when it came to his brief-telling of Nitze's early years and the influences on his life – something sprang off the pages.

"Talbott says that Nitze was travelling in Germany with his family when World War I broke out. He also says the family name derives from the Greek goddess of victory Nike, and that the family migrated to Germany from the Russian steppe centuries ago. He went to Harvard and Wall Street, made lots of money, then took an "intellectual sabbatical" back at Harvard. He was so drawn to Oswald Spengler's *Decline of the West* and the Russian mystic Ouspensksy he almost chucked Wall Street for philosophy. He went back to Wall Street for the rest of the depression then got invited into the Roosevelt administration by colleague James Forrestal."

"The one who jumped out the window James Forrestal?"

"The first secretary of defense after they changed it from 'War' to Defense." I responded. "He also visited Germany and met with Hitler after the Nazis came to power. He referred to them as damned impressive."

"So Paul Nitze is where the ancient story meets the 20th century – the Grail romances, the Greek gods, World War II, Nazi Germany and the Cold War." Liz said with a curious grin.

"He's almost mythical. He started his own school of international relations at Johns Hopkins. He moved policy through four administrations at the highest levels then went to work for Ronald Reagan as an Arms Control negotiator. *He is* the Master of the Game. What are the chances he knows all about Afghanistan and what's been going on there?"

***

Paul Nitze opened new doors into those unexplored German connections I'd dreamt about – Wewelsburg, Himmler, Grail legends? There's no way he didn't know the secret – the old secret going back through the centuries, the connections to the Greek gods, family intrigues through medieval Europe and Frederick Barbarossa long before there was a Soviet Union or even a United States. The pieces were falling into place. And then came a message from somewhere I hadn't expected.

"You woke me up before he got to tell me his name." I heard Alissa cry out from her bedroom next door as Liz tried to wake her up for school.

"Who's name?" Liz asked. "I was dreaming with dad's father and this guy in a funny suit and hat and he said he was eight hundred years old."

As I woke up I felt a sharp pain in my back and shoulder, almost as if Alissa's dream had shot through me like a bolt of lightning. By the time I joined the conversation she was already at the kitchen table and halfway through breakfast.

"Tell it to me again." I asked. "And fill in all the details. Please?"

"We were all staying in a house by a lake. I had gone to a local dance school and was asked to perform in their recital. Backstage between performances these two men approached me. At first I thought it was you with red hair," she said looking suspiciously at my head. "You looked so alike. But the longer I stared the more he started to look like that picture of your father in the living room."

"Then what happened." I asked.

"He reached down and gave me a hug and said, 'do you know who I am?' And I said I think you're my grandfather. Then he asked. 'Did my son marry a nice woman?' And I said yes."

"You said there was someone with him." I added.

"He had dark hair and was very tanned and muscular and was wearing an orange and red plaid suit with bellbottom pants and a matching golf cap. I asked him how old he was and he said 'Oh about eight hundred years.' Your father then turned to me and said 'Alissa, I'd like to introduce my friend…' And mom woke me up."

"Ahh, I see. And that's why you were yelling."

"I was mad because I didn't get to find out his name."

***

"So who do you think it was?" Liz asked after Alissa had gone off to school.

"I don't know. A spirit guide? A plaid bellbottomed suit and matching golf hat? I don't think my father knew anyone who dressed like that. I certainly don't."

"But he's obviously a messenger from your father." Liz said.

"So what's the message?"

"Eight hundred years. He came to tell you you're on the right track. But he wants you to know you haven't finished. You're not done because you haven't put yourself into the story yet. That story goes back eight hundred years and it's not just history. It's personal to you.

Chapter 13

So we took Alissa's dream as a signal beacon and followed it.

"Didn't the Fitzgeralds come to Ireland eight hundred years ago?" Liz asked.

"The first expedition began in 1169, but the full invasion with Strongbow came in 1170." I said.

"Either way it's still the twelfth century. You're family has been in Ireland that long. In fact your family had been in Ireland for exactly eight hundred years the year we met in 1970. AND your father asked about me."

I'd never thought of it that way. "So you think Alissa's dream is about that?"

"I do. I think someone is calling from the past. I mean really calling. Your father is reconnecting to you through Alissa and his mysterious eight hundred year old friend is his messenger."

"So do we write another screenplay – a book? I don't know how to write about something like that." I said, realizing I was hitting an invisible wall.

"Umberto Eco did it with *Foucault's Pendulum*. He went back to the fourteenth century with *The Name of the Rose*. We're just going back a little further." Liz said.

"Yea. But that was as a novel. Our research on the background of the Fitzgeralds and William Rufus is real." I said thinking about it. "And we know that the Mithraic rituals were brought to Britain by the Romans."

"But it's still all a narrative. And you dreamt about black knights and now we've found this Teutonic connection to Paul Nitze." Liz said. "Don't you see, it's a mystery. There's this whole storm of events spiraling around that started in the twelfth century with the marriage of Gerald and Nest and Alissa just met a rider on the storm."

"So it's like a calling from the past." I said. "Then let's put all the research together in one place. We'll make an outline of all the stuff we've found and what we think is going on." I offered.

"I like that." Liz said, smiling sweetly. "And we'll call it 'The Voice.'"

By the end of 1991 there really was nowhere left for us to turn but to dream. We'd left our Afghan experience behind and dug into writing and researching about the merging fields of militarized wonder-drugs, bio technology and computers. The future looked like it was coming to an end the way it had begun – with a big bang. The analogue world of cause and effect was transforming to digital before our eyes. We were entering a world where anything goes and we could see it had no place to go but wrong.

The Cold War was getting shaky in Eastern Europe. What Paul Warnke had told us he'd discovered about the Soviet system running out of steam in 1968 was playing itself out. Afghanistan was tearing itself apart. The scripts we'd written were praised by producers but were way outside of Hollywood's narrow vision. The material world we'd come from seemed to be following some preset plan for self-annihilation. And that's when we came upon another book written during World War II by a man named Paul Winkler titled *The Thousand Year Conspiracy.* And it all started to make sense.

"None of the various theories of sociology which have inspired Western thought in the last 80 years makes possible a complete explanation of what is happening in the world today. This is due to the fact that most of these doctrines have regarded the evolution of mankind as an organic whole. They have neglected to take into consideration an anachronistic survival of a creation of the Middle Ages, which is arising out of the distant past."

Winkler's words were like manna from heaven. Here was a guy writing fifty years before our time who'd figured out there was an ancient esoteric agenda running events from behind the scenes.

Although he was focused on blaming Nazi Germany and absolved the West of any responsibility there was no way the Germans were alone in maintaining a thousand year occult conspiracy. He even admitted the whole thing began in the twelfth century because of the bitter competition between the Papacy and the Holy Roman Empire and that Emperor Frederick Barbarossa's prestige suffered a heavy blow with the Pope's success in the first Crusade. The subsequent consecration of the Knights of the Temple of King Solomon (the Templars) and the Order of St. John (the Hospitallers) as Papal armies only exacerbated the rivalry and made the creation of an exclusively German Knighthood, inevitable.

"So why was the Teutonic Knighthood such a problem?" Liz asked. "Weren't they all under the control of the Pope?"

"That was the idea but Winkler claims that Frederick subverted it for his own purposes and that is where the conspiracy began." I said. "He explains it right here: under 'Imperial Monks, a skillful manoeuvre: to allow establishment of a Knights' Order, at first of solely religious appearance so that it would have the consecration by the Pope indispensable to its prestige. It was not until its existence was quite secure, that the Teutonic Order more openly put itself at the service of the Imperial plans for expansion.'"

"So it all goes back to Frederick Barbarossa." Liz said.

"Or Barbarossa's ego. He was of the Hohenstaufen family and had himself proclaimed *Dominus Mundi* 'Master of the World.' Winkler claims that because the other two Knighthoods were older and more respected it "was preferable to turn to other lands in order to secure actual conquests.'"

Liz laughed. "And the Germans never stopped securing other conquests. I think I get it. But where do the Fitzgeralds fit in?"

"I'm coming to it. You remember that statement in the *Expugnatio* where Reimund gives the speech about descending from Troy? Well Gerald of Wales claimed that the Fitzgeralds who wound up in Ireland *did* descend from the Trojans who founded Rome. During the Papal wars with Barbarosa in the twelfth century they found themselves on the losing side and had to get out of town."

"So that's the Italian connection your Uncle Harold is always talking about."

"He's done a lot of research. JFK even talked about it on a trip to Italy when he was President." I said.

"So how does it work?" Liz asked.

"There's two variations. "One goes back to Otho. Remember that Walter is Gerald's father. This mysterious Otho is Gerald's grandfather. According to this one Otho descended from the dukes of Tuscany, who moved from Florence to Normandy and was already an English Baron by the time of the conquest in 1066. Nothing is really known about Otho except the name derives from the Old Norse Óttárr and that he had some very special status with the Normans. But he is real."

"And what's the other variation?" Liz asked smiling.

"That the Geraldines are related to the Gherardini family of Florence. Three brothers named Gherardo, Maurizio and Tommaso arrived in Wales from Italy just in time for the Norman invasion of Ireland. After the invasion the names became anglicized into Gerald, Maurice and Thomas who founded the Fitzgerald dynasty."

"And who are the Gherardinis?"

"Feudal lords of Florence – Supported Frederick during the Ghibelline wars against the Guelphs."

"There's Frederick Barbarosa again."

"Became Holy Roman emperor in 1152. Cambrensis mentions Frederick Barbarosa and the Third Crusade. Harold told me Fredrick struggled with the Pope for control of the empire. The Gherardinis wound up on the losing side."

Liz was stunned. "So the Geraldines are connected to the Holy Roman Empire."

"It's just a theory. But the mythology of the Earls of Desmond *is* the same as the mythology as Barbarosa and King Arthur. They never really died but were taken to some magical place to rest and heal before returning to save their people at the end time."

"Saving their people at the end of time. That could come in handy." Liz admitted. "So tell me about the Knights Templar."

"I think Baigent and Leigh described it the best. After the first Crusade (1066 to 1099) the European nobility saw the need to create militant Holy Orders to maintain their control of the Holy Land."

"Right – the Knights Templars and the Hospitallers." Liz said.

"Some joined to get their sins forgiven – remember these guys were already out there killing and robbing on behalf of their feudal barons. Some joined out of religious zeal."

"And the others?" Liz asked.

"Some people believe the Priory of Sion families pushed the Crusades because they wanted to get back the control of Jerusalem."

"What do you mean by get back?" Liz asked.

"That's where it gets complicated. The Merovingian Kings of France (AD 451-751) traced their lineage back to the House of David. According to Laurence Gardner a Grail researcher, they believed King Solomon was the model of earthly kingship. And their descendants had a lot of influence with the Pope."

"So these families created the Templars?"

"The Hospitallers were already providing protection and lodging to Catholic Pilgrims. The Templars weren't necessary."

"So what did they do there?" Liz asked.

"They set up shop at the Al Aqsa Mosque on the site of Solomon's Temple and started digging."

"What's digging under Solomon's Temple's got to do with Jesus Christ?" Liz observed.

"Nothing. And therein lies the first problem with the Knights Templar. Some say they were looking for the Ark of the Covenant, others say it was treasure. Whatever it was they immediately established contacts with some pre-Christian Gnostic sects – Essene/Zadokite/Nazarean mystery schools. Liz grew intrigued as I continued. "Nazareans?"

"According to Baigent and Leigh these groups in Palestine had knowledge of all the ancient mysteries – Egyptian, Greek, Zoroastrian, Mithraic and everything in between. And that's where we come to the second problem with the Templars."

Liz caught on before I could say it. "The Fitzgeralds."

"Oh, are they ever. And that's where our thesis, JFK and the reason why he was murdered starts to come alive."

Templars (brother-minister, brother-knight and brother-priest. *Münchener Bilderbogen*, 1870.

Chapter 14

"So how did this mystique about the Templars come about?" Liz asked.

"Narrative creation." I responded. "Their backers created the story they wanted people to believe. In 1118 the whole idea of warrior monks was anathema to Christianity. Murder was a mortal sin for which you went to hell."

"How did they get around that?" Liz asked.

"*De Laude Novae Militiae, In Praise of the New Knighthood.* At the behest of a French noble, St. Bernard of Clairvaux redefined killing infidels from homicide to malicide and lobbied the Pope on the Templar's behalf."

"And the Pope accepted it?" She asked, shocked.

"And then some. Listen to this."

> *Indeed, the knights of Christ fight the battles of their lord in safety...The soldier of Christ kills safely: he dies the more safely. He serves his own interests in dying and Christ's interests in killing!.. He is the instrument of God for the punishment of malefactors and the defence of the just. Indeed, when he kills a malefactor this is not homicide but malicide, and he is accounted Christ's legal executioner against evildoers.*

"So he wrote up a blanket pardon ahead of time. How did that go over in the Christian countries?" Liz asked.

"Like a charm. The Templars got rich and famous as their ranks swelled with the sons of noble families. Eventually everybody, including the Hospitallers and Teutonic Knights got into the act, even Strongbow."

"Richard de Clare? The Earl of Pembroke became a Templar?"

"Richard and Gilbert de Clare were patrons of the Hospitallers and the Templars. Strongbow's support was so generous he was named an honorary member. The Templars got to invent the first ever banking empire with branches stretching from Europe to the Middle East."

"And put Europe's royalty in their debt by loaning them money for wars against each other, I'll bet." Liz added with a smirk.

"At the time it was forbidden for Christian money lenders to charge interest. Only the Jews could do that. So the Pope allowed the Templars a special dispensation and within a few years they were the wealthiest and most powerful institution in the Christian world." I said.

"Who interfaced and traded with Jewish and Moslem bankers in the Holy Land." Liz added, taking it one step further.

"Think BCCI, the Bank of Commerce and Credit International that funded the Afghan 'holy warriors' and created al Qaeda. That's the model BCCI followed – the warrior Knights of the Temple with their white robes and red crosses got to break the law at will because they were fighting infidels." I concluded. "God's bankers."

"I didn't realize the corruption went that far back." Liz said, shaking her head in disbelief.

"Baigent and Leigh think the whole Templar raison d'étre was just a front for St. Bernard's Cistercian Order and the Duke of Champagne's secret plot to rule Europe."

"Is that what you think?" Liz asked.

"The monasteries acted like mini-states in the Middle Ages. But the Templars were a cut above even that. Innocent II issued a Papal bull – *Omne datum optimum* – granting them 'Every great gift' which exempted them from all authority on earth – secular or temporal – except for the pope himself. Henry I didn't like Pope Innocent but Clairvaux persuaded him to go along. The Templars did pretty much whatever they wanted in Europe and the Holy Land until the French King – Philip IV – who was deeply in debt to them – ordered them arrested and charged with heretical practices. Then on November 22, 1307 under pressure from Philip, Pope Clement V issued the papal bull *Pastoralis Praeeminentiae* instructing all the monarchs of Europe to seize their assets. And then the Holy War really began."

"So if the Templars were really just corrupt bankers like BCCI, why are they still revered as these pure spiritual guardians of the Holy Grail?"

"Popular fiction – twelfth century Angevin propaganda, eighteenth century Masonic myth-making and Sir Walter Scott's nineteenth century romantic stories. There was no Christian *Grail* until Chretien de Troyes composed the narrative poem *Le Conte du Graal* in the late twelfth century."

"It didn't begin until the Twelfth century?"

"William Nitze and Tom Peete Cross wrote about it on page one of *Lancelot and Guenevere*. 'The story of Lancelot and Guenevere makes its first appearance as literature in the Roman de la Charrete (Lancelot) by

Chrétien sometime around 1177. But the theme of the story, under different names, was current in Ireland centuries earlier. Chrétien composed the poem at the behest of his patroness, Marie of Champagne, and to please her he made it the vehicle of a system of Courtly Love.'"

"Ah. So we have another reference to the Court of Champagne."

"And their role in spreading 'Courtly Love.'"

"Meaning Troubadour and Cathar." Liz observed.

"Baigent and Leigh draw a direct line from the Templars to Wolfram von Eschenbach's *Parzival* a few years later. Parzival is an Arthurian hero who sets out to find the Holy Grail and portrays the Templars as the 'guardians of the Grail and of the Grail Family.' He established the Templar Grail narrative. Eschenbach claimed to have heard the story from one 'Guiot de Provins, a Templar scribe and propagandist' they write. They believe another version of the story called Perlesvaus was actually written by a Templar soldier."

"So explain to me how they get to claim they're the guardians of the Grail, based on a French retelling of an *Irish story* that has absolutely nothing to do with Solomon's Temple?" Liz asked.

"Because, according to Baigent and Lee, they possess a secret and whoever possesses the secret gets magical powers."

"Well that makes perfect sense." Liz said, exasperated.

"I know it sounds ridiculous but there is something that raised my curiosity." I said as Liz looked at me suspiciously. "He actually puts the responsibility onto the Scots and Robert the Bruce." I told her. "Let me read it to you. 'By Bruce's time, Celtic tradition, Grail mystique and Templar values had fused into a single, often confusing, amalgam. Thus, for example, there is the well-known Celtic 'cult of the head' – the ancient Celtic belief that the head contained the soul, and that the heads of vanquished adversaries should therefore be severed and preserved."

"And what about it?" Liz asked, confused.

"Severed heads were central to Masonic rituals and the Masons claim descent from the Templars. Skull and Bones? The last earl of Desmond's head was sent to Queen Elizabeth and piked on London Bridge after she communed with it. And then there's that day in Dallas in Dealey Plaza at a Masonic triangle when JFK suffered the Celtic triple death – strangled by a shot through the throat, shot in the back and then decapitated with the third shot. Researchers claim his brain is missing."

"You said the power of the Templars had something to do with magical powers."

"The Templars were tortured to reveal their secret. Baigent and Leigh write 'the Templars had their own *cult of the head.* Among the charges preferred against them, and one to which a number of knights pleaded guilty, was that of worshipping a mysterious severed head sometimes known as *Baphomet.*'"

Liz grimaced. "This is getting bizarre."

"It gets better. When the king's officers raided the Paris Temple on October 13, 1307, they found a silver reliquary containing the skull of a woman. When the formal charges were drawn up against them they listed that in each provincial Templar headquarters they worshipped severed heads as idols."

"Worshipped them to do what?" Liz asked.

"The Templars testified that the heads could, make riches, make a tree flower and the land germinate. And if that wasn't enough it could save them."

"Well they couldn't have been found guilty of being saved, given they were all burned at the stake."

"Not all of them. Some of the Templars lived to tell the tale of what the Papal machinery had done to them. Some were absorbed into the other knighthoods. But there were others. The Templars had their own fleet of ships, a vast treasure and connections all over the known world."

"So they could have bought their way out of it." Liz realized.

"Easily and that's where the revenge motif comes in. The Pope confiscated their properties and delivered them to the Hospitallers. After being expelled from the Holy Land the Hospitallers relocated to Malta and changed their name to the Knights of Malta. Over the centuries a lot of prominent Catholics became members including Allen Dulles, Alexandre de Marenches and Joe Kennedy." I said.

"Grounds for revenge?" Liz asked.

"Holy vengeance. The last grand master of the Paris Temple, Jacques de Molay promised that God would get even and some believe the cause was passed down to the Templar's successors."

"You mean the Masons."

"Baigent and Leigh claim there's no actual proof the Templars transformed into Masonic secret societies, but don' tell that to a Mason. The Reformation stoked hatred for the Catholic Church. JFK was hated for being a Catholic when he ran for President and you didn't have to be a Mason to feel that way."

"But why do the Masons emulate the Templars?"

"I think the men of the Enlightenment liked the narrative of mystical illumination. They liked the idea of an ancient secret guiding them to rule the world."

"You're kidding."

"No, really. It's a brotherhood – a secret society. Men get to prove themselves and the girls couldn't join. The Templars were vehemently anti-female, dedicated to celibacy and forbidden to so much as touch a woman including their mothers. They considered men who consorted with women to be evil. I read in this book written by a Mason that sex was considered so evil the Templars were given their own cemeteries so that even in death they wouldn't have to mix with men who consorted with women."

"No wonder they hated JFK." Liz said.

"The Elizabethan roaring boys who wiped out the Desmond Fitzgeralds hated them for being Catholics. But I think they hated them for loving women more."

He's a District Attorney.
He will risk his life,
the lives of his family,
everything he holds dear
for the one thing he holds sacred....
the truth.

KEVIN COSTNER

AN OLIVER STONE FILM

JFK

The Story That Won't Go Away

WARNER BROS. PRESENTS

IN ASSOCIATION WITH LE STUDIO CANAL+, REGENCY ENTERPRISES AND ALCOR FILMS AN IXTLAN CORPORATION AND AN A. KITMAN HO PRODUCTION AN OLIVER STONE FILM KEVIN COSTNER

KEVIN BACON TOMMY LEE JONES LAURIE METCALF GARY OLDMAN MICHAEL ROOKER JAY O. SANDERS AND SISSY SPACEK CO-PRODUCER CLAYTON TOWNSEND PRODUCTION DESIGNER VICTOR KEMPSTER

DIRECTOR OF PHOTOGRAPHY ROBERT RICHARDSON MUSIC BY JOHN WILLIAMS EXECUTIVE PRODUCER ARNON MILCHAN BASED ON THE BOOKS "ON THE TRAIL OF THE ASSASSINS" BY JIM GARRISON AND "CROSSFIRE: THE PLOT THAT KILLED KENNEDY" BY JIM MARRS

SCREENPLAY BY OLIVER STONE & ZACHARY SKLAR PRODUCED BY A. KITMAN HO AND OLIVER STONE DIRECTED BY OLIVER STONE

DOLBY STEREO

SOUNDTRACK ALBUM ON ELEKTRA RECORDS, CASSETTES & CD'S

Chapter 15

"I just read a review of Oliver Stone's *JFK* movie in the Globe and we're going to have to see it." Liz said, putting down the paper. "The review says it opens a lot of new doors."

"Oliver Stone and JFK. That's an interesting combination." I said, flashing back to our frustrating experiences in Hollywood. "Maybe we should have gone to see him instead of ABC News back in 1987 and made a feature film of it. Now that would have been a kick."

By a strange coincidence, the collapse of the Soviet Union in December 1991 and the debut of Oliver Stone's movie *JFK* occurred simultaneously. Stone was one of the biggest A-list directors of the 1980s with hits like *Wall Street, Platoon, Born on the Fourth of July* and *The Doors*. He was asking a lot of questions about America that people wanted answered but despite our shared interest in controversial politics, we'd never thought of contacting him.

***

"He really got it with this one." Liz said, the morning after the screening. "I didn't know anything about David Ferrie being a priest in an underground religious cult. That changes everything."

"I read where he trained for the priesthood but was dismissed by two seminaries. But he became a bishop in something called the Orthodox Old Catholic Church of North America."

"And what about that scene with him, Kevin Bacon and Tommy Lee Jones playing Greek gods? You know they do that stuff in these secret societies. And they take it very seriously."

"They don't need secret societies to do *that*." I said. "And speaking of *that* I had a very unusual dream last night with Kevin Bacon."

"Unusual how?" Liz asked, her curiosity piqued.

"Well I heard they once tried putting subliminal advertising in movies to get you to buy Coca Cola but I've never heard anybody getting pitched in a dream by an actor playing a role."

Liz was shocked. "What?"

"There's a lot of memorable things in that movie." I said. "But there was nothing in Kevin Bacon's performance that might cause that. It was like I picked up on him doing an acting exercise – fooling around to get into character. And it was very real."

"Sounds like some of that mind control stuff we researched for the X-File script we wrote." Liz said, laughing. "Maybe there's another book on screenwriting you didn't come across."

"The idea that secret societies were behind that day in Dallas makes sense – given what we've learned about the Templars – the Orphic mysteries and their contempt for Rome." I replied.

"I think Oliver Stone would love the idea behind *The Voice* and the way the Fitzgeralds fit into the thousand year conspiracy." Liz added.

"Yea. They're all over it from Rufus to Queen Elizabeth I." I said, thinking about the overlapping events and personalities. "Actually Winkler believes the conspiracy traces back to Egypt and was brought to Greece and contained in the Eleusinian Mysteries."

"That's a lot of mysteries." Liz said smirking.

"Well it's no mystery that whatever they were was exclusively male and secret. Winkler writes that Plato mentioned them several times with reverence and his teachings appear in many ways to have been inspired by them. Listen to this. 'While *the secret* of the Mysteries was carefully guarded and their exposure punishable by death it is written they were held by an Orphic brotherhood who brought the secrets of the Pharaohs from Egypt and that they involved a great number of ascetic rules in which the mysteries were revealed in Seven Degrees.'"

"Just like the Mithraic mysteries." Liz said as I handed her the Winkler book. "And here I thought of Plato as purely rational."

"Plato's secrets are hidden in the rational." I pointed out. "He explains it right here. 'Western civilization with its uncompromising rationalism has always refused to believe in anything that was beyond pure reason – except when it comes to the strictly religious domain. But religion, the purely mystical content of religion, is for us today entirely separate from science and philosophy. For the Greeks, science and philosophy were closely connected with the Mysteries."

Liz read on further. "Some Greek authors actually credit the teachings of the Mysteries with having brought forth civilization itself. The reason for the secrecy was justified in the following manner by the ancient Greeks. 'Truth is of divine origin and is revealed only to the few who are willing to work for it ... having received the truth with no effort they would not appreciate it and might misuse it.'"

Winkler was an eye opener. "So what if they did appreciate it and still misused it?" I said. "Western civilization rationalized the esoteric out of existence and doesn't see the evil it does anymore."

"It sounds like an early formulation of Burnham's formal and the real." Liz said, scratching her head. "The formal to keep the peasants in line and real for the elites."

***

Whatever the ultimate purpose of the Mysteries, they had served to establish an exclusive esoteric religion for the few and a simple exoteric religion for the uninitiated masses. *Do what you're told or you'll go to hell.* Maintaining this secret created the need to give "civilization" an outward appearance that "gave rise to a widespread illusion," according to Winkler – that "mankind was moving slowly but surely in the direction of progress."

But the truth was – mankind wasn't.

"Western man thought that *decency* and *cooperation* had been accepted as everlasting principles for the guidance of humanity." Winkler wrote. "Our fathers and ourselves did not realize that the lupine brand of thought which had once characterized feudal Europe lived on..." and would spread far beyond Nazi Germany after World War II.

***

I'd spent the last four years perfecting my screenwriting skills and we'd developed some solid scripts. Taking a story spun off the movie *JFK* seemed like a good idea and like a miracle by mid-January we'd secured a meeting in New York for April 20, 1992. There was plenty of time to prepare but where to begin?

"It's becoming clear." I said to Liz after thinking it through. "Over the centuries the public's been sold a romantic fiction of the Knights Templar as a Christian Knighthood protecting something elusive and mystical called the Holy Grail. But it's also clear that the public has no idea what the Templars had really been founded to do. The OSS and CIA used them as an inspiration for their agents just the way the Nazi SS had used the Teutonic Knights. Everybody knows now what the SS had been created to do. But if the CIA had also been modeled on an extremist life-denying Orphic cult, what had the CIA been created to do?"

"Do you think Oliver Stone knows about the Knights Templar and how their reputation evolved over the centuries into a self-fulfilling myth?" Liz asked.

"Well if he doesn't he's going to know it by the time we've finished putting our research together." I said.

***

In addition to Baigent, Leigh and Lincoln and the Grail researcher Lawrence Gardner, the Italian medievalist and philosopher Umberto Eco brought the Templars back to life in his 1988 novel *Foucault's Pendulum.* Dispensing with the romantic legends, Eco had taken the suspicions about their purpose and given it a twentieth century reality check.

"According to Eco," I told Liz. "The Templars were created as an elite vanguard to obtain and secure occult secrets in the Holy Land and make ready the return of the true Messiah. As structured by their Cathar backers in France and England, they'd become a powerful autonomous deep-state within medieval society with an apocalyptic plan to fulfill biblical prophecy and remove anybody who stood in the way."

"That sound like the CIA to me." Liz said.

"Exactly. A rigid, orthodox Church was no match for their diabolical ingenuity and life-denying doctrine. The Cathars' focus on the cosmic battle between good and evil and God's time-ending judgement of the material world was a powerful seduction. And over the centuries they positioned themselves for victory as the second millennium neared."

"It's not like what Umberto Eco is saying isn't true." Liz said when I told her what he was revealing. "But it is a novel."

"It is," I admitted. "But the eighteenth century Frenchman who wrote a pamphlet about it, Charles-Louis Cadet de Gassicourt is real and apparently the illegitimate son of Louis XV."

"So what are you saying?"

"That whether Eco's or de Gassicourt's story is true or not, the idea that the French Revolution was the work of a long term conspiracy makes sense. It also makes sense that if such a conspiracy existed, the Catholic John Fitzgerald Kennedy would be viewed as a major obstacle to their plans."

***

As with our experience in Afghanistan, the more we probed the more the official narrative fell apart. And now that I knew what clues to look for, a powerful alternative narrative began to emerge.

"I found this definition of the Templars in that encyclopedia of Freemasonry we bought at that old bookstore on Venice Beach," I told Liz.

"The sect of Ishmaelites, which goes back into the history of Islam, gave birth in the last quarter of the 11th century to that of the ASSASSINS. Its political and philosophical doctrine is supposed to have been unfolded slowly and with great circumspection in nine degrees. The Assassins were content with 7. On this sect, order or society it has been affirmed that Hugh de Payens modeled the Knights Templar. A.E. Waite *A New Encyclopedia of Freemasonry*, 1925."

"Ah. And so the truth is revealed," Liz said, smiling.

Baptism of Clovis. Clovis was the son of Childeric I, a Merovingian king of the Salian Franks, and Basina, a Thuringian princess. The dynasty he founded is named after his supposed ancestor, Merovich. Clovis succeeded his father to become king at the age of 15 in 481. By Jacob van Maerlant, circa 1325.

Chapter 16

And so the truth about the origin of the Knights Templar was coming into focus. But how did the transfer to Masonry take place?

"So are the Freemasons the modern carriers of what the Templars were created to do?" Liz asked.

"Umberto Eco wasn't the first to draw the connection between the Templars and Freemasonry. A lot of authors over the years tried to nail it down and failed – but there are some clues. Look here. De Gassicourt's 1797 pamphlet *Le Tombeau De Jacques Molai* traced the French Revolution, as 'the work of a long line of conspirators from the Templars and Assassins through Cromwell and the Jesuits 'to Robespierre and Babeuf.' It's a matter of record that Napoleon was a member of the Templars extreme Illuminated lodge of Lyons and Gassicourt later became Napoleon's personal pharmacist."

"So Gassicourt should have known the inside story." Liz added.

"You'd think. But it's still meaningless unless you find the common purpose to tie it together. And that's where a book published in Dublin in 1884 titled *Grand Orient Freemasonry Unmasked* by Monsignor George F. Dillon comes in. If the Knights Templars were agents for the Merovingian line of the House of David and wanted their Jewish King to be the King of Kings wouldn't they want all the other kingdoms under their control?"

"Of course." Liz said.

"So what would they do?" I asked.

Liz smiled. "Bring in the Jews."

"The Kabbalistic Jews. Look at this footnote on page14. 'The Jewish writer, Bernard Lazare, so remarkable for his hatred of Our Divine and Catholic Church, writes it is certain that there were Jews at the cradle of Freemasonry – Kabbalistic Jews, as is proved by some of the rites that have been preserved. During the years that preceded the French Revolution, they probably entered in greater numbers still into the councils of society and founded secret societies themselves. The Jews have swarmed into it (Freemasonry) from the earliest times and controlled the higher grades and councils of the ancient and accepted Scottish rite since the beginning of the 19th century. There were Jews around Weishaupt, and Martinez de Pasqualis, a Jew of Portuguese origin, organized numerous groups of Illuminati in France."

"And who is Weishaupt?" Liz asked.

"Adam Weishaupt – founder of the Bavarian Illuminati – former Jesuit. Wanted to replace Christianity with a religion of reason. Inspired the French Revolution and some say the American."

"Illuminati?" Liz said, thinking. "They're supposed to be behind everything."

"The hidden controllers. It's been written they go all the way back to Zoroaster in ancient Persia six thousand years before Plato. Split off from his priesthood – the Magi to act and direct the course of human civilization. Established the sacred Kingship rituals to control the royal bloodlines and programmed people to accept it."

"Like with Rufus." Liz said. So how does that get us back to the Templars?"

"Look at page 42." I said, reading on. "Monsignor Segur, Bishop of Grenoble informs us that the real secret of Freemasonry consisted even then (1747) in disbelief in the Divinity of Christ, and a determination to replace that doctrine which is the very foundation of Christianity, by Naturalism or Rationalism. Mgr. Segur tells us that Laelius Socinus, the heresiarch and founder of Unitarians gave his followers the title of Freemasons, and invented the allegory of the Temple of Solomon. This temple, destroyed by Christ for the Christian order, was to be restored by Freemasonry after the Christ and the Christian order should be obliterated by conspiracy and revolution. The state of Nature was the 'Hiram' whose murder Masonry was to avenge; and which, having previously removed Christ was to resuscitate Hiram, by re-building the Temple of Nature as it had been before."

Liz stood for a moment, transfixed before motioning for the book.

"Mgr. Segur moreover," She said, reading, "connects the modern Freemasonry with the Jews and the Templars, as well as Socinus. The Jews for many centuries previous to the Reformation had formed secret societies for their own protection and for the destruction of Christianity which persecuted them, and which they much hated. The rebuilding of the Temple of Solomon was the dream of their lives. They had special reason to welcome with joy such heretics as were cast off by Catholicism. It is therefore, not at all improbable that they admitted into their secret conclaves some – at least – of the discontented Templars, burning for revenge upon those who dispossessed and suppressed the order." Liz shook her head in wonder. "So they didn't accept the divinity of Jesus and claimed that he destroyed the Temple of Solomon," Liz said. "But they considered his blood line to be the Sangreal? How did they reconcile that?"

"They didn't. The Sangreal is a nineteenth century invention perpetuated by the Priory of Sion. The pagan rituals had nothing to do with Jesus, Jerusalem, rebuilding the Temple of Solomon or the Knights Templar. It's a belief system manufactured to justify the illuminati's objective. And the illuminati's objective is to direct human destiny toward the Demiurge, the leader of the Archon."

"Also known as Yahweh or Ahriman. I get it." Liz added. "So where were the Fitzgeralds in this cosmic war of light against dark?"

"Right in the middle of it and for four hundred years." I said. "With all these Masonic lodges incubating discontented Templars, Gnostics, Manicheans and Cathars all they needed was an illuminati front man. Martin Luther showed up and the Protestant Reformation was underway." I added.

"So the Protestant Reformation brought on a struggle between the King of England and the Papacy and the Fitzgerald family sided with the Papacy."

"In 1534, the English Parliament declared Henry VIII 'Supreme Head on earth of the Church of England' and in 1559, his daughter Queen Elizabeth I became the Church's 'Supreme Governor.'"

"And what happened in France?" Liz asked.

"The Huguenots rose from exactly the same ground where the Cathars had been suppressed by the Albigensian Crusade two hundred years before. Queen Elizabeth I's deep-state Earl of Leicester, Francis Walsingham and Philip Sydney sent soldiers, guns and money. Protestant armies waged holy war against the Pope across Europe and in Ireland they targeted the Desmond Fitzgeralds."

"So before we finish putting this thing together for Stone, let's recap what we've got." Liz said, staring at the pile of books we'd accumulated. The Fitzgeralds came to England from Normandy during the Norman Conquest in the eleventh century in the person of someone named Otho. Over the next thirty years Otho's son Walter became successful building and managing castles for the new royal family of England. He was rewarded with estates and became a trusted member of the Familia Regis. Walter's son Gerald was among the advance guard of King William II's (Rufus) march into Wales and somewhere around 1097 Gerald married the Welsh princess Nest."

"That's a good start," I said as Liz proceeded.

"Gerald of Wales made clear in his book, the *Expugnatio Hibernica* that by 1170, his family was fed up with Henry II and his children and wanted to strike out under their own banner in Ireland. Despite repeated efforts to stop them from London, they embraced Irish culture and grew to be the most powerful political force in Ireland as the Dukes of Leinster and Earls of Desmond."

"And that's when they got into trouble." I added as Liz continued.

"Forsaking the English language, English customs and English law, the Fitzgeralds married the land and became 'more Irish than the Irish themselves' as the Seanghaill. Their ongoing intermarriage with Irish clans produced furious resentment from London, while the coming of the Protestant Reformation with Henry VIII produced outright hatred. How am I doing so far?" Liz asked.

"Sounds good to me." I said. "Continue."

"Known for their loyalty to Rome the family became feared and hated as agents of the Counter Reformation. And London's response came from a variety of Protestant factions. But the most interesting response came from something known as the Sidney Circle – an ancient 'stream of religious consciousness,' that had been suppressed for centuries and committed to ridding the world of the Roman church."

"And that goes without saying is where the revenge for the Albigensian Crusade and the destruction of the Knights Templar comes in." I offered.

Liz was rolling now. "The Sidney Circle and its primary operatives, Francis Walsingham, Edmund Spencer, Walter Raleigh, and John Dee, represented the militarized edge of Renaissance Neoplatonism. The goal was not just to replace Catholic Spain as a global empire but to restore an ancient belief system suppressed by the church. That system would encompass both the physical and the astral realms and fulfill a biblical prophecy subverted by Rome. And the first step to that destiny was the conquest of Ireland. Their plan required taking on the Fitzgerald Earl of Desmond in a genocidal war of extermination – which continued on to November 22, 1963." Liz said, finishing off.

"Remember that part about Spencer and *The Faerie Queene* in Richard Berleth's book." I added. "There was a magical element to the Elizabethan war against the Fitzgeralds that I never knew about. I read the *Faerie Queene* when I was a freshman at B.U. just before I auditioned for HAIR. Spencer, Marlowe, Sidney and Raleigh were a part of my life as an English major. I had the Norton Anthology in my dressing room at the Wilber

Theatre when I met you. I had no idea that Spencer's *Faerie Queene* was an allegory for their war against the Earl of Desmond. And then there's the Just War Doctrine of the Catholic Church which the Pope granted the last Earl in desperation to defend his family. I was drawn to Afghanistan because of the Just War Doctrine. Colin Grey and Keith Paine. Remember? They wanted to use it to justify a preemptive nuclear strike on the Soviet Union. Camelot and Just War – might makes right. I think that's what the war on JFK was really about. I think that's what Camelot is all about. Back in the twelfth century, the Fitzgeralds had been inducted into something very ancient and powerful. The Elizabethans were jealous of that power and were willing to destroy Ireland to get it. And there's no way JFK isn't connected."

Oliver Stone, Oscar winning American cinema screenwriter and director, (1946-) Stone at the 2016 San Diego Comic-Con by Gage Skidmore.

Chapter 17

The months we'd spent preparing to meet Oliver Stone had gone so quickly we'd barely noticed that our 1988 screenplay depicting the collapse of the Soviet Union had actually come to pass. The Cold War era we'd grown up in and become deeply involved with had vanished almost as I had written it and as if on cue, Oliver Stone had stepped in out of a dream to fill the void. Stepped out of a dream wasn't an exaggeration.

"I don't believe the dream I had last night with Stone," Liz said at breakfast. "It was like really being there with him in this French palace."

"And what was he like?" I asked.

"He was being very nice. He wanted to know all about me, where I came from. And you know what was funny? I felt as if I already knew him."

And that's where it began. The dream with Kevin Bacon was only a hint of things to come – opening an exchange that put me and especially Liz into an ongoing lucid dream communication. From the moment he'd said yes to meeting us, Liz had been on the receiving end of an open channel and it never stopped. Materializing in three-dimensional hologram-like dreams, Liz found herself suddenly awake in Greek Temples, French Chateaus and Park Avenue apartments – meetings with actors Oliver had directed like Tom Cruise, Michael Douglas and Kevin Costner.

In my searching, I'd read a little bit about Kabala and how it was important to have reached maturity before practicing it. I'd turned forty on my last birthday but I now understood how important the advice was. Dealing with this kind of stuff could make you crazy.

Fortunately my dreams were business-like – production somewhere in Afghanistan, discussing the risks of the adventure but always testing and probing for answers. I'd read where Stone had taken his cast and crew of *Platoon* into the jungle before shooting to get them ready for what he planned to put them through. That made sense, I thought. Rough 'em up ahead of time so you don't waste money when the camera rolls. But did he do this in dreams as well? And if he did, how the hell did he do it? It didn't take much digging to find out that Stone took an avid interest in the power of dreams. He'd even named his company IXTLAN after Carlos Castaneda's book on the subject. Apparently dreams were more powerful than I'd ever imagined. But if it wasn't just our imaginations, it sure as hell raised a lot of questions. Was this real or even possible? And if it was possible did he know he was doing it?

***

The April 20th meeting in New York arrived before we knew it – the Stanhope Hotel was on the corner of Fifth and East 82nd facing Central Park and the Metropolitan Museum of Art. A very impressive hotel in a very impressive neighborhood. But as we parked the car and headed West I was struck by a strange set of coincidences.

"You know, the last time I was in this neighborhood was in 1972 when I was in Superstar." I said to Liz. "I lived on the corner of East 82nd and Rap Avenue."

"That's just a few blocks away." Liz answered. "How strange."

"This is also the day my father died in 1968. April 20th. I hadn't thought about it until now. You had those dreams of Oliver with your family and now this."

"What do you think it means?" Liz asked.

"I hope we find out."

The lobby of the Stanhope was small and busy with lots of people coming and going. I wondered how many of them had come to see our famous host.

"We have a two o'clock with Oliver Stone," Liz said to the desk clerk as I checked out a place to wait.

"He'll be down as soon as he's finished with his meeting." The young woman said after calling upstairs. "Just take a seat."

In the growing shadow of our dreams, the meeting began strangely when a young woman – dressed in black cape and hood – sat down across from us and stared as if she had something to tell us.

"Hello." I said, breaking the silence.

"It's busy in here." She responded, looking around. "Are you Oliver Stone?"

"Do I look like Oliver Stone?" I answered as she continued to stare at me.

"I have something to tell him." She said.

"They told us he'd be down in a minute."

"Then I'll wait."

It was impossible NOT to see the woman staring at us and for a brief moment I wondered if this wasn't part of Stone's psychological staging for the interview – like some *Strange Days* scene from his Jim Morrison movie he hadn't used. The feeling ended only a few minutes later when Stone appeared and the young woman rushed to greet him.

"What do you think she was doing?" Liz asked under her breath. "She seemed kind of witchy."

"Maybe she was doing some kind of energy reading on us." I said, watching Stone nod as she delivered her message.

"I guess we'll soon find out," Liz said as he thanked the woman after no more than a minute and then turned toward us with a smile on his face.

"Thanks for getting in touch," he said as he extended a hand. "You're one of those Fitzgeralds."

"Yes. It goes a long way back in Ireland." I said smiling.

"Well let's sit and tell me about it."

"We found your take on the secret societies surrounding the JFK assassination to fit in with some research we were doing." I told him as he sat down in a chair off to our left. "We put all the research together in something we call *The Voice*. It's just an outline but you can begin to see there's something about the history of the Fitzgerald family and the Camelot legends that stretch way back beyond JFK." I said handing him the research paper. "The Reformation brought it to the surface in the 16th century, but it had been there for centuries before that – back before the Norman Conquest in 1066."

"I'll take a look at it," he said taking the paper. "I am interested in the JFK background but I've already done that. What I'm really interested in is your experience in Afghanistan. You know – the biggest CIA operation in history – bringing down the Soviet Empire and ending the Cold War? Do you think you could give me a treatment about that?"

"A treatment on Afghanistan." I mumbled, realizing I should have expected him to ask for Afghanistan but didn't want to think about it.

"Yes, of course," I stammered in shock. "It was back on the front page of the *Times* this morning. But it's not really what you read in the papers. It's very different."

"That's O.K." Stone said. "Surprise me."

I'd spent five years trying to separate myself from Afghanistan. The high level PDPA government connections I'd once had ceased to exist after Boris Yeltsin cut the funding from Moscow. The crazy Peshawar Seven Mujahideen groups – Rabbani, Gailani, Hekmatyar – who'd done nothing but fight with each other for ten years – were now fighting it out in the streets of Kabul and the future looked grim. But if Oliver Stone wanted a story about Afghanistan, that was worth trying to get done.

"We'll put something together and get it to you," I said after he walked us out the front door of the hotel and onto the sidewalk.

"Good. I'll be looking forward to seeing it. I am interested in this angle you've got on JFK, too," he said glancing at our research paper.

"Have you read Umberto Eco's *Foucault's Pendulum*?" I asked.

"I tried," Stone said. "But I couldn't get into it."

"Well. I know it's mystical," I added. "But it's kind of like that. His sources are real. And so are these ancient heresies. The Inquisition left a lot of grudges and the grudges went underground. And I think that's where the answer to JFK might be."

The meeting was over as quickly as it began with Oliver Stone bidding us farewell from the sidewalk as we headed back to our car.

"So how difficult is it going to be to give him an Afghanistan treatment?" Liz asked.

"A couple of weeks. I've always dreaded the idea of trying to write about our experience. So much of it was just intellectual, piecing things together. How do you tell a story about the biggest secret operation in CIA history and bring it to life?"

"Well I think you're about to find out." Liz said as we reached the car.

Chapter 18

Oliver Stone, IXTLAN Productions
3110 Main Street, 3rd Floor
Santa Monica, CA 90405
April 27, 1992

Dear Oliver,
Thanks for the generous amount of time you allowed for us to present our ideas. I hope they proved helpful. As you mentioned, there are hundreds of conspiracy theories, most of which are at some level, truthful. But even if you tracked them all down with a budget the size of the Pentagon's you'd still be missing the deeper reasons connecting the events and personalities, the "pattern" that ties the threads together.

This is why we've stopped chasing News stories and taken the path we're on. The 24 pages of Voice research condenses an enormous body of work and may at times inadequately express the connectivity of the 1000 year conspiracy. But I assure you it is there. The deeper we go, the thicker the ties become and I have highlighted only those things I thought would be most meaningful to you.

Our experience with Afghanistan led us into a bizarre web of intelligence agencies, private relief groups, political contradictions and media cover ups that should make for a fascinating screenplay. But what drove us to Afghanistan also revealed to us, the deeper mystery didn't reside in that tiny poverty stricken nation, but in the machinations of that secret bureaucracy in Washington. This quest has been the subject of all our screenplays and will be the subject of the Voice. Tying the mystical and the historical together in a one thousand year quest to find the reason why.

Jim Morrison was connected to it and tried to reject it. Ironically he succumbed to it by embracing death. I am sure there are many others like him who hear the call and simply can't handle the responsibility it entails.

The Voice is therefore the calling to the Mystic warrior to leave the path that others tread and answer it no matter what the consequences. The quest can take many forms and many years. But eventually all these paths lead to the truth. As we near the end of the millennium the quest takes on a particular urgency and I suspect from the condition of the world today, it involves nothing less than our survival.

We are preparing treatments for both an Afghanistan screenplay and the Voice. If you have any questions regarding the material we have already provided, we will be more than happy to discuss them with you. For your information I have provided a page from Frank Donner's AGE OF SURVEILLANCE on the media-CIA connections. As you'll see, CBS and the New York Times have always figured prominently. In regards to the reference I made about the Masons, Jim Marrs notes on p. 462 of his book that both Earl Warren and Harry Truman were members. So were Lyndon Johnson, Gerald Ford, Ronald Reagan and George Bush.

If it walks like a duck and talks like a duck … …

Thanks again and best regards,
Paul Fitzgerald

The Oliver Stone meeting was enough to get me up and running and within a few weeks I'd hashed out a 21 page screenplay treatment that told the whole sad Afghanistan story as best I understood it.

Using Stone's JFK for inspiration I opened with a three page prologue introducing my two main protagonists, Leo Cherne and Paul Nitze and why they were key to understanding the big picture.

"In 1976 a man named Leo Cherne approached then CIA director George Bush with a proposition. Cherne, a man at the center of the intelligence community for nearly forty years, had been the primary lobbyist in the 1950s for American involvement in Vietnam. But now, as head of the Gerald Ford's Foreign Intelligence Advisory Board this angry Cold Warrior wanted an extraordinary favor. Permit a small group of former CIA and military officials to review the CIA's 'Defense Analysis' the Gospel of Soviet capabilities used to determine the level of Soviet threat and the awesome weapons needed to respond to it. Known as Team-B, this group of bitter ex-Truman/Kennedy/Johnson hard liners led by Paul Nitze, embarked on a bloody confrontation with the CIA regulars. Denouncing their analysis of Soviet intentions as completely naïve, they recommended hundreds of new weapons systems and a massive escalation of the arms race. And in a move that rocked the intelligence community, the Team-B reassessment was accepted by Bush."

With the collapse of the Soviet Union in 1991, word spread quickly that everything Team-B had said about Soviet intentions was a flat out lie. The Soviets had not been running out of oil as the CIA had claimed and had had no intentions of invading the Middle East. Their main concern had been for the regime of Afghan President Hafizullah Amin going over to the U.S. and having a new enemy on their southern border. The Soviets had been conned into invading and the Carter administration had used the invasion to drop détente and SALT. But the neoconservative effort to politicize American intelligence – and create a permanent war economy – had worked.

I'd made a bet with myself that centering the Afghanistan story on Leo Cherne and Paul Nitze would give Oliver Stone the historical sweep needed to move the work he'd done with JFK to the next level. That day we'd met in New York, Kabul had been overrun by the Mujahideen. A week later Los Angeles had been consumed by riots following the beating of Rodney King by four police officers. Here was Washington celebrating the collapse of Soviet society through the destruction of Afghanistan and the second largest city in America was tearing itself apart. It was an irony I wanted Americans to know that went back generations.

Leo Cherne and his protégé – future CIA director William Casey – had written the book on how to militarize the U.S. economy in the run up to World War II by re-conceptualizing America as "The Arsenal of Democracy." Cherne had been the genius behind the U.S.'s psychological warfare effort. He'd helped establish Freedom House in 1941 to promote America's entry into World War II on the model of the Nazi Brown House. Then in 1946 he'd joined the International Rescue Committee (IRC) to capitalize on the refugee crisis created by that war. Cherne had personally helped to stoke the 1956 Hungarian uprising – was rarely seen in public but quietly moved behind the scenes influencing the lives of powerful men including JFK, whom he'd introduced to Marilyn Monroe.

Paul Nitze went back before World War II as well, but Nitze's influence provided a direct and sympathetic link to Nazi Germany, Wall Street and Big Business. As a stockbroker Nitze had seen first-hand how Nazi Germany had shaken off the depression with military spending – had met personally with Adolph Hitler – drafted the Cold War NSC-68 in 1950 and been in on every run up to defense budget ever since. If anybody was the daddy of the Cold War, it was Paul Nitze. The possibility that he and his Team-B had had nothing to do with Afghanistan was impossible. But there was also a mystical side to Nitze that drew me in. Strobe Talbot had touched on Nitze's interest in the Russian mystic Ouspensksy. But it was his study of the German author Oswald Spengler's *Decline of the West* that bordered on the magical for me. Nitze was no ordinary government bureaucrat. He was a true blue zealot.

Because of Nitze an entire generation of agreements between the Soviets and the U.S. had come undone while the loyal officials who'd negotiated the treaties over six years and under three presidents found their loyalty questioned.

Because of Nitze an ugly agenda had emerged to revive the Cold War and it built like a volcano toward the 1980 Presidential election. All that was needed to make the plan fully operational was a major incident – an event that could be painted so nakedly uncivilized it would alter everyone's perceptions of Soviet behavior and crush any Congressional opposition to a massive three trillion dollar rearming of America. And that was where Afghanistan came in.

In fifty one scenes I told how the whole thing had come about based on our experience. It told how we'd connected to the Afghan Ambassador Farid Zarif at the United Nations, gone to Afghanistan and got a preview of how the world would end. I wanted Stone to know how the same people who'd framed the Reagan agenda of the 80s had used Afghanistan as a fuse to restart the Cold War and that these were the same people who'd convinced the Eisenhower and Kennedy administrations to commit to Vietnam.

> Oliver Stone, IXTLAN Productions – May 21, 1992
>
> Dear Oliver,
> Enclosed is the Treatment for AFGHANISTAN you requested during our meeting 4 weeks ago. 90% of what is there actually occurred to me and all of what is there is true; I have condensed and combined incidents, personalities and time to dramatize what was a ten year process. I had put off even thinking of the story until now for the very reason I have [the character] "Hartigan" describe in the treatment; namely that it simply became impossible for Liz and I to carry the story alone any longer. In the heady days of Reaganomics, people just couldn't understand and more importantly, didn't want to. And as you may be discovering with JFK, institutional pressure can be brought to bear against any efforts to alter "official wisdom" with amazing coordination and swiftness.
>
> But as I pulled my thoughts together these last few weeks, the bloody events occurring simultaneously in Kabul and Los Angeles

convinced me that perhaps Americans were ready to understand the inside workings of the machine. Afghanistan is a key to that machine.

I hope our simple treatment puts the events in a sequence you feel is cinematic. As always we look forward to your comments.

Best regards,
Paul Fitzgerald

It was an epic story and on May 21, 1992 we mailed it to Oliver Stone at his IXTLAN office in Los Angeles and waited. And while we waited the dreams got even more intense.

Liz at Christ Church Dublin 1997

Chapter 19

"I dreamed Oliver Stone came up the back steps and stood on the deck last night." I said to Liz at breakfast. "He told me it's all going to work out just the way you want. You're going to be very happy."

Liz gave me the look. "Knowing that it's all going to work out how long do we wait to call him?" She asked impatiently. "It's already been a month."

This was the hardest part of all. "I'd hoped this wouldn't happen." I said, feeling that tightness in my solar plexus again. "We met with him and gave him what he asked for."

"So what do you want to do?" Liz asked.

"Give me the number." I said, reluctantly.

This was the part I always hated about show business – did I get the part? Am I still in the running? Did he like it or does he even care. This was the part where the dedicated agent was supposed to step in and go to bat for you. But we didn't have a dedicated agent.

I waited until after lunch to call California and reached Oliver's assistant.

"Azita. Do you know if Oliver intends to do anything about the Afghanistan treatment I sent him?"

"No. I'm sorry. I meant to call you." She said. "He's been through so much with JFK. There's been so much criticism he needs a break."

It went without saying that we were disappointed. The Hollywood system was virtually impenetrable. Getting to someone as high on the ladder as Oliver Stone required luck. Getting him to want your work was more like a miracle.

"So that's it?" Liz asked when I told her.

"Afghanistan is an albatross." I said. "It's been like that since we started. I had to do the first trip without you because you were pregnant. CBS basically disowned it. I had to research, write, produce and edit the PBS documentary on my own. Ted Koppel's ABC Nightline undermined Roger's efforts at negotiation in 1983 and just when we got ABC's Peter Jennings support for a third trip, the Afghans opened up to the entire Western media. Alexander the Great must have put a curse on the place."

"So what do we do now?" Liz asked.

"Throw in the towel." I said. I know how Oliver Stone feels. He wants relief from the bullshit and so do I. I just wish he hadn't pulled me back into it in the first place."

"Then why don't you tell him that." Liz said as if challenging me to a duel.

"I will. Just so long as I don't have to call him again. You know how much I hate talking on the phone."

I'd already written three letters to Oliver Stone and writing him a fourth felt like the right thing to do.

> Dear Oliver,
>
> I called and spoke to Azita and she told me of your decision regarding Afghanistan. After the service you've done on JFK I can see why you don't wish to take on another fight. Afghanistan was always a tough story to do, even before the Russians. You are right though. It is the biggest story of a generation and it should be done by someone who can bring its historical importance to the big screen. If there is anyone you think who might be interested in that challenge we'd very much like to approach them. In the meantime keep up the good work. I don't know anyone who hasn't been deeply moved by your films. You are an inspiration to us all.
>
> Best regards, Paul Fitzgerald

And that was it. If Oliver Stone, the one and only man in Hollywood willing to buck the system was afraid of taking on Afghanistan then the time had come to do something else. I had reached the point where I felt I could finally wash my hands of the whole business and live a normal life. And that was when on the last Friday afternoon in July – while I was mopping the kitchen floor – the phone rang.

"Hello, Paul?" The now familiar voice of Azita said at the other end of the line. "Oliver asked me to call and give you a message. He said if you can turn the Afghanistan treatment you sent him into a screenplay in four weeks, he'll consider taking out an option on it."

"Oliver said he'll take out an option if I can write the screenplay in four weeks?" I repeated.

"Oliver said, *he'll consider* taking an option out on your Afghanistan story if you can finish the screenplay in four weeks." She repeated.

The idea momentarily stopped my breath. "But there's no guarantee." I stammered.

"Oliver said he strongly encourages you to write the screenplay."

"What does that mean?"

"He said he strongly encourages you to write the screenplay."

"So If I write the screenplay he might option it, but he might not?" I countered.

"He strongly encourages you. That's all he said."

The call was brief but I got the message. "Thank you Azita." I said, taking a deep breath. "Tell Oliver I'll start on it right away."

I hung up the phone and turned to the calendar on the kitchen wall with numbers running through my head. I had 27 days to write a 120 page screenplay – counting an overnight delivery. The treatment was already twenty four pages long leaving me at least ninety six pages to summarize twenty years of covert history. That was about twenty five pages a week. The characters were real and the twists and turns were already worked out. I had been a sprinter at school. I'd run against Olympic athletes at Boston University and paid the price in pulled muscles. I'd used that experience to tackle Afghanistan but I was now ten years older. I also knew it hurt. I turned to the task at hand and finished mopping the kitchen floor before Liz got home after picking up Devon at summer camp.

"Guess who called?" I said to Liz as she walked in the door.

"Olive Stone." She said with a look of amusement on her face.

"No, Azita." I said. "He wants a script in four weeks and maybe he'll option it."

"Maybe?" Liz said with a skeptical look on her face. "Can you do it?"

"Do I have a choice? It's the payoff we've been looking for."

I'd had pressure before in my life and dealt with it. I'd delivered a devil's bargain to CBS News and ABC Nightline they couldn't refuse and they'd accepted. Now the devil was on *my* back and I knew exactly how Bill Lord and Peter Larkin must have felt.

"You pinged him with that letter you sent." Liz said. "You knew, didn't you?"

"And he just pinged me back. Now I have to fulfill my part of the bargain."

"The devil's bargain, you mean." Liz said, smiling.

I decided to wait until Monday to start and use the weekend to clear the deck and think. There were so many different ways this story could be told – characters added – context, but I'd just have to deal with that later. There was no time to wander from the treatment and every reason to stick to what I'd set down.

The first week came and went without incident as did the second – five pages a day, sometimes six. It was all in the treatment. By the third I was beginning to feel the pressure and found myself getting sick after dinner one night."

"What's going on? Liz asked.

"I'm having doubts. Oliver's JFK created a firestorm and that was thirty years after the assassination. Afghanistan is still smoking. The people who made it happen are still very much alive and a lot of the facts aren't really known. I've got a feeling they're not done with the place."

"They're never done with any place. You know that. Do you think they're going to be bothered by a film?" Liz said, scrunching up her lip.

"*Yes.* If Theodore Eliot thought it necessary to destroy our little documentary, how would he feel about a feature film from Hollywood's most controversial director?" I said. "This film will explode like a bomb over New York and Washington and make a lot of people angry. If Oliver Stone is still reeling from JFK, how's he gonna handle our take on Jimmy Carter's imaginary greatest threat to peace since World War II?"

It was all happening so fast it was making me dizzy. At that moment my decision to accept the challenge finally got to me. But as I turned back to Liz, I saw that I wasn't alone.

"I had another Oliver dream last night." Liz said, smiling. "There was a family gathering at my house in New Jersey and Oliver was making himself right at home. I saw him with his back to me talking to my cousin in Yiddish. I realized he was playing a trick on her so I rushed over. And then I realized I knew who he really was. And I was so excited I knew his name I tapped him on the back and it made a loud sound because his back was so dense. It was so loud it woke me up but I still remembered his name. It was the Trickster, Hermes, the communicator between man and the gods. "

"So you're saying he's trying to trick us?" I asked.

"With the four week offer. I figured it out. If we don't get it to him in exactly four weeks he doesn't have to take it. That's the trick."

"I guess I'd better hurry up and finish the screenplay then." I said.

Chapter 20

So Liz realized we were dealing with the Trickster right off the bat and she got it from a dream. "I know they call Hollywood a dream factory." I said, trying to make light of it. "But I never took it literally."

"It all does kind of fit. Doesn't it?" Liz asked. "The dreams have been there from the start. But I don't know if I'm prepared to deal with a Greek god messing around with my family."

"Maybe the gods aren't what we think they are." I added. "Maybe that's where the gods have always lived, in our dreams."

"I hadn't thought of it that way." Liz said thinking hard. "Well whether it's a dream or not, I'm calling Azita this week to make sure when our screenplay gets to Oliver's office Friday morning it's in his hands by that afternoon. Four weeks to the day."

The final scenes came together smoothly and as the day approached, Liz made the call.

"I don't think Oliver meant literally four weeks Azita told me." Liz said at dinner that night. "She said I'm sure it will be fine if it's later."

"Of course she's wrong." I said.

"We know the script has to be on his desk by Friday afternoon." Liz said, finishing up. "It's part of the deal. My Trickster dream confirmed it."

***

We didn't have to check with Azita again to ensure the screenplay arrived on time. At around 2:P.M on Friday the phone rang with someone from Oliver's office to tell us that page 7 was missing and that we should send it via fax.

"I'm absolutely sure I had all the pages in there." I said to Liz as she yelled out from the living room. "Ask them to call over to the local CIA station and see if someone left it in their Xerox machine."

We spent the weekend on pins and needles wondering what was happening in Santa Monica. Then a call from Azita on Monday confirmed that Oliver's business partner would be getting back to us with an offer. "Congratulations." She said. "You did it."

Great. If only I knew what the "it" was. Something about our families and their connection to Oliver wasn't confined to dreams. From the start coincidence had seemed to rule. He had scheduled that first meeting on the anniversary of my father's death and then Liz had the dream with him meeting *her* family. The warning signs were blinking red. What were we dealing with? There was no way he could have known any of that.

Then on Friday, just as we were sitting down to dinner Oliver's partner and President of Ixtlan, Janet Yang called and asked flat out. "How do you know Oliver? Were you in Vietnam together?"

I explained that I'd only met him that once in New York, but she was suspicious.

"You seem to know him so well." She said, obviously bewildered. "He asked for the screenplay in four weeks and we all said. There's no way anyone can deliver a screenplay in four weeks. Certainly not one that highly developed. And four weeks later like clockwork, there's the screenplay on his desk like it came out of nowhere."

And so it was – as if by magic. On our drive down to New York in April we'd played little else but the Doors' *Morrison Hotel* and the Irish singer Enya's music. At the time it certainly sounded magical. Had we found some mysterious frequency on which to communicate with Oliver Stone? At any rate we now had a Hollywood deal to deliver Afghanistan and the fun was just beginning.

***

It would take months for the final legal agreement to come through that gave Oliver a three year option on our Afghanistan story. That gave us time to do further research while delving into the mystical aspects of Carlos Castaneda and his journey to Ixtlan.

With the Cold War officially over, some old CIA spooks had delved into the history books and written about the first Americans to venture to Afghanistan. One book written by an ex-CIA agent named John H. Waller contained some old photographs and low and behold who did I find.

"Liz. Do you remember that old book you found at the UMass library ten years ago when we were working on the documentary – the one about the first American to go to Afghanistan?"

"*The Memoirs of Colonel Alexander Gardner Soldier and Traveler,*" she said.

"Colonel of Artillery" I added, reading from the Waller book *Beyond the Khyber Pass.*

"What about it?" Liz asked.

"That book I ordered from Barnes and Noble has his picture in it. I didn't realize until now it matches Alissa's dream with my father to a T."

Liz entered the room and scanned the picture. "Yes it does." She said as her mouth dropped. "Alexander Gardner, Irish American mercenary in a uniform of his own design, who commanded Maharaja Ranjit Singh's well-trained artillery in its battles with the Afghans. He also served as a British agent." Liz said in amazement while staring at the picture. "You always said people suspected you were the agent in the room."

"Yea – Bond, James Bond." I said joking. "But who is this guy? He has to be the eight hundred year old soldier from Alissa's dream. Who else dresses like that?"

Liz was ecstatic. "You're right. He's the role model for *Flashman* and Rudyard Kipling's *The Man Who Would Be King*. You loved those stories. But what's he doing with your father?"

"Afghanistan. What else?" I said.

Gardner's unusual picture – holding a sword while posing in a Tartan plaid suit of his own design with matching turban, leapt off the page when I'd first seen it. I had connected with Kipling and Flashman from early on. Now I realized, Gardner had leapt into my life.

Afghanistan had come with its own peculiar mystical power that brought me into an ancient crossroads and then brought my daughter together with my father. Life didn't get stranger than that and Alissa confirmed what I suspected when she came home for lunch.

"Does this picture remind you of anyone?" I asked.

"Yea. That's the eight hundred year old man from my dream," she said in less than a New York second.

By teaming up with Oliver Stone we seemed to have joined in his journey to Ixtlan and crossed over from a fact based reality into something else. But what was the else?

"Maybe we're learning how to see through our third eye." Liz said one morning in October after we'd purchased some of the Castaneda books. "Oliver's teaching us."

"And how would you know that?"

"Because of a dream I had last night." Liz said giving me the look. "I was at Oliver's beautiful French Rococo style palace waiting with hundreds of others to see him. I was sitting on a couch alone and suddenly he appeared in front of me. He placed his thumbs in the middle of my forehead – my third eye – and pressed down firmly and told me 'this is good.' I felt very relaxed and after he was done we talked and he was very sincere and thoughtful."

"And then what?" I asked growing curious.

"Just as he was going to leave I felt disappointed. He stopped and continued where he left off and stayed with me."

A "Journey to Ixtlan" was a journey I hadn't expected. But once I realized what was happening, I felt the freedom to explore the possibilities. The gist of Castaneda's Don Juan story *was* self- exploration and often involved the need to "trick" yourself into getting answers through sorcery. Yes, *sorcery*. His books were filled with it. "Listen to this," I said to Liz reading from *The Power of Silence*. "It is called the trickery of the spirit, or the trickery of the abstract, or stalking oneself, don Juan said in. After all, the spirit had resolved previous impasses with trickery. It was obvious that if it wanted to make an impact on this man it had to cajole him. So the spirit began to instruct the man on the mysteries of sorcery. And the sorcery apprenticeship became what it is: a route of artifice and subterfuge."

I knew all about artifice and subterfuge from Afghanistan. Covert action was built on it – trickery, bluff and dishonesty. So this experience was not new. But coming through dreams was new and Oliver Stone *was* teaching us how to do it. He'd opened a channel – a very personal channel – whether he knew it or not. But it took some getting used to.

"I had no idea the narrative process was so mystical." Liz said when I told her what I'd learned about Castaneda.

"Most of the writers I studied in school had mystical experiences." I said. "You couldn't be a writer in the nineteenth or even twentieth century without engaging the mystical. Kipling used it. W.B Yeats thrived on it – the communion of the living and the dead."

"But that still doesn't explain Alexander Gardner and why he appeared to Alissa." Liz countered. "He didn't come from Oliver Stone. He came from your father."

"Then he's got to have something to do with my family's experience in Ireland." I said. "He's the inspiration I've been trying to find to rewrite the screenplay. He walked into the story and he's important. But right at the moment I don't know how he fits in."

"Then we're going to have to figure that out.

Chapter 21

The information coming through the dreams was so mind altering we decided to keep a log hoping there would come a time when we could figure them out. At times it felt as if we were living in both a dream and a reality and wondering which one was more important. What a tool! There were also telltale signs that our minds were being explored as we experienced our lives being reassembled by something that didn't quite know how it all fit together.

By the third week in February the contract had been signed, sealed and delivered and we were on our way to Washington for interviews. SALT negotiator Paul Warnke was at the top of the list. Afghanistan expert Selig Harrison was next. Warnke's Law partner Clark Clifford had helped to found the Safari Club, but that day's discussion was about Paul Nitze and the collapse of the Soviet Union.

The previous fall, a version of the 1976 Team B report had been declassified and old friend Ron had sent me a copy from Washington. Even though redacted, the trumped up nature of the accusations against the Soviet Union were as obvious as its prophecies. The Team B report wasn't an intelligence analysis. It was a Manichean religious edict intended to damn the Soviet Union regardless of the facts. The objective had been to win over the Washington bureaucracy for unlimited defense spending and provoke America's Cold War enemy into doing something stupid and they'd succeeded. Paul Warnke expressed amazement at how Nitze had turned the government against SALT with Team B and what Brzezinski had done with Afghanistan to fulfill its dire prophecies.

"I decided when I was in the government in the Johnson administration that the Soviet Union had already concluded by the late 1960s. There was no way in the world they were going to become the dominant power. I think we were aware at that point of the fragility of their overall system. But they did not know how to get out of it. McNamara's major concern was that there'd be an unending offensive nuclear arms race. So he asked me to meet regularly with the Russians. And it was clear to me that they were as anxious as I was to find some way of resolving our differences. And that was the fundamental difference between us and Paul Nitze. The Team B members ignored an awful lot of evidence in order to support their preconception that there was an unending and intractable hostility between the United States and Soviet Union. But Brzezinski was obsessed. It was basically that inbred Polish attitude toward the Russians. It was almost an ethnic thing with Zbig."

"And what if SALT II had occurred?" I asked.

"I don't think there would have been any Afghanistan invasion by the Soviet Union. And I think we could have reached an agreement twenty years before we finally did. " Warnke added.

"There may be a deeper reason for Nitze's behavior," I suggested.

"Well, I admit. He's an enigma to me." Warnke said.

"Have you ever read Oswald Spengler?" I asked.

"No."

"It was written just after the German defeat in World War I. According to Strobe Talbot's biography of Nitze, Spengler's *Decline of the West* was a great influence on him. I got an old copy and it's interesting to speculate what might have caught his attention – Western Teutonic Man as the Parzival searching for the Holy Grail and that only in this expression of lonely, single-mindedness can he find the true meaning of life. It's not twentieth century. It's purely mystical. Am I approaching the true meaning…"

"Could be." Warnke laughed, concluding.

Paul Warnke confirmed what we'd suspected from the very beginning. The Soviets would never have invaded Afghanistan had they not been targeted by Zbigniew Brzezinski and tricked into believing they were coming under attack.

"It *was* Brzezinski," I told Liz. "Paul Nitze created the official narrative with Team B for the old line establishment, but it was Brzezinski and the neoconservatives that made it happen."

"It's going to be interesting to see what Selig Harrison says about it when we see him tomorrow." Liz responded.

We'd decided to stay with old friends Ron and his wife who lived in downtown D.C. and as so often happened, Ron made me an offer I couldn't refuse.

"Clinton's state of the Union address is tonight." He said after dinner. "My supervisor asked me to go down to the White House and answer the phones after the speech. I told her I had out-of-town guests but she said you were welcome to come along. She could use the extra hands."

Use the extra hands was putting it mildly. After checking in at the Executive Office building across the street from the White House it became clear how desperate the Clinton team really was.

"I'm sorry your clearance took so long, the woman said as she returned my driver's license. The Bush people took everything they could get their hands on when they left, including the lightbulbs and the toilet paper. We knew they'd probably bugged the old phone system so we decided to replace it. We hope the new one gets installed in time for the speech, but it's going to be a close call."

"Spending the evening of February 17, 1993 in the basement of the White House, fielding phone calls after Bill Clinton's first State of the Union address was an experience I couldn't have imagined. It was also a firsthand look at the desperate state of American politics. The country was split down the middle but nobody in authority would admit to it.

***

The next day Liz and I headed off to visit Afghan expert Selig Harrison at the Carnegie Endowment.

"Paul Warnke stated yesterday that if SALT had been passed by 1978 there would have been no Afghanistan." I said, throwing out the first question.

"Well that certainly was one of the factors that contributed to their state of mind at the end of 1979. But it was broader than that." He said, beginning an in-depth recap of how the Soviets blundered into Afghanistan. "And I have argued that the situation that led to the Soviet intervention was the internal situation which got out of control. They had created this well armed Afghan leadership that by the end of 1979 they feared were going over to China or the United States or Pakistan or all of them combined. Hafizullah Amin was regarded as CIA, not by everyone in the Soviet system, but by certain elements, particularly elements in the KGB."

Harrison confirmed our suspicions about the role of Zbigniew Brzezinski and the U.S Ambassador Adolph Dubs and that for some reason he believed Brzezinski was being protected.

"We're focusing on the time period leading up to Afghanistan and the influence of Zbigniew Brzezinski." I said.

"It's funny you'd say that because my book is being published by Oxford and I haven't had any direct discussions with them. But I gather they think I'm too rough on Brzezinski and so I'm kind of amused at that. I can only tell you that my interpretation – what I'm writing is that Brzezinski had a struggle for American policy toward Afghanistan in 1978 and 79 with Ambassador Dubs. Dubs believed he could try to make Amin into a Tito – or the closest thing to a Tito – detach him. And Brzezinski of course thought that it was all nonsense."

We had heard from the beginning that Brzezinski was a major factor in the Afghan saga. His Russophobia was legendary. Had I been a police detective, his secret dealings under President Carter would have made him a person of interest. He'd have done anything to undermine the Soviet Union. But hearing from someone as high up as Harrison about his direct conflict with the assassinated ambassador made the story explosive.

"It's all bending toward Brzezinski." I said to Liz after saying our farewells. "We've got to get these interviews to Oliver as soon as we get home and try to frame the rewrite to match it."

"I meant to tell you." Liz said. "Ron said he located the *Counterspy* magazine publisher Conrad Ege. He's here in Washington. You've got to call him when we get back to their house. Maybe you could go see him."

With the use of Ron's borrowed Yugo I embarked on an exploration of the Washington suburbs and a test drive of Yugoslavian automotive technology.

"Is that thing safe?" Ege asked as the door nearly fell off the hinges when I reached his place.

"How *could* it be?" I answered trying to get out of the car without breaking it. "It helps to put the Cold War in perspective. Doesn't it?"

Added to the fact that I thought I'd been tailed all the way from Ron's building, the effort to meet Conrad Ege face to face was proving very interesting.

Ege had published some of the best research of the 1980s on Afghanistan and a lot of other covert actions. Along the way he'd divulged the names of some active CIA agents and found himself in deep trouble. By the time I met up with him he'd taken a job with a German periodical. Getting his help was a stroke of luck.

"How did it go with Ege?" Liz asked when I got back to Ron's.

"Aside from the fact that I think I was being followed, it went great.

"You were being followed?" Liz asked her jaw dropping.

"I don't know the streets so I had to keep driving around and I kept seeing this black Porsche. It was hard to miss. You know what Goldfinger said when James Bond kept showing up. 'Once is happenstance. Twice is coincidence, the third time is enemy action." I admitted reluctantly. "Either that or there's a lot of people in D.C. driving black Porsches.

"Well it's a spooky city." Liz replied.

"And then some. But when I told him about the film project he turned his entire Afghan archive over to me. And that alone made it worth the risk."

The Washington Monument located on the National Mall in Washington, D.C. (APK 2009)

Chapter 22

Washington *was* a spooky city. But when we got back to Boston, things only got spookier.

"I had this wild dream last night." Liz said waking up one morning a week later. "We were in the old house on Chesterford Road. Oliver was upstairs with us working on the story when I heard someone coming. I looked out the window and a very happy Zbigniew Brzezinski had pulled into the driveway and was waving to me as he got out of his Dodge Dart."

"A very happy Brzezinski?" I said, pondering the idea.

"Yeah. In a Dodge Dart. Remember them?" Liz asked. "So I rushed down to greet him through the kitchen at the backdoor. I escorted him through the dining room and he asked why there were so many people here. I explained it was a holiday and there are always people here on the holidays. So we walked into the hallway but it was now turned into a grand hallway with stairs that were under repair leading up to the bedroom where you and Oliver were working. I started to take him up but suddenly the stairs became a ladder. It was obvious work was being done and paint started to drip on my head and he stopped. I told him he should go up alone but he couldn't seem to negotiate it. I knew you and Oliver were still working upstairs, but because the house was being transformed into a mansion Brzezinski couldn't get to you."

The dream was packed with symbolism and a warning. What did it mean? Our small, personal story was being transformed into a grander one. That was easy enough. But why was a key figure like Brzezinski being discouraged from getting to me and Oliver when he had clearly come to meet with us? And why was he so happy to see us in the first place when we were trying to expose him? The dreams were becoming a very important source of information.

The very day before Liz's dream, a car bomb had been detonated in the basement of the World Trade Towers in New York, sending shockwaves through the establishment. The suspects were unknown. Was it possible it had something to do with Brzezinski's secret operation?

Brzezinski's policies had spread Islamic terrorism far beyond Afghanistan. Had his project come back to the United States and blown up in his face? Nobody in the U.S. knew what Brzezinski had really done to win the war against the Soviets. Even fewer cared. If the bombing *was* connected it would shine a beacon on a story that had been absolutely invisible. It would also put pressure on Oliver to want us to dig as deeply as we could into telling how it happened.

By mid-March I'd finished transcribing the Washington interviews with Warnke and Harrison and Liz called LA asking for a meeting. With Oliver about to cast a new movie called *Natural Born Killers* in New York, a date was set to fly down for early April, and I set out to draft a new treatment.

In the meantime word had surfaced that it was the Brzezinski-backed Islamic clergy that had set off the bomb at the World Trade Towers and it made my visit to Oliver even more urgent.

The limo ride to Billy Hopkins Casting in the West Village brought back memories I'd have rather forgotten. I empathized with the half dozen or so young actors waiting to be sized up by Oliver Stone. I also wondered if any of them would ever make it to the big time before getting thrown under the bus they'd just got off of. I knew first hand that showbiz held an allure that almost never paid off. And when it did you were always looking over your shoulder to see who was waiting to grab your spot on your day off. Writing about Afghanistan was hard. But it was better than sitting in a New York casting office waiting to audition for a very busy Oliver Stone.

The wait was brief. "You wanted to see me?" He asked after sitting down at the desk in his office.

"I wanted to tell you about our trip to Washington and the research we're doing on Afghanistan."

"Yea – tell me something good. What is going on with Afghanistan?" He said, gruffly.

"I've been hearing that the Trade Tower bombing might have been done by the Mujahideen guys the U.S. used to get the Soviets." I responded.

The news seemed to deflate Oliver like pulling the plug on a balloon. "Oh, no. Not that." He moaned as he put his hands on his head and slumped onto the desk, rolling it back and forth. "They're going to kill me."

It *was* JFK. Oliver Stone was a wounded veteran and he'd been wounded again by JFK.

"I wanted to give you these." I said, handing him the interviews with Warnke and Harrison. "Warnke was adamant. The Soviets wouldn't have invaded Afghanistan if Carter and Brzezinski had gone ahead with SALT II. Harrison claimed it was all Brzezinski's doing and that he wanted them in Afghanistan to give them their Vietnam."

"He said that?"

"In so many words. Afghanistan was a throwaway. It was always in the Soviet Sphere of influence. The U.S. didn't want it. They had Pakistan and Iran. Brzezinski wanted to bait the Russians there. The U.S. ambassador wanted to calm it down and keep them out. They had a big fight. The ambassador lost. It's all in there." I said, wondering what was going to happen next.

Oliver paused and nodded thoughtfully. "Then thanks for coming down. You know I told Azita, Liz could have come too." He said, lightening up slightly.

"It's a busy week day. Somebody has to handle the home front." I said.

Oliver smiled. "Well give her my best."

And that was it. Ten minutes with Oliver Stone and it was over. Back in the limousine. Back to the airport and back at home by six o'clock.

"You're home already?" Liz asked as I shut the garage door and set my briefcase down on the kitchen floor.

"Quick and dirty."

"Where did he take you to lunch?"

"He didn't take me to lunch." I said. "I ate the peanuts they served on the flight."

"But Azita said he would."

"I guess Azita didn't tell him."

At that moment the phone rang and Liz went to the living room to answer it.

"Paul. It's Azita. She wants you to get on the phone."

"Yes Azita. I just walked in."

"I have good news for you." She said in a sort of happy sing-song voice. "Oliver wants to meet with you."

I was dumbfounded. "But I just met with him in New York."

"No. He wants you to come out to California and meet with him at his office. He wants to know when can you come?"

Talk about a surprise. "The vacation week is coming up and we'd planned to go there for the third week in April. Let us know what day works for you."

Only two hours before I had met an Oliver Stone that seemed not at all happy to see me and left with a bag of peanuts for my trouble. Now I was asked to come to California as soon as possible. I was genuinely confused.

"So what does he want?" Liz asked as she came back into the kitchen.

"He wants to see us in L.A. I guess the interviews must have worked." I said.

Liz gave me a big smile. "Well, as Jake Gittes says to Curly in *Chinatown*. 'When you're right, you're right. And you're right."

***

To me going to L.A. *was* Disneyland. Something prevented people who had moved there from ever coming back to New England. It was like heroin must have been to an addict. Maybe it was the weather – the outdoor lifestyle – never having to worry about snow on the roof, or frozen car batteries or too much rust on the rocker panels. A writer friend of mine called it ennui – where one day blended so flawlessly with the next you just got lost in the sameness – and died of boredom. L.A. was Hollywood, pretense and make-believe. It was a glitzy cartoon cutout pasted over a desert town and now we had to bring the reality of our Afghanistan to it and make it work. Could we do it?

***

There was no point in starting the rewrite until after California so we continued on developing *The Voice* and sending Oliver chapters as they were written. Word came from Azita that he loved getting the installments and the meeting was set for April 20th with enthusiasm. Once again it had been up to Oliver to fit us into his insane schedule and once again we had been scheduled a year to the day we'd first met him on the anniversary of my father's death. The coincidence this time was too strong to ignore and I found myself once again drawn to Carlos Castaneda for guidance.

"Death is the only wise advisor that we have. Whenever you feel, as you always do, that everything is going wrong and you're about to be annihilated, turn to your death and ask if that is so. Your death will tell you that you're wrong; that nothing really matters outside its touch. Your death will tell you, 'I haven't touched you yet.'" Liz said reading from our copy of Castaneda's *Journey to Ixtlan*. "There are references to death all over the book. Here's another. 'A warrior must focus his attention on the link between himself and his death… He must let each of his acts be his last battle on earth. Only under those conditions will his acts be his last battle on earth. Only under those conditions will his acts have their rightful power.'"

"Death is a character to Castaneda." I said trying to sort out in my mind what was happening. "He uses death to find his warrior. My father is obviously a door to finding my warrior." I said, responding to Liz. "This is the third time my father has been brought to my attention by Oliver Stone. Makes me wonder."

Alexander Haughton Campbell Gardner (1785-1877), also known as Gordana Khan, was an American traveller, soldier, and mercenary. He appeared to Paul's daughter Alissa in a dream with his father.

Chapter 23

The dreams were forcing both of us to reconsider what we'd been doing in Afghanistan and what had happened with my father's visit to Alissa with the eight hundred year old man. They also made us realize there had been a deep mystical component to Afghanistan that I'd simply overlooked. I had not gone off to war in Vietnam like Oliver Stone. I had made my war, Afghanistan, but as a story teller. My mother thought he was interested in me because I hadn't gone off to fight the war like him. But little did she know I'd been fighting the war of light against dark for most of my life. Afghanistan was the most significant geopolitical event of the late twentieth century. As the storehouse of ancient knowledge and the seat of human civilization Afghanistan connected everyone to the deep past whether they knew it or not. Kipling had written about its mystical allure and a Senate Select Committee on narcotics had even acknowledged the unseen powers of its drug dealing holy warriors in a report dated January 3, 1985.

The Mujahideen leadership, through their mystical tribal communications network, should put an end to the production of opium, morphine base and heroin in their territory. It read.

I had secured the document years before but at that moment I saw in it a power I hadn't recognized. The Fitzgerald family had started out in Wales as Christian holy warriors in the eleventh century – an area steeped in the original Grail mythology. The family chronicler Gerald of Wales was an authority on dreams and visions and Merlin's prophecies. If the Mujahideen holy warriors were connected to a mystical communication network acknowledged by an intelligence community in the twentieth century, why wouldn't the Fitzgeralds have been connected to one in the eleventh? And if they had, couldn't it still be active and used to communicate with its tribal members today – like my father had done with Alissa in her dream?

The idea was obviously stretching the rational, but the more I looked at it the more I realized how profoundly limited the rational could be. I was beginning to understand what the intelligence community wanted with the esoteric powers of Muslim holy warriors and why a fourteenth century French King and a Pope would get so worried about the holy warriors known as the Knights Templar. Yea, they'd had the King's money to be sure, but they also held secrets that made them extremely powerful esoteric warriors – and so did the Fitzgeralds. Everything seemed to be connecting me to the past, linking me with some distant voice to fulfill an ancient purpose.

Because of Oliver Stone I was now on alert to the hidden aspects of everything I'd come to know and not just Afghanistan but Ireland too.

***

As we researched, the dreams intensified. Just after I'd met with Stone in New York, I found myself mysteriously transported to a rustic farm house somewhere in Texas. Two young women dressed in satin dresses entered the room accompanied by a man with a rifle who stood guard while they spoke to me. "We are here to invite you on a mission from our lord and master David Koresh to fight the growing evil and power of Satan in our land." One of them said amid the sound of electronic static in the room. "There are many benefits to joining our group and many lovely ladies here to attend to you and your needs."

I was suspicious. "Yes, the power of evil is growing." I replied. "And I support anyone's effort to change the world for the good. But I would never, never, never support any effort that required violence against others to succeed."

At that moment men dressed in black Nazi style helmets and black uniforms burst through the door and began to shoot while the guard behind the women started shooting back. Afraid, I turned toward an open window in the side of the room and jumped through, then rolled to safety onto the grass outside. As I escaped I impressed myself at how fast I could travel through the empty pastureland. I even noted as I ran how much it reminded me of rural Texas.

The next morning I told Liz about the dream and how I felt I'd somehow been summoned to it. I told her about the strange holographic nature of the encounter – about the electronic squawking in the background and how the women's voices kept cutting in and out. I thought nothing more of it until two weeks later when I opened the front page of the Boston Globe and read about the Branch Davidian standoff with Federal Agents of the ATF at Waco and realized that's where I'd been.

Faces from the distant past began to appear right in our living room. A BBC program on the ancient Celts presented the reconstructed face of a two thousand-year-old bog body found in Manchester England. Thought to be a royal sacrifice called "Lindow Man," the face could have been my own. The dreams even overlapped with reality as I'd found myself discussing production issues with Oliver, only to receive a fax unexpectedly the next day regarding the same subject.

Liz's dreams overlapped as well and became deeply personal. On April 12th she told me, "I got a call from Elizabeth Stone asking when I start my job with Oliver. She told me that she is concerned about him carrying this burden alone and is anxious for my work to begin."

But despite my suspicions and the dreams, the vibe established by Oliver and his partner Janet Yang was positive. As we arrived at the Main Street Santa Monica office we immediately found ourselves face to face with a popular Hollywood icon.

"Isn't that Woody Harrelson?" Liz whispered as we were ushered into a work area near his office.

"Yea. He's doing a script written by Quentin Tarantino and Woody's the star." I said.

Harrelson smiled and said hello as we drew closer and the thought struck me immediately, that everything Oliver did was a test. Harrelson's father Charlie was a convicted hitman and gangster. There was a rumor he'd even been one of shooters that got away that day in Dallas disguised as one of the three tramps. Was Oliver testing me to see how I reacted to the son of a potential assassin of JFK or was he testing Woody Harrelson to see how he'd react to me? We hadn't even started yet and it was already making me crazy.

In a few minutes I'd forgotten all about Harrelson and got down to the subject at hand as we were ushered into the big kahuna's presence with Janet and Azita bringing up the rear. And that was when the fun began.

"Azita. Bring in the shoes." Oliver said shouting out to his assistant.

"You want them now?" She asked politely.

"Yea. Bring em in. I want to try them on."

And so we sat and watched as Azita marched a half dozen boxes of men's shoes and placed them beside Oliver's chair in front of us.

"Go on Paul." He said as he proceeded to try on one pair and then another. "You were going to say something."

I wasn't going to say anything. So I waited for a long thirty seconds for Oliver to finish and then we began in earnest.

"And so where do we go from here?" Oliver asked.

"There's a lot of options." I said, deciding to wing it for fun. "How about Paul Newman as Paul Nitze organizing the Team-B to undermine the CIA."

"Hey who's the director here?" Oliver answered, half joking. "I do the casting."

"O.K. So it's someone who looks like Paul Newman. It opens with a symphony orchestra playing Bach. Nitze loves Bach. Nitze's the conductor, swirling his baton – commanding all the stars in the universe to conform to his will. He's got a mystical streak. His father's an expert on Grail mythology. He studied Spengler and Ouspenski and Swedenborg when he went on sabbatical from Dillon Read. Went to Germany in the 1930s and met with Hitler. He is the Great Architect of the Cold War – the father of the Cold War. A vast imagination and the power of will. The triumph of will. And if he wants the Soviet Union destroyed, thy will be done."

Janet smiled at me and then looked at Oliver. "That's a really good pitch. How'd you do that? Are you in the business?"

"I was inspired." I said. Because of Oliver's shoe routine, I knew there were no rules.

Oliver was intrigued. "You said something about the mystical. What's mystical about Afghanistan?"

"What isn't?" I replied. "It's ancient. Maybe the most ancient – home of Gandaran Buddhism – Greco-Buddhism. Alexander the Great stopped off there looking for the Philosopher's Stone. His men stayed and founded cities. And then there's this." I said reaching into my briefcase.

"It's from the Senate Select Committee on Narcotics requesting the Mujahideen to use their mystical communications network to stop the drug trafficking. It says so right here."

"Where? Show me." He said as I got up to hand him the report.

"Right here." I said, pointing it out. "You can keep this."

Oliver was more than intrigued with the document and especially the implications.

"I want you to put this in the rewrite – the mystical. Get it into the treatment. You always work it out in the treatment."

Oh Jeeze. There it was again. Another treatment. Zero to sixty. I didn't know what to say, but it wasn't no. Could I do this? I'd gone to Broadway for Jesus Christ Superstar – done Afghanistan before anyone else, been to one world fair, a rodeo and a picnic and got an A-list director to want my screenplay. Why should this be any different?

"I will certainly try." I said, taking a very deep breath.

"Can you do it?" Liz asked as we headed out of the office into the warm Santa Monica sunshine.

"I don't know." I said, basking in the glow of our momentary victory. "But I sure as hell am going to try."

"By the way." Liz said. "After the meeting, Azita told me Oliver just separated from his wife Elizabeth. So my dream with her was a real message for help."

"It wasn't just *your* dream that was real." I countered. "Somebody had a TV tuned to CNN in Oliver's office. Remember the dream I had in Waco Texas about the shootout with David Koresh and the Branch Davidians? Well it happened last night. Janet Reno ordered an attack and the Feds burned the place to the ground with everybody in it."

I noticed the impact of weaving the mystical into our story-telling almost immediately when on May 5th Liz told me about an awake-vision she'd had that morning. "I woke up at 4:30 and saw a white horse standing over your side of the bed." She said. "He looked so real I had to reach over to scratch his head and nose and he responded to me. The horse hairs felt VERY real – rough like a wild horse whose mane was never combed."

"Maybe that's a signal from the last earl of Desmond, Geroid Iarla." I said laughing. "As the story goes he rides a white stallion around Lough Gur once every seven years until the end of time. Something we're writing is stirring his spirit."

It took me three more weeks to craft a new treatment called *Afghanistan – Three Knights of Desmond* that wove a mystical character into the story with a name central to our research on the Fitzgerald family in Ireland – Desmond FitzMaurice.

> *This story evolves like a double helix, a caduceus; one representing day the other night. Day is the rational – represented in the telling of the conflicting historical events of Afghanistan, through flashbacks and Paul's flashes of insight gained by sticking with the story for so long. The night is the mystical, where the day's events and the history preceding them take on a different, nightmarish meaning interwoven with Paul's past as a Geraldine. The vehicle for this mystic chord is provided by the mysterious character Desmond Fitz Maurice, whom Paul encounters in the garden of the Kabul Hotel one night, and continues to discuss events with for three consecutive nights.*

Liz was contrite. "So Desmond is the area your branch of the family controlled in Munster. How clever."

"It's a composite. Desmond means South Munster." I said.

"And FitzMaurice means the son of Maurice." She added.

"And Maurice is the father of the Desmond Fitzgeralds – the son of Gerald and Nesta and the brother of William Fitzgerald, David the Bishop of St. David's in Wales and Angharad de Barry. Liz's interest was growing. "And your father's name is William and your great grandmother is a Barry."

"And that takes us back eight hundred years into the mists of Medieval Ireland through three nights in Afghanistan and a stop at the Kabul Hotel."

"Wow. That really is mystical." Liz said, genuinely impressed.

We dated the thirteen page treatment May 27, 1993 and over-nighted it to L.A. before the ink was dry.

"Oliver loved the new treatment." Liz said after getting off the phone with Janet. "He's going to call this afternoon at 4:30 and give us some notes on how we should handle the rewrite."

I was beginning to think there was something more about our mystical connection with Oliver Stone that couldn't be explained.

"It's brilliant." He said as we listened to his call. "Especially this character you've got, Desmond Fitz Maurice. There's so much I can do with a character like that. If you can get the draft done on time I can make it my next project. You and Liz can come out to Aspen and we can work on it together."

Somehow I'd passed every test Oliver had thrown at me and moved onto the next stage only to find myself moving further on. And here I was at the final stage being called brilliant by one of Hollywood's top directors. The writing gods were smiling on my efforts. All that was left to do was to draft a polished version of the screenplay I'd already written with a mystical slant and my job would be complete. What could possibly go wrong that could stop me from finally getting my Afghan story told?

Chapter 24

Before getting off the phone, Oliver handed it over to Janet Yang to tell us that they'd been asked by a staffer for Congressman Lee Hamilton – who'd helped out with the JFK film – to come to work in L.A. and "Would he be an asset to our Afghanistan project?"

To which I immediately answered – "Yes. That would be a great help," thinking a seasoned staffer could get us some of the needed documentation that was only then being declassified. I had no way of knowing that this Washington insider was the son of a powerful deep state player and would eventually reveal that he wanted nothing to do with the story we were delivering.

At first "Eric" didn't seem like a problem I couldn't overcome. Both Oliver and Janet were enthusiastic about our Afghan project. What *was* a problem – and one that became more apparent as I moved into the rewrite – was a question I had been avoiding from the beginning. *What had drawn me to Afghanistan in the first place?* What had possessed me to go to such lengths to uncover the truth behind the largest covert operation in American history? And how was it connected to Ireland and the tragic story of the Desmond Fitzgeralds?

That was something I had avoided. Something I had built a wall around – something about myself that came rushing at me as soon as I'd finished the new treatment. And it seemed to speak to me in the voice of the black knight from my dream. "Are you ready to join us?"

In the original treatment I had put a distance between myself and the story. I had tricked myself into thinking I could tell it without making it personal. Now I had to write about THAT experience with the help of my mystical alter ego Desmond FitzMaurice and for the first time in my life, I was lost. I was now on my own journey to IXTLAN and I didn't know where it would take me.

To complicate matters, my request to Eric for research on Zbigniew Brzezinski as a main character got absolutely no response. Was this just a lack of interest or something more? His sole contribution up to that point was a useless transcript from a Congressional hearing but he had never addressed our central thesis – the secret war orchestrated by Paul Nitze's Team B and implemented by national security advisor Brzezinski.

As I sailed into uncharted waters I realized I couldn't make the drama work without knowing more details about what Brzezinski had done. How were the Saudis involved? Who had ordered up frontline Stinger missiles for the Mujahideen holy warriors? What role were the Chinese playing before the invasion? I knew for certain Brzezinski had enrolled both of them in his plans in 1978 and that a high level Chinese operative was working with the Shah's SAVAK. Did the Maoists in Kabul have a hand in kidnapping the American ambassador? Did they do it at the behest of Beijing to provoke a "situation" the Russians could be blamed for? And what about the Safari Club? Brzezinski had put himself in charge of the CIA's covert operations at the National Security Council. The Dubs kidnapping was manna from heaven for his agenda. Did he know about it ahead of time?

I picked up a copy of the book *Crossfire* by Jim Marrs on which Oliver's JFK was based. I also picked up Oliver and Zachary Sklar's *The Book of the Film,* documenting the volumes of research supporting the movie. Both books relied on thirty years of discovery, interviews and detective work by dozens of researchers. Afghanistan was based on my personal experience and the first-hand knowledge that the Soviets had been tricked into invading. And most of Washington had thought it was a good thing – not a bad one. If Oliver Stone still got raked over the coals for a heavily documented *JFK.* What was going to happen because of Afghanistan?

In the meantime things began to get rough. In late May, Oliver's wife Elizabeth filed for divorce and as the summer progressed changes started to happen with new people brought in at IXTLAN. Rumors circulated that *Natural Born Killers* was so violent it wasn't going to be released and that Oliver's third Vietnam movie *Heaven and Earth* was struggling. We learned that Eric had been working on Oliver and was pushing a script on Richard Nixon which would require all of Oliver's attention and a huge budget.

June turned into July turned into August as I struggled alone to pull the pieces together and make Afghanistan work as a film. Following the February bombing of the World Trade Towers the FBI had uncovered a vast terror network linked to Brzezinski's "heroic" Freedom Fighters. Afghanistan was now a *big* and controversial story about CIA blowback which continued to absorb every minute of my day. But as I wrestled on with the geopolitical story well into the fall, the implications of mixing my role in Afghanistan with the mysticism of Ireland were crossing over to Liz in real time.

"I woke up very suddenly." Liz told me on September 9th. "There were bright lights dancing on your side of the bed – multicolored lights. I kept staring at them as they got closer and closer until they began to take form and turn into little people dancing and rocking back and forth."

"Little people? Do you mean *Those* little people?" I asked.

"Yes. Those little people – the Fairy Folk and they were very busy. Their dancing seemed to be bringing them into my reality. Then I realized they were celebrating something when a man who looked like Henry VIII started to wave at me."

"Henry the VIII? With the Fairy Folk?" I asked, skeptically.

"He just looked like that with a beard. Anyway, I was surprised that he could see me so I waved back. Then I noticed a huge blond lady hovering over you and the Fairy Folk with her long hair hanging down to my level. She was smiling and watching the celebration. I noticed the clock indicated it was 12:40 on the bureau across from the bed. I just kept watching and then I realized I felt wrapped in a frequency with a hum surrounding the whole room."

"Sounds like you dreamt of Aine, the goddess of Munster and mother of Geroid Iarla." I said.

"But this wasn't a dream." Liz added. "As the scene began to fade the Fairy Folk dissolved back into the original beams of colorful lights that I saw at the beginning. Then it finally faded, the hum was gone and the room was back to normal."

"But you were awake?"

"Yes." Liz said emphatically. "I was awake the whole time."

By October twenty fifth I'd produced a one hundred and fifty four page epic that we overnighted to L.A. And that was when things got seriously weird when five days later on the eve of our sixteenth wedding anniversary Liz received a visit from Oliver Stone in a dream.

"I found myself in the vestibule of an ancient Temple. I was sitting on a stone bench looking out into a dimly lit room with an altar surrounded by large Greek columns." Liz told me the next morning with a strained look on her face. "It was unlike any dream I've had with him. I watched as he serenely floated in with his feet suspended off the ground and sat down next to me. His eyes were black and hypnotic and surrounded me in warmth. He was smiling and I was pleased to see him. We were both dressed in long ceremonial robes and we talked of things."

"What kind of things? I asked, growing concerned.

"I can't remember." Liz said thinking hard. "Then suddenly I found myself alone and wrapped in a blanket on the bench. Next to me was a drawing of myself and I realized some kind of ceremony had taken place, but I couldn't remember it. *You* rushed in holding a small paint brush announcing, 'You did it. You did it! Did you fall in love with him?' But I couldn't remember what happened. I just took the brush and started painting stars on your back."

"Stars on *my* back?" I said, finding myself growing angry and wondering what was going on.

"What kind of power are we dealing with here?" I asked.

Liz gave me the look. "Actually it made me nervous. I don't like the fact that I can't remember what happened?"

I was tense enough waiting for a response to the screenplay but this was pushing me to the limit. Liz's dream had blurred the division between waking reality and sleeping so profoundly I was feeling it as a threat.

"Remember the dream with him when I called him the Trickster?" Liz asked. "That was the first one. But this was so real when I think about it now, it scares me."

"All that sorcery and trickery and not remembering what happened sounds like Castaneda." I said.

As the days passed I could feel the darkness growing. Then on the night of November 3rd I revisited a dream I'd had in Afghanistan ten years before in the medieval church with the Black Knights. By that time I knew the location because I'd stumbled across a picture of it. It was Wewelsburg, the castle of the Black Sun – Himmler's esoteric headquarters in the North Rhine-Westphalia region of Germany.

The Black Sun symbol was a pagan rune, used in Nazi mysticism to conduct unknown rituals, which I now suspected had something to do with the mystical communication network of holy warriors. I had performed the Mithraic renunciation ritual in my first dream there. The Mithraic rituals represented the Aryan, Indo-European foundation of the Grail quest going back to Afghanistan and Zoroaster. But in this dream I found myself helping to unload small wooden crates into the aisle of the church. As I brushed the snow from them and saw the markings, I realized they contained the remains of SS soldiers who had died fighting on the Eastern front. Himmler had intended the war in the East to be a Teutonic Crusade and named the operation Barbarosa in honor of the Holy Roman Emperor Frederick I's third crusade who had drowned crossing a river on his way to fight it.

I now accepted the dreams as a regular form of communication. So far they'd actually produced some concrete results. But Liz's dream had crossed a threshold for both of us.

Driven by suspicion and the need to know I read up on everything I could find about dreaming. A huge volume by Oxford fellow Robin Lane Fox on ancient pagan religious practices revealed a long and detailed history of dream communication between gods and men. He even referred to Sorcerers who "offered spells for conjuring up prophetic dreams and considered the arts of 'dream-seeking' and 'dream-sending' to be a central part of their business."

Sorcerers conjuring up spells to seek-dreams and send-dreams sounded an awful lot like Castaneda to me. And when I found a newly published copy of his book *The Art of Dreaming,* I decided that I would try to send a dream to our favorite director and see what would happen.

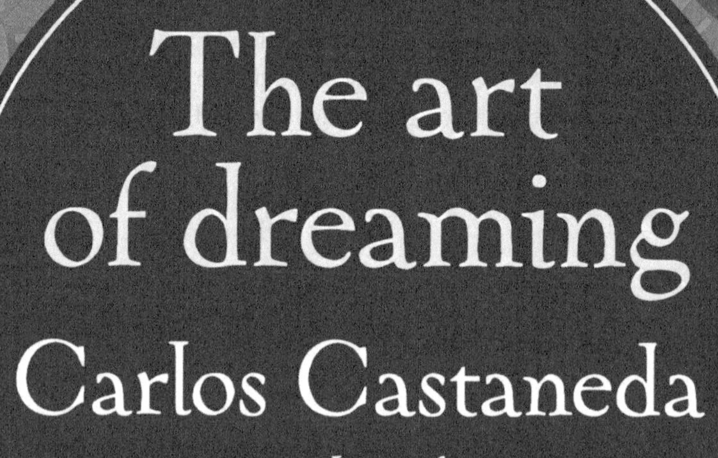

author of

The Teachings of Don Juan

Chapter 25

Revelations were just then emerging about the military's use of what they called "remote viewing." Ageless techniques for immersing into trance states were simple enough for anyone to master. The scientific basis for viewing something or someone in a faraway place had recently been researched and documented by Michael Talbot in his 1991 book *The Holographic Universe*. Communicating on such a frequency was no secret to the Mujahideen holy warriors. Castaneda's work indicated that South American shamans had been doing it for millennia. So on the fifteenth of November in the dwindling light of the day, I decided to lie back on the couch in my office, close my eyes and wait for the red image to turn blue. I then concentrated on reaching my target by repeating his name three times with intent, and the result was almost immediate.

I quickly drifted through a cloud-like haze then found myself in an outdoor café facing a Cathedral across the plaza in what looked like Mexico. I was sitting with a pretty young woman who was trying her best to distract me from interfering with Liz and Oliver who were sitting nearby having an intense conversation. I was totally aware at that moment that I had had other experiences like this where Oliver set me up with someone while he focused on Liz and I was getting annoyed with it.

"Tell me what he thinks of me." I asked the young woman.

"He told me that you were deceitful – a house of mirrors." She said. "And every time he gets inside the house and thinks he knows who you are, another door opens and someone else steps out."

The encounter was meaningful. I shook myself awake and went downstairs at 5:30 p.m. but before I could tell Liz what I had done, the phone rang.

"That will be Oliver." I told her as she stopped in her tracks.

"What did you do?" She asked suspiciously.

"I accessed the mystical communication network." I said, surprised to see the result materialize so quickly.

"Hold on, I'll put Paul on." Liz said, putting her hand over the receiver. "He's annoyed." She whispered.

"Stay on the line. I'll take it on the extension." I said.

"Hello Oliver. How are you?"

"I'm calling from South America." He said backing off slightly when he heard my voice. "I'm scouting locations. I had to move on with plans for another production so I'm putting the Afghanistan film on the shelf temporarily."

"So what does that mean?" I ask.

"I am going to do your film. Just not right now."

"Well what about the script?" I asked.

"It's getting there, but it needs more."

"More what?" I asked, hoping for a clear direction.

"I need a book. Something that lays out the whole thing from beginning to end."

"But that book hasn't been written." I said. "Why don't you let me write an annotated version and put background notes in it. You know. Things that back up the story. Would that help?"

"Yes. It would. But look, I've got to go. Do it again and put the notes in and I'll look at it."

And that was it.

"He agreed that you should write it again." Liz said, hanging up the phone.

"Yea. You heard what I told him and he said yes."

"Well that's something I suppose."

"This is frustrating. He's the director. I'm looking for a dialogue. And this is what I get?"

So after months of laboring to improve our Afghan story and add the mystical, I embarked on revising the screenplay again.

Afghanistan had been a fruitless effort for seven long years. We'd done all the heavy lifting and had nothing to show for it but hostility. Oliver had dragged us back into the soup and we'd gone willingly solely because of him. But this latest setback had hit something in me the wrong way and by the night of November seventeenth, it wanted out.

"You've been acting strange all night. What's going on?" Liz asked just before bedtime.

"This writing thing is making me crazy." I said, feeling angry and paranoid. "Someone is conspiring against me. I can feel it pressuring me to reveal myself as if I'm some kind of cutout."

That night, before I drifted to sleep I told Liz I'd be gone by morning. "They've been with me all my life. I've lost some of them over the years but the last of them will leave because they can't stay. I don't know who'll be left, but I can feel them departing."

I was more than angry. I was furious. My spirit guides had delivered me to this place and they were now deserting me when I needed them the most. Apparently these were the archons I'd appeased by throwing myself into Afghanistan. Now that I was exposing them, they were leaving.

At 2:22 exactly I awoke from a nightmare with a feeling of having been eviscerated. Liz heard me struggling in the dream and was already awake.

"What's going on?" She asked.

"I was frantically building and rebuilding this wall of black blocks." I said, barely able to catch my breath. "I finally realized something was grinding them down faster than I could rebuild them, so I stopped. Then I heard the sound of a chorus of voices wailing in minor scale, like falling angels. As the wall I was working on began to disappear I looked back and saw what I'd been struggling with was a black pyramid. It kept disintegrating until all that was left was this empty room underneath. I thought it was empty. Then I noticed this two dimensional shadow figure pressed up against the back and as that wall disintegrated the figure floated up and out toward a mirror at the other end of the room. I gazed into the mirror and I could see the face of an entity that looked just like Rudolph Steiner's bust of Ahriman. He stared back at me and bellowed, "You cannot live without me. For thousands of years I have given you direction and meaning and now you throw it all away."

"You just encountered Ahriman, the father of lies and the god of the material world – the demiurge." Liz said. "Wow. Then what happened?" She asked.

"I reached out and broke the mirror. I smashed it and at that moment I felt as if I'd been expelled from heaven and thrown down to earth. That I had died. It's this damn work for Oliver Stone. It's killing me."

Liz was sympathetic. "Paul you got the message in your remote view. Didn't the woman tell you Oliver thought you were a house of mirrors? Well you just broke the mirror. Oliver Stone didn't do this to you. He just tricked you into doing it to yourself because you wanted it done."

I fell back to sleep and was immediately back in the dream. All the walls were lowered now. The pyramid was gone and even the room underneath. All that was left was the broken mirror in the middle of a blank square. The only black was the reflection of darkness in it. But as I watched, the mirror began to re-form, pieces pulling themselves back together as if challenging me to stop them. Some part of me wanted that mirror back together. Some part of me wanted that black pyramid. Some part of me wanted the power that Ahriman had brought to it. I had to decide and I did by pulling the mirror off the wall and shattering it once again, only this time I set the mirror on fire.

As the smoke cleared I could see the glowing white ball that I had tried to free in a dream a year before had been released. And as it burst into flame, it filled the blank square with light and I fell into a deep sleep.

***

Janet Yang called a week later and told Liz that Oliver had changed his mind. "They don't want us to rewrite the draft, and she emphasized they won't pay us." She said.

"And what did you tell her?" I asked.

"I said we're going to write it even if we don't get paid."

Something had changed in our relationship to both Oliver and Janet. There was tension now where before there had been harmony. And as the December debut of *Heaven and Earth* approached, our access to Oliver's mystical communication dream network brought our journey to IXTLAN into places we could never have imagined.

***

It was November 29/30 1993 – one full moon after Liz's ceremony dream. I was exhausted and wanted a break. But I also wanted to know where Liz was going in her dreams. So I tried an experiment. As I fell off to sleep I again expressed an intention, but this time to go to the land where Liz had had her most important dreams. I knew it was a long shot but as I fell into the white clouds I soon found myself in a large indoor arena with a dirt floor and actor Tommy Lee Jones reenacting a scene. Shirtless, he walked toward me and I introduced myself as someone who had written material for Oliver. Suddenly Oliver appeared from behind with a broad grin.

"What are you doing here?" He asked.

"I'm just poking around searching for answers." I told him.

"Meet me in the old white house in the valley when we're done. I think you'll find some answers there," he said.

And so I found Liz and we went to this ramshackled old white House in the valley which resembled the Bates Motel. And our latest dream adventure with Oliver Stone began.

Chapter 26

Back downstairs I was ready to leave but I saw that Liz had become the life of the party explaining to a couple of startled guests how ancient women had created all the realms of existence we knew. Liz possessed a kind of wild energy in this realm that I had never witnessed in her before. I also wondered whether I was losing my mind.

As we left she told me she'd been invited back later that night and I mentioned the unsavory characters I'd found upstairs.

"I don't think you'll want to have to deal with them at 2 o'clock in the morning," I said.

"Then I'll wait till morning to return." She said, agreeably.

I woke up in the bedroom and told Liz what I had seen.

"I visited Oliver too." She said. "He was cordial and friendly but wouldn't escort me from tent to tent."

"What does that mean?" I asked. But before she could answer I woke up again and realized my conversation with her had also been a dream – a dream inside a dream. It was 7:15 and she entered the room already dressed.

Oliver had invited us to the Boston premier of *Heaven and Earth* for Monday the sixth of December. Over the weekend immediately prior to the event I dreamt that I had asked that the fog be lifted from Liz's dreams. As premier day arrived I dreamt of visiting Oliver in Cambodia – camped out in a black tent – while he shot the movie *Heaven and Earth*. In the dream I remembered Liz telling me he wouldn't take her from tent to tent. Was this the tent Liz had spoken of in her dream?

The dream log revealed numerous encounters with Oliver and Janet Yang and how the tone was changing.

On December thirteenth I dreamt that things weren't going well between them at IXTLAN. I watched as Janet attempted to navigate a dangerous bridge. I yelled out to her that it wasn't safe but she insisted it was OK. I repeated the warning but she continued to insist "it's like it was before." Finally as I turned away I heard her say. "Wait a minute. It is different – very different." I then saw the bridge fold in on itself and heard a crashing sound as it collapsed. I interpreted the message to mean that Janet's time at IXTLAN was over.

Both Liz and I loved *Heaven and Earth* – beautifully shot and beautifully acted. Oliver's direction was sensitive and powerful and represented a profound shift in his filmmaking. But American audiences didn't go for it and it lost $27 million of its $33 million dollar budget. The movie had been a gamble for Oliver and his reputation and I sensed from my dream that it was Janet Yang that paid the price.

***

On January 10, 1994 an option check arrived from Oliver's producer Arnon Milchen completing the first year of our three year contract. Where it went from there we didn't know but it reminded us – however much Oliver might like our work, it was Milchen who wrote the checks.

Money was always an issue but it hadn't stopped us in the 1980s and it wasn't going to stop us now. So on the very next day – my birthday – we crossed our fingers and overnighted version 3.0 of Three Knights of Desmond – contained in an empty Laphroaig Scotch container I'd bought for my birthday.

The dream response was almost immediate. But instead of meeting the A-list director who'd helped define American film for the 1980s, I now found a man who seemed to have lost his own way.

"I dreamed with Oliver again last night." I told Liz as we settled down to breakfast.

"How's he taking it?" Liz asked.

"Not well. He called and I answered the phone. I said, 'Hello Oliver,' and he said, 'That's not my name anymore.' When I asked what his name was he told me that hasn't been decided yet. Then he told me.... 'I called to explain why I stopped the film." But he didn't finish. You came into the office and we walked out into a corridor to discover we were in a set of empty offices being cleared. I walked down the hall and found a vacant sound stage with Oliver sitting amid some folding chairs, smoking a cigarette, listening intensely to three men. I yelled. 'Are you going to explain it to me or not,' and I woke up."

The next weeks were filled with vivid dreams and on January 22nd I dreamt I met Le Li Hayslip – the subject of *Heaven and Earth* – outside a collapsed mine shaft. Dust filled the air. Her body was trapped in the rubble but her spirit buzzed around my ears like a bee and I could hear her voice loud and clear.

"Where is Oliver?" I asked her. "Can't he help you?"

"Oliver is gone. He not here. But he took my names of power."

"What names of power?" I asked.

"Queen of Heaven." She said. "He took my names of power and ... and left."

It seemed that Oliver had shifted dimensions since we'd met him. The dream quality had changed. Were we now just another project waiting for the big guy's attention? Two weeks later we found out.

"I read the script and it's the best one yet." Oliver said in a warm voice. "It's getting much closer but I need a hit to do Afghanistan. In the meantime keep sending me the chapters you're writing on *The Voice*. I'm finding this background to be fascinating. And by the way. I ran into Sean Connery at a film festival. I told him about Desmond Fitz Maurice in Kabul and he loved the idea."

We were pleased to get Oliver's call and duly impressed with Sean Connery. But since our project was on hold we came to rely more on the regular stream of dreams than direct communication about what he was thinking. Fortunately they were usually right.

"I arrived at Oliver's private office last night," Liz said on the morning of March 19th. "The Laphroaig box we sent him must have struck a chord. He was sitting chuckling over a box of Boston Scotch. He told me he bought it because it reminded him of his youth. He offered me a glass and I started to drink it. You know I don't like scotch and I didn't drink much but I liked the taste. Then I noticed he was pitching ice cubes behind my back as we spoke. I realized the ice cubes would melt and make a mess so I started picking them up. Then he started to pick them up too. So I thought to myself. "Oh great, all we have to do to get Oliver to make our movie is too make it ourselves and I laughed. Oliver stood up and you were just observing. And he asked me if I could be his 'Right Hand Man.'"

With that dream Liz said she understood how difficult it was for Oliver to absorb all the criticisms projected at him after JFK and that this was what prompted his wife Elizabeth to request her assistance in the dream. The warrior part of him could take the hit. But the creative part absorbed it and it hurt too much.

"I told Oliver I understood what a person must do for him." Liz said. "Let the anger pass through and not project it at him. That's the hard part for people. They think he's a lot tougher than he really is."

***

As the writing progressed over the next few months we continued to send Oliver chapters of *The Voice*. I also rewrote the Afghan screenplay again to update what we'd been reading in the papers. Between the bombing at the World Trade Towers and the Mujahideen's unending struggle for control of Kabul, Afghanistan was setting the stage for a coming apocalypse. I'd reimagined the whole concept and sent it on May 12th, 1994.

The latest effort was an entirely new way to treat the Afghan story – mythical as well as mystical – opening with Zoroastrian fire dancers invoking the wrath of the ancient god Mithra in the mountains of Nuristan and ending with him delivering fiery destruction to the World Trade Towers in lower Manhattan. And so we waited once again. And on June 6th I dreamt that Oliver called from a nearby hotel and told Alissa I should come down to see him. "Tarantino is HOT and the movie is testing well." He said. And it was there in that phantom dream hotel where the inspiration to fuse *The Voice* and Afghanistan came together and where the character of Desmond Fitz Maurice began to take on the form of the resurrected Irish Earl Geroid Iarla – in a life of his own.

CHAPTER 27

There was a lot of action at the dream hotel. Oliver and I talked in a conference room as his people fielded calls. It seemed like business as usual with him. But as we were leaving he surprised me by saying. "I spoke to your father and he has a message for you. He said he's very concerned about you leading that hard Irish life."

"If Oliver got a message from your father," Liz said contemplating the possibilities. "He had visited the land of the dead."

"And visiting the land of the dead is dangerous." I said telling Liz more about the dream. "You might not be able to come back, so I told him how really pleased I was that he returned safely."

"But I wonder what your father meant by a 'hard Irish life"? Liz asked.

"I can't even imagine." I responded.

***

In July of 1994 we met with Oliver in L.A. and it was clear that IXTLAN was in transition. Where it was transitioning *to* wasn't clear. Oliver requested that we expand the role of the rebel, drug-dealing Gulbuddin Hekmatyar in the latest rewrite and to my great surprise requested that we look into going back with him to Afghanistan. With the fighting around Kabul out of control and Iran completely off limits to Americans I couldn't imagine how that was going to happen. The triumph of the Mujahideen over the Soviet backed PDPA government had left most of our contacts swinging from the lampposts. I told Oliver we would look into it. But when I mentioned the idea to Eric, it became clear that Afghanistan was going nowhere.

"That's not a good idea at all. I don't want Oliver going to Afghanistan." Eric said, grumbling over dinner a few nights later in Santa Monica. "I have plans for the future and *that's* not something I want him to do."

It was no surprise that Eric's plans were to advance his own film project but his open warning about travelling to Afghanistan made it clear he was undermining ours.

In addition, *Nixon* was proving to be a burden from the start. We learned that Oliver's producer Arnon Milchen never believed the production warranted a $40 million dollar budget. The problem wasn't Eric or the scriptwriters he'd brought in. The problem was Richard Nixon. Oliver's powerful and dynamic *JFK* had lifted the nation and helped to heal an open wound in the American psyche. Eric's *Nixon* revived wounds Americans wanted forgotten.

The struggle over *Nixon* created a crisis inside IXTLAN and sucked the air out of Afghanistan but the bright spot for us was Oliver's growing interest in *The Voice.* And so as his focus shifted we found ourselves returning to the reason we'd contacted him in the first place – the mystical. And that was when Alissa's dreams with my father began to lead us to the answers we'd been looking for.

***

"Over the last two years Alissa has received two dream messages from my father." I said to Liz. "One came through an eight hundred year old man connected to Afghanistan and another through Oliver Stone. How are they connected?"

"Through the mystical communications network. What else?" Liz said.

"Okay. But what's the common thread?" I asked.

"Your father was a soldier in World War II and so was Oliver's. Oliver was in Vietnam. Soldiers face death as a matter of course. That makes every soldier a Holy Warrior and you risked your life by going to a war in Afghanistan. Your father's connecting to you on that channel."

"So what is it about Irish life that's so hard? And why is my father so concerned about it in the afterlife he keeps sending me messages through it?" I asked Liz.

"I don't know yet. But I'm working on it." Liz said.

I went back to the beginning and retraced my moves before writing *The Voice* research paper – the one we'd given Oliver that April 20th 1992. In my first conversation with Janet Yang, she had asked me how I'd known Oliver so well and whether there was something she could read that would help her understand. I told her that I'd been reading W.B. Yeats' *A Vision* and recommended it. So I dug out my copy and poured over the pages again and for the first time realized what I had done. I wasn't only tuned into the holy warrior network. I was also on W.B. Yeats' communication network, the ancient one he'd uncovered with his wife Georgie back in the 1930s.

"So we were already primed and ready to go for Oliver Stone." A shocked Liz said when I told her.

"*A Vision* is more than just a spiritual guide book. Apparently *A Vision* is a work of sacred geometry. We were already working magic with *The Voice* and didn't even know it." I said turning to the book. Listen to this:

> *I have heard my wife in the broken speech of some quite ordinary dream use tricks of speech characteristic of the philosophic voices. Sometimes the philosophic voices themselves have become vague and trivial or have in some other way reminded me of dreams.... For one said in the first month of communication, 'We are often but created forms', and another, that the spirits do not tell a man what is true but create such conditions, such a crisis of fate, that the man is compelled to listen to his Daimon.*

"His Daimon?" Liz said, grasping it immediately. The Daimon was the ancient Greek word for destiny or fate. So we were already in a conversation with *our own* fate when we met with Oliver?"

"And his too, I assume. The Daimons were tricking all of us into going places we didn't necessarily know existed."

"So we created a Trinity." Liz said.

"Exactly. Your Daimon already knew what we were doing. Listen."

> *And again and again they have insisted that the whole system is the creation of my wife's Daimon and of mine, and that it is as startling to them as it to us. Mere 'spirits' my teachers say are the 'objective', a reflection and distortion; reality itself is found by the Daimon in what they call – in commemoration of the Third Person of the Trinity – the Ghostly Self.*
>
> *Much that has happened, much that has been said, suggests that the communicators are the personalities of a dream shared by my wife, by myself, [and] occasionally by others.*

Liz was astonished. "And so the ceremony dream. We were all making it official."

"Through a *sacred* ceremony." Look at this," I said, pointing to another discovery. "I found this quote from Yeats in another work."

> *I think it was Heraclitus who said: the Daimon is our destiny... I am persuaded that the Daimon delivers and deceives us, and that he wove the netting from the stars and threw the net from his shoulder. Then my imagination runs from Daimon to sweetheart... I even wonder if there may not be some secret communion, some whispering in the dark between the Daimon and the sweetheart.*

"Do you see what he's saying?" I asked. "You started painting the stars on my back after I gave you the paint brush. Remember?" Yeats wrote that *The Daimon wove the netting from the stars and threw the net from his shoulder.*

"You're a painter, not a weaver." I said. "So your Daimon used the metaphor of a paintbrush to create the stars. Then he wrote, *Then my imagination runs from Daimon to sweetheart.* You said I asked if you fell in love with him. That was your Daimon talking to you. Not me."

"So the chapters from *The Voice* you've been writing are channeling the philosophic voices of the Daimons." Liz said.

"I don't know how it works but writing *The Voice* opened us up to the voices of the gods, or our fates, or maybe the earth's fate. I don't know. But it all happens in dreams. Yeats described it later on as a 'Communion of the Living and the Dead.' He cited Swedenborg describing all the entities 'between the celestial state and death – the dramatis personae of our dreams – as plastic, fantastic and deceitful.' Now that I understand it I feel compelled to finish it and God knows what role Afghanistan will play."

I was just beginning to understand the power that the writing had unleashed. Liz and I were experiencing an ancient practice that Yeats and his wife had rediscovered back in the early part of the 20th century. And it was directly connected to the Fairy Faith in Celtic countries. It really didn't matter what Oliver or Janet or Eric really thought about it. It was what it was, and I'd reached the point where I didn't care what they thought.

In addition to that the Irish legends and myths used by Yeats in his plays and stories were those that corresponded directly to Gerald of Windsor and his family, and what he'd engaged when first going to Ireland in 1102. Reading *A Vision* was like stumbling onto a secret cipher that decoded the destiny of Western civilization from its beginning until its end. But I knew I hadn't just stumbled on it. The Voice had called out to me and I'd answered it. Now I just had to figure out what it was trying to say.

Chapter 28

As we reached the fall of 1994 our experience in the mythic realm began to resemble what Yeats called "the arbitrary, harsh, and difficult symbolism" of mingling reality with the dream world. He recalled the struggles he'd had grappling with his mythic heroes and wrote that "It was only by watching my own plays that I came to understand this reverie, this twilight between sleeping and waking, this bout of fencing, alike on stage and in the mind, between man and phantom... is the condition of tragic pleasure."

There was no "tragic pleasure" in our effort with Afghanistan – tragic maybe – pleasure no. Yes we finally had a Hollywood deal but it literally sucked. Our life's work was in the hands of people we didn't know and with the exception of Oliver, couldn't trust. What we did have was a twilight realm – a perfect place in which to struggle with the messages we'd been receiving. And so I soldiered on to finish *The Voice* as the dreams persisted relentlessly.

We were now more than halfway through our contract but the nature of the dream experience was evolving beyond our relationship with Oliver Stone. On October 15, I told Liz about a dream that reminded me of the Koresh experience from over a year before.

"I found myself walking with a group of men dressed in black suits and white shirts through the ruins of a city." I said. "We came to a courtyard with a bronze statue of a horse and rider surrounded by bombed-out buildings with broken classical columns. The rooves of the buildings had been torn off as if by war. Debris filled the streets. Small explosions could still be heard from around the area as we climbed the white marble steps of a building. Inside a technician was working unsuccessfully at a broken console. He told me, 'We even made a new key for it, but it won't turn in the lock.' I reached over and turned the key clockwise and it gave with a loud click. A panel rose from the console which revealed a moving three-dimensional map of instructions encased in a diamond-shaped object."

"Where was it?" Liz asked.

"I'm coming to that. The map looked like a series of Rorschach tests when suddenly the words *on the signal push the left button* appeared across the map. I pushed the button but nothing happened. The technician sitting next to me then said, 'Now I know what to do.' He then reached down inside the cabinet and touched a glass dome causing a screen to appear. On the screen were skin divers in wet suits hauling something from the ocean-bottom. A voice from the screen said, 'the discovery was brought to Brookhaven National Laboratory for analysis.' I then saw a van pulling up to the lab and the dream ended."

"What was the discovery in the van?" Liz asked.

"I don't know." I said. "But it must have been something connected to the explosion. I looked up Brookhaven Lab this morning. The place is a nuclear physics laboratory. They have this huge circular particle accelerator there."
"What does that do?"

"Searches for the Holy Grail of physics." I said.

"Which is?"

"Proof that large bodies – like the planets – can bend spacetime. It said there had been some kind of incident there back in April. Something about a High Beam Flux Reactor that caught fire."

"Wasn't there some kind of Flux Reactor in that movie *Back to The Future*?" Liz asked.

"The Flux capacitor. It was the device that made time travel possible."

Liz laughed. "So you think somebody was trying to travel back in time?"

"It was just a dream." I said. "But it was a lot like the Koresh dream. Realistic with a lot of technical details and very specific."

I was coming to the conclusion that there was much more to Hollywood's role than just making movies. There appeared to be a vast network of information ready to draw from that had nothing to do with entertainment and I had found myself connected to it.

"To William Butler Yeats, metaphors were the language of dreams and dreams were metaphors for a truth we couldn't understand." Liz said. "Dreams were metaphors for the Otherworld, beyond our senses."

"But what if the metaphors aren't beyond our senses. And what if the act of writing brings the metaphors to life?" I added.

On October 17, I revisited a Nazi dream I'd had years before but this time I could make more sense of it.

"You remember that dream I had years ago where I found myself in Germany with a bunch of American and British commandos at night?" I asked Liz the next morning.

"The one where you told the German officer you were descended from the Norman-Hibernian king of Ireland."

"But this time I was aware that it had something to do with the Grail. Remember all that stuff in Raiders of the Lost Ark? How they made the Nazis out to be so evil because they were looking for the Grail? Well the Germans and the Americans started out searching for it together in Central Asia."

Liz smiled. "What they don't tell you."

"The focus was around Tibet but they went through Afghanistan and explored the entire region looking for clues – three times. A mainline guy from Philadelphia – Brooke Dolan and a German named Ernst Schäfer left Berlin in January 1931for Moscow and then Siberia, Manchuria and down to Peking. The two did it again in 1934 and Dolan helped to finance the 1938 SS expedition which Schäfer led."

"The SS expedition?"

"The U.S. wasn't at war until 1941. A lot of American businessmen were in favor of an alliance with the Germans, not the British. Himmler was searching for the Holy Grail and anyone connected to it. He had a whole esoteric department called the Ahnenerbe (Ancestral Heritage) organized to look for it."

"So how does that fit in with your dream about the High Beam Flux Reactor?" Liz asked.

"Time – or spacetime to be exact. The chronology of death and rebirth – Sunrise and Sunset – Resurrection. The God of time is a space god located in the heavens – in the Cosmos. As it is above so it is below."

"And the Mithraic mysteries are the steps necessary to know man's relationship to that God." Liz added.

"It's too much information to learn all at once. But to know God is to know time and to know time is to become one with it."

"Then the real Holy Grail of physics is the perfection of humanity through time? Of course. Rudolph Steiner identified it in his writings. Let me see if I can find it." Liz said as she ran off to the bookshelf. "Here it is. *Christ And the Spiritual World – The Search for the Holy Grail,* Lecture IV 31 December 1913, Leipzig. *Yesterday we spoke of how preparation was made for that which had to come about for the evolution of humanity. We spoke of the three permeations of a Being of the higher Hierarchies by the Christ. The first post-Atlantean world picture to show a direct effect of the threefold Christ-event was that which arose from the Zarathustrian impulse. From the point of view relevant here I should like to associate the Zarathustrian world-picture with "Chronology." It looks beyond the two Beings, Ahura Mazda and Ahriman, to the workings of Time – Zervan Akarana. From this Being proceed the rulers of Time.*

"Ruling time. That's where the Grail ritual crosses over into alchemy. It takes time for all that to happen." I said. "The Grail ritual is about the evolution of humanity – all humanity – the striving for perfection over time. It's a fucking metaphor. I don't know if the Nazis were looking for the Ark of the Covenant. But their search for the Holy Grail suggests they sure as hell wanted the control of time."

***

February 1995. As we entered the third year of our contract, the dreams continued relentlessly. But the tone of our real-world contacts with Oliver and his staff had changed dramatically. A visit to his office in late February revealed an altered landscape at IXTLAN with Janet Yang out of the picture on our project and a former talent agent and producer now in charge.

"It looks like Oliver's got a new sidekick." Liz said after a brief meeting. "He strikes me as a Hollywood deal maker – you know the type."

"Yea. I do. *If you want to send a message don't go to Hollywood go to Western Union.*"

It was pretty clear from our first encounter with "Danny", that the emphasis at IXTLAN was now less on making statements than on making money. The change in tone was stark.

"Azita told me that Milchen wouldn't give Oliver the money for Nixon so he brought Danny in to find him another financier." Liz said.

"And who did he find?" I asked.

"A guy named Andrew Vanja. He's producing another *Die Hard* Film coming out this summer with Bruce Willis. *Die Hard with a Vengeance.*"

It was now my turn to be shocked. "I had a dream with Azita and Bruce Willis just a few weeks ago on my birthday." I said. "We were in Oliver's new offices somewhere. Azita went off to get a file or something and I saw Bruce Willis. He came right over and asked me to please help him get back into Oliver's good graces now that he knew Tarentino was a prick. He pleaded with me that he didn't mean to get on the wrong side of Oliver."

"What did you tell him?" Liz asked.

"That I had no influence with Oliver to do that – no influence at all."

Chapter 29

I didn't know at that moment in 1994 that Bruce Willis had been desperate for the John Travolta role in Quentin Tarantino's *Pulp Fiction*. Willis only got into the film as a last minute replacement for Matt Dillon who'd pissed off Tarentino and got fired. Tarentino had written *Natural Born Killers* around the same time so I must have stumbled onto Oliver's Tarentino channel and picked up on Willis's angst. I had forgotten from my years in show business how desperate actors were to keep working and how far they'd go to curry favor. Dreaming about someone else's angst was taking it to a new extreme. But this was the kind of thing that was happening on a regular basis and by the spring of 1995 I was getting used to it. As the year progressed though it appeared that we had no influence with Oliver to do much of anything. Our encounters at IXTLAN with Danny and Eric were a waste of time. And when it came to advice on our screenplay we'd have been better off talking to the wall. To recap; Afghanistan had been engineered to lure the Soviet Union away from détente and arms control into a Vietnam quagmire. The forces behind it were the same right wing fascists who'd launched World War II. Under the CIA's auspices they had been successfully integrated into a worldwide covert network (under the cover of being pro-democracy) and infiltrated into governments around the world. They had operated a global narcotics racket during the Vietnam occupation and facilitated its migration from Southeast Asia to Afghanistan's lawless borders after the fall of Saigon. Some oil rich Arab states had joined in to help out the operation while spreading their explosive brand of radical Islam into Europe, the U.S. and Central Asia. The fallout was already terrorizing the world. A mysterious new group called the Taliban had emerged to do battle with the remnants of the Afghan Mujahideen and the only person who had the sense to care about any of it was now committed to doing a film about a president who was universally loathed.

When Azita told us that Vanja had been the guy to bring *Rambo* to the screen and would now own our project, it nearly tossed me over the edge.

"This is not good news." I practically shouted. "Rambo is a comic book hero. He represents everything that's wrong with Hollywood."

Oliver was obviously not going to turn our Afghanistan story into Rambo IV. But when he responded to my most recent effort to rewrite Afghanistan as a political thriller by saying, "I'm not Costa Gavras," it all went downhill.

Initially I feared the switchover from Milchen to Vanja meant our project would enter some kind of twilight zone with Milchen taking it and Oliver losing control. His decision to buy it from Milchen outright solved that at the get go. But the uncertainty of not knowing which way to go with the screenplay was now growing.

The one bright spot was with Oliver's enthusiasm for *The Voice* and we would spend the next months laboring to transform some medieval mysticism and the Fitzgeralds use of it into a twentieth century story.

The more we researched the more it became clear that an occult conspiracy had been moving behind the scenes for millennia, starting wars, assassinating leaders and secretly directing the flow of history towards its goal. A guy named Michael Howard had even written a book about it and made the idea sound plausible. When you added the outright destruction of the Fitzgerald dynasty in 1583 and JFK to the mix, you might even have called it an invisible history.

> While occultism, like all religious systems, has its fair share of eccentrics it also boasts members who are respectable people of high social standing. A dyed-in-the-wool materialist who dismisses the occult as pure fantasy will be even more shocked by the central thesis of this book… that many famous historical personalities of the last 2,000 years, including statesmen, politicians, religious leaders and royalty, were actively involved in the occult, mysticism and magical practices. In addition it will show that many of the major historical events of the period have a hidden significance which can only be explained in terms of an occult conspiracy.

We had encountered evidence of numerous secret societies and hidden agendas in our dealings with Afghanistan. The world's intelligence services were by definition occult conspiracies and those were just the so called "legal ones." The word occult simply meant hidden, but what were they hiding and why keep it a secret? JFK had come up against an occult conspiracy in his quest for world peace. But why did he need to be so brutally slain? To act as an example for those who would follow in his path? Or was his murder another in an ancient tradition of sacrifice demanded by an ancient priesthood that ruled beyond the material world?

I knew that getting to the bottom of this mystery was probably impossible. I would need guides to an underworld I barely knew existed. I would also have to work my way through it by myself and I didn't know which would be more difficult. So I decided to dig into the mystical experiences I'd had while working with Oliver and that was when the darkness began to come alive.

"Don't you love me the best?" The Black Knight said to me one night as a full moon shown through the skylight. "The time has come for you to know yourself."

Ahh. There he was. That voice I'd confronted in the dream in the cathedral – the voice that had revealed itself that day in the hospital as I came out of the anesthesia – had come to life as my mystical guide. And from what I'd been reading about the Fitzgerald family and its past, I knew he would have plenty to say.

***

"We're in a position to give people a background story to history that nobody's ever even thought about." Liz said, excitedly. "The Holy Grail, JFK, the origins of the British Empire and not just the dry facts. The ancestors of JFK were involved in the mystical underpinnings of Western civilization. It's mythic. Your bloodline was actually there challenging the authority of the kings and queens in mystical ways that people don't see."

"Well the Angevin kings saw it." I said. "Right from the beginning. And they didn't like it either."

There was something about the Fitzgerald family history in Ireland that had "RESERVED FOR THE END OF TIME" written all over it – Something about both the beginning and the end of things. I could sense it all my life just hanging there, that other shoe just waiting to drop. Geraldus Cambrensis (Gerald of Wales) gave a hint of it with his dreams and visions at the opening to his 1189 book *The Expugnatio Hibernica* (The, Storming of Ireland). The Fitzgerald family were the riders on that storm. There was no doubt about it. They had most likely cooked up the motives for doing it in the first place and the Black Knight had arrived to tell me how it all began.

"Where do you want to start?" He said in a voice that reminded me of someone stepping on crushed glass.

"At the beginning" I suggested.

"Well, there are things you will need to know. The Fitzgeralds who arrived in Ireland came from Wales and had arrived with a mission to establish a kingdom of their own." He said, holding back.

"I already figured that out." I responded. "But there's something more to it isn't there?"

The Black Knight feigned surprise. "Something more?"

"The struggle between light and dark – between good and evil?" I replied. "The prophecies and visions of the End Time. Connecting the beginning to the end. It began in Afghanistan with Zoroaster didn't it?"

"In the beginning there was a void." The Black Knight said smiling knowingly.

"And then Ahura-Mazda, the all-good and all-knowing god appeared to the Zoroaster who taught 'the great idea that all history is a unity.'" I responded.

"Yes. It began with Zoroaster before the flood." The Black Knight admitted quietly.

"Then begin there." I said. "Before the Flood."

The Black Knight drew a long breath and then began.

"Zoroaster looked back to the 'eternity past,' and the beginning of time and forward to the Last Judgement and the 'eternity to come'. He saw everything that came in between as a cosmic struggle between good and evil, until at the end evil is finally overthrown in a great apocalypse and the accomplishment of God's purposes."

"So Zoroaster is the Prophet." I said.

"And Zoroaster's son – born of a virgin mother – will become the Savior, the Saošyant, Astvat. ereta – He who embodies truth. He will drive the Drug of Falsehood out from the world of Truth. Truth will conquer the evil Drug, hideous, dark. He will gaze with eyes of wisdom, he will behold all creation… he will gaze with eyes of sacrifice on the whole material world, and he will make the whole material world undying."

***

"Sounds like you had a great conversation with the Black Knight." Liz said when I told her the revelations. "Did you remote view him?"

"I found a bunch of old research papers from the 1930s and 40s and just slipped into character. I got the impression they were far more into this sort of thing back then."

"Why do you think that?" Liz asked.

"Because the perspective changed after World War II. You can see it in the writing. The tone is different. These people were looking at it as a matter of faith that had legitimacy, not as science. 'Ahura Mazda created many and good creatures… in order that they shall make the world perfect, in order that the dead shall rise up.' Zoroaster preached the divinity of man. Science doesn't preach that. Science is the new Magi, the celibate priestly class who inserted themselves between God and man, then merged with the warrior class to give themselves a tradition of bravery and courage. And you know who the warrior class worshipped."

"I'm all ears." Liz said.

"Mithra" I said triumphantly "the mediator between God and man. The Magi created a trinity with Ahura Mazda, the sun god Mithras and the archangel Spenta Mainyu (holy spirit)."

"And the Mithraic rituals are the Grail rituals. I think I'm getting the picture." Liz admitted.

"The Black Knight is a much better instructor than I could have imagined."

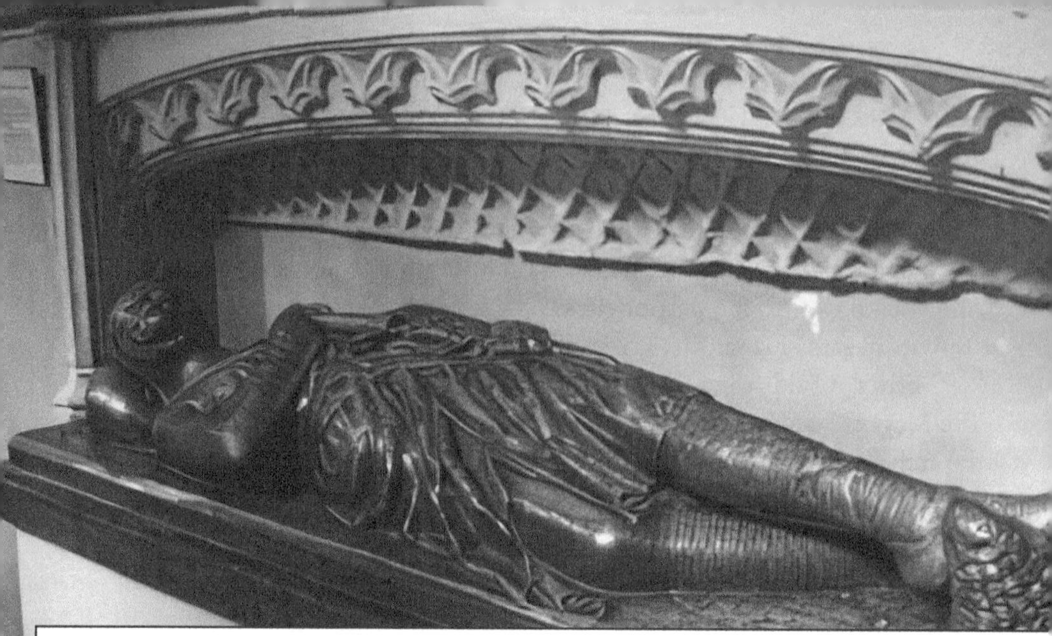

Crossed legs of British knights symbolized the Roman Labarum, the Pax Romana or the Chi R According to one source: "The Chi-Rho is the first two letters of the name of Christ in Greek. C stantine saw these letters interlocked along with the phrase 'in hoc signo vinces' the night bef the Battle of the Milvian Bridge (312 A.D.), which inspired Constantine to embrace the Christ faith. This is the symbol Paul saw out the window under the moonlight. ☧

None of this would have been of any importance to Paul had he not noticed the morning t his father died before the undertaker came that he was calmly lying stretched out on the liv room floor with his legs crossed like the knight above. He thought it odd at the time and a noticed how peaceful his face looked not yet knowing the status of such a symbol. Knights wh fought in the Albigensian Crusade were also memorialized with crossed legs.

Strongbow's effigy at Christ Church (below) also has his legs crossed. Strongbow is on recorc having lavishly supported both the Templars and the Hospitallers.

Chapter 30

April 16, 1995 I got up from bed at 3:20 a.m. after a strange messianic dream and stood at the window looking out onto the patio. It was Easter Sunday Morning and the moon had cast a shadow from the tall pine tree in the shape of the Chi-Rho symbol – the Roman labarum used by the Emperor Constantine as his military standard. If anyone would have known about the legacy of the Black Knight it would have been the first Holy Roman Emperor and I took it as a sign.

"The dream stood out to me as predictive," I said to Liz later that morning – a premonition of how Judgement Day would look."

"So what does it look like?"

"It started out with me having an argument with someone in the kitchen of a farmhouse." I said. "I told the person in charge I did not want to stay the night and would not be there for breakfast in the morning. The person threatened to call the police on me if I didn't stay but I left anyway with a friend. We went to a nearby town to eat and then on to his house to watch television. It was very late and we were sitting in the dark watching a movie when I heard the doorbell ring. The guy's mother came to the door and told me the police had come for me and I realized I had no choice. They brought me back to the farm in a police car. On the way we passed crowds of people walking on the highway but there were only a few policemen directing the people and no cars."

"That's unusual." Liz said.

"Back inside the farmhouse everything was quiet. But there was this large pantry with chains wrapped around it that had been rolled over to block the double door from the kitchen. From that spot I could hear a commotion outside and I saw through the window a Cadillac convertible approaching with a man in a white robe with blood on his face sitting in the back seat."

"This is getting creepy." Liz said, giving me the look. "Did you know him?"

"He looked like Johnny Depp playing Jesus Christ." I said. "Next, I heard a knock on the double door. It was Depp and he was calling me by name. 'Paul, unlock the door and let me in.' He said. I noticed the door was padlocked with a cable so I told him, 'I will if I can."

"Did you have the key?" Liz asked.

"No. But just then I touched the lock and it fell away and he came in – followed by throngs of people who quietly swarmed through. And that was when I realized that this was the Resurrection and that Johnny Depp was the Christ." I said.

"My God," Liz gasped. "And on Easter Sunday – the day of the risen dead."

"I don't know why I'm dreaming these things. But I am definitely connected to something."

"Was there more?" Liz asked.

"I didn't know what to do next so I sat down at one of the long tables that had been set up in the dining room. The people were calm and still pouring in but they weren't saying anything. And then I thought, *what do the dead eat?* The only thing that came to mind was *the living*. So while everything was still calm I decided to leave and was joined by some of the people who'd been hiding out at the farm. The Highway Patrol was still guarding the empty road but was too busy adding up numbers to their clipboards to notice. So we passed out of the courtyard onto the empty highway and I woke up."

***

As spring rolled into summer and the esoteric history behind *The Voice* fell into place, my case for an ancient and mystical grudge behind the Kennedy assassinations began to grow. Added to the apocalyptic fever that was building in Afghanistan with the rise of the Taliban it was becoming clear that the West was on the verge of a mystical explosion. But nobody seemed to understand what was happening. Washington had fallen under a spell of its own making. In order to defeat the atheist Soviet Union, America's high priests had entered into a spiritual Holy War. Washington was now seeing results that didn't make sense in a rational world. But it didn't seem to matter. The West had kick-started a spiritual uprising for the first time since the Crusades. The Crusades coincided directly with the Fitzgeralds origin story in Ireland. As we approached the millennium the similarities between the magical world of Merlin's prophecies and the scientific dilemmas of the modern world were converging. As we added them into *The Voice* and sent out chapters to our director, Oliver began to realize the time had come to secure an option on our Grail story to incorporate into Afghanistan. But as the summer of our third year came to a close both the dreams and the realities of dealing with Danny and Eric were telling us it was time to move on.

Having to tell Oliver Stone we did not want to give him an option on *The Voice* was *not* the way I wanted to end our professional relationship. After three years of involvement we had hoped to advance what we'd begun that day in1992. We had wanted Oliver to have *The Voice* but not the way his new partners wanted. When he told us now he could not do Afghanistan without optioning it we sadly allowed our Hollywood contract to drift away.

***

It seemed logical to believe that withdrawing from the contract would end the dreaming. The end of 1995 meant that we were done. But as the deadline neared I discovered the opposite was occurring. Removed from the binding legal obligations, the dreaming continued – only less business-like and more personal. When I told Liz the next morning she said it sounded like what she'd experienced at the beginning.

"I found myself with Oliver, Azita and you in the dining room in Stoneham where I grew up with Azita on the phone to the Pentagon." I said.

"I can't get through to the right number," Azita said.

"As Oliver barked out suggestions, I remembered that Ron had given me a Pentagon phone book and I ran upstairs to my room to get it. As I rifled through my bookcase I realized it was here at home in my office and then all of a sudden Oliver was there, sitting on my bed."

"Why did you do this Afghan thing?" He asked.

"Because of the overwhelming danger and the overwhelming moral need to prevent what I saw as a terrible future coming." I replied.

"When I said that he got very warm and started to glow. Then I told him 'I came to you because there was nothing left for me to do except deliver a message to the public. Something bad is going to happen if we don't mend our ways and you are the only person capable of doing that."

"I then told him that if he could complete that mission, to tie this spiritual world into the physical one, he had my blessing and my thanks."

***

With Oliver gone, there was nothing left to do but finish *The Voice*. It struck me at first that someone in Hollywood might want to pick up where Oliver had left off with Afghanistan, but without a major director connected to the project, it was no longer a project. And so as we entered 1996, we once again found ourselves alone.

"There's something about Afghanistan that's caused me to break free of the material world." I said to Liz as we started to pick up the broken pieces. "Was it Doctor Afghani who told me that God had sent me as a messenger? Or was it that Greco-Buddhist Temple at Hadda that drew me into the mystical? I haven't seen Alexander the Great lurking in my dreams."

"We know that the Grail rituals are connected to the sun god Mithra from thousands of years ago in and around Iran and Afghanistan." Liz said summarizing what we knew. 'We know that Mithraism was the soldier's religion and linked to the apocalypse by the Zoroastrian priesthood. We know that it was brought back to Rome by the legions and spread to Wales with the invasion of Britain. And we know that the Apostle Paul was a convert to the cult and infused Christianity with many of its rituals."

I thought about it. "We also know that the Fitzgerald family was involved with those rituals." I said, recapping.

"So where does it all connect, and the magic begin?" Liz asked.

"I think the real magic begins when they touch down on the beaches of Ireland in 1169, and the Black Knight finds himself in the hands of a power that his destiny required him to marry."

Chapter 31

"There's a lot of mythology surrounding the Fitzgerald family in Ireland." I said as we began to formulate a thesis. "Some of it's been mixed in with ancient Irish legends but it's also mixed in with European ones too."

"You're referring to the Barbarosa legends about the long dead hero rising from a lake at the end of time?" Liz asked.

"Yea, but those legends are older as well," I said having dug into the research material I'd found. "The Fitzgerald myths and the European ones all borrowed from the same Indo/Aryan and Zoroastrian mythologies. I found this origin myth about Geroid Iarla in a French study published in 1879, *Revue Celtique*. According to the folklore, Maurice was walking on the banks of the river Camogue when he saw the beautiful Aine Chliar the goddess of Munster bathing. He seized her cloak, which magically put her under his power, and then lay with her. Aine told Maurice that she would bear him a son Geroid Iarla (Gerald the Earl) but cautioned him not to show surprise at anything strange his son should do. The boy was born at Lough Gur and grew into a handsome young man. One night there was a gathering at the castle and none of the ladies could compete with Geroid's dancing. Then one young woman challenged him by leaping back and forth over the guests, the tables and the chairs. The old Earl turned to his son and said 'Can you do anything like that?' To great applause, Geroid rose and leaped into a bottle and out again. At that moment the Old Earl made the mistake of looking shocked at his son's performance…"

"And triggered the spell," Liz said, guessing.

"Were you not warned, said the young Earl, never to show surprise at anything I might do? The Old Earl's shocked display forced his son to leave his father's world because from then on he would be seen as a demi-god and not a human and have to go with his mother to the otherworld. "You have forced me to leave you" were his last words to his father as he entered the lake and swam away in the form of a goose."

"So how does that compare to the other legends?" Liz asked.

"The story about Maurice Fitzgerald stealing Aine's cloak is universal. Aine is the goddess of the land that Maurice wishes to possess. He can't just steal her cloak and violate her. That undermines the meaning of the encounter completely because he wants her to love him. She's a goddess and he's a mortal. She's way too experienced to be taken that easily. She's seen his kind before."

"So the cloak is a test." Liz said, smiling.

"And Maurice had to pass it to show he was the rightful human consort of the land." I said.

Liz found the idea amusing. "Of course it's not easy being married to a goddess. Ok. Go on."

"Another telling of the legend goes, once every seven years Lough Gur appears dry revealing a tree covered with a green cloak. The beautiful Aine sits under the cloak knitting. Her suitor, in this case Maurice gallops in on his horse and seizes the cloak before the water rushes in and drowns him and he barely makes it out. Water always plays a big role in the ancient mysteries. In the Zoroastrian story the virgin mother of the Saošyant, Vispa.taurvairī (She who conquers all) conceives him "after bathing in a lake where the prophet's seed is miraculously preserved."

Liz smiled again. "So these stories are metaphors for a sacred creation ritual every seven years and the rushing of birth waters."

"Every seven years the cycle is renewed, just like with Rufus and Becket. The river represents the flow of Time and the birth-lake represents the Universe into which Time delivers the child and all under the signs of the Zodiac." I said. "The numbers seven and twelve are repeated in all the ancient mythologies; seven planets and twelve signs of the Zodiac. As it is above so is it below. That's Plato's Astral magic – the magic practiced by the Elizabethans – the correspondence between the world of divine intelligence (the Ideal realm) and the material world."

"Seven has always been my lucky number." Liz added.

"Mine too. But that's where the Magi come in again because they're the ones who introduced the god of time into the Zoroastrian system. And you can't have time without a time god."

"And what's *his* name?" Liz asked.

"Zurvān Akarāna. Not much is known about the Zurvanite religion but aspects of it show up in all the ancient initiation rituals. To Plato the initiate needed Time to recollect all that he'd experienced in his past lives not to mention the Time to experience it. Time was the lord of everything that happened under the Zodiac."

"And the Zodiac is where the gods of the heavens come into play." Liz added.

"The French book says, Aine, Anu is an Irish divinity in whom lunar characteristics are easily recognizable. The reader will have noticed the significant belief about the necessity for observing the moon when ascending the hill on Saint John's Night (June 23rd). Aine here appears as the mermaid love of the Earl of Desmond, and the ancestress of certain families, like the Mélusine of French tradition."

"And what's a Mélusine?" Liz asked.

"Let me look it up." I said, grabbing the encyclopedia. "Here it is 'A legendary figure from European folklore depicted as a mermaid, sometimes with two tails, as a serpent from the waist down, or as a dragon. She is associated with the ruling houses of Anjou, Lusignan, and Plantagenet.'"

Liz sat back with a look of wonder on her face. "So the Fitzgeralds have their own Mélusine in Aine who is connected to the all the royal mythologies. Wasn't Guy de Lusignan the king of Jerusalem?" Liz asked.

"Just about the same time the Fitzgeralds came to Ireland. Aine's mythology connects the phases of the moon to the birth waters which then links Geroid's mother to the Oceanids of ancient Greece."

"Can I see that paper?" Liz asked, amazed at what I was telling her. "The Tree in the Lake, at whose base a Woman sits knitting, seems to correspond to the Eastern world- fire- or soma-tree, springing out of a lake and also with the Old Norse Yggdrasill. The Irish woman knitting, who is clearly connected in some way to Geroid's fate, seems to answer the Norse three Fates, Past, Present, and Future."

"This shows the similarities going all the way back in history." Liz said, continuing to read. "'The Geroid Iarla legend's chief elements seem to be his birth from a waterwoman, who has been allied to a mortal lover; (b) the alliance of Geroid, himself a being of the waters, with a mortal wife; (c) the young earl's leap into and out of a bottle; (d) his disappearance as a goose; (e) and his present enchantment among the Sidhfir, whence he is to return. The tradition of Geroid's origin recalls classical legends of the birth of heroes on the banks of rivers.'"

Liz put the paper down. "So that explains the water metaphor. But what's this part about his disappearance as a goose all about?"

I took the paper back. "It says here under additional notes, "the tale is probably connected to myths of ancient India and Greece and the Garuda – 'a fabulous being, half man, half bird, appears in the Vedas, the Mahabharata, and the Ramayana. The Garuda approximates to that of the swan. Students of the Swan-Knight legend have frequently recognized the fact that it is from the other world that the mysterious stranger, Lohengrin, Helias, Salvius, arrives. Geroid 'Iarla is directly connected with the same world. He is a king among the Sidhfir and will arise mounted on a black steed with white face to join in the final war, shouting out 'I am the Sidhe prince of the Gaill, and my name is Geroid 'Iarla."

"Sounds like your dream with the German when you told him you were descended from the Norman-Hibernian kings of Ireland. And that's where the deepest secret of the mysteries reveals itself, doesn't it?" Liz surmised.

"Exactly" I said. "There's a fundamental schism about the material world among the believers in the ancient religions. Some say that material creation was divine and can be purified by human experience to a higher level while others claim that all matter is evil – made by an inferior god and should be destroyed."

Liz nodded. "Yes the demiurge, Yahweh, Ahriman, the demon of the lie."

"But I think the deepest secret that the Magian priesthood wants to conceal is that all men and women contain the seeds of divinity and can become gods, or at least god-like." I added.

"Wow. That would threaten the priesthood wouldn't it? So that explains the Albigensian Crusade against the Gnostic Manicheans." Liz said.

"Humans becoming gods is a very old idea and there are traces of it in all religions down through the ages. I think it's safe to say that the Fitzgeralds thought female creation was a good thing. They connected to it when they went to Ireland but they couldn't avoid Zoroaster's war of the light against the dark – of good versus evil and it came looking for them."

"That's because they hadn't reached the end of time. But we're getting close aren't we." Liz said.

"We saw the Ahrimanic nature of the war of light against dark in the Neocons Team B Report. Remember? They defined the Soviets as being Manichean just the way the Elizabethans had defined the Fitzgeralds. But they were the ones being Manichean. They were the ones employing the Demon of the Lie to commit genocide, not the other way around. That was the issue that drew me into studying the arms race and then Afghanistan. Remember the Just War Doctrine? The Pope invoked it for the Fitzgeralds in their war against the Elizabethans because *it was* a genocide. It just rang true to me at the time. The Team B was using an ancient heresy to justify a war of extermination against the Soviet Union and I knew it."

"As Zoroaster wrote, they were using 'the evil Drug, hideous dark,' to cloak their lie." Liz said. "In my opinion that means the unconscious darkness is humanity's biggest enemy."

Chapter 32

By the end of 1996 the mysterious Islamic extremists known as the Taliban were in possession of most of Afghanistan's provinces and had taken Kabul. One of their first official actions as Afghanistan's new leaders was to drag the former Afghan Prime Minister Najibullah from the United Nations compound, castrate him and then hang him from a construction crane.

With the help and urging of the C.I.A and the U.S. government's Freedom House, Saudi Arabia's extreme Al Qaeda network had consumed Afghanistan and was ready to take on any comers to its Puritan Holy War of divine vengeance. There was certainly nothing to go back for now.

Given the circumstances there was little left for us to do but finish *The Voice* – and so we planned an expedition to Ireland to revisit the site of another Holy War – one that had created an empire by consuming the Fitzgerald family in a life and death struggle for its existence.

Dublin Airport – Monday August 1, 1997 – 8:15 a.m.

The last time I'd landed in Dublin was on a midnight flight from London in June of 1971. Back then the airport was a lifeless backwater with a four story passenger terminal and a single, dark Aer Lingus plane parked at the gate. London had been sucking the wealth out of Ireland's land and its people for eight hundred years. Despite the creation of the Irish Free State in 1922 they still hadn't given up complete control of the Irish economy and I was startled to see that it showed. I had just spent the last hour in conversation with a thirty something married couple – Conor and Maeve on their way home from a London weekend who'd given me a quick education on "the troubles." And as I listened I realized I had a lot to learn.

"What do you know about Ireland?" The man sitting next to me asked with a curious Irish lilt. "What do you really know?"

"I know a little about the history." I said. "My father's family owns a farm in the south. My mother's been on about the British all my life."

"Well you're going to learn a lot of things you might not have heard before." He continued as he proceeded.

"Ireland has been officially neutral since 1922. We didn't take sides in World War II or the Cold War and we're not a member of NATO. We trade with the Soviet Union. Aeroflot contracts with Aer Lingus to service their international flights to the West at Shannon. We buy busses from Czechoslovakia, hams from Poland, wheat from Russia."

"I never knew that." I admitted.

"Then I'll bet you didn't know we were not exactly enemies to Germany during World War II."

What they don't tell you. "No. I hadn't heard that either."

"The Luftwaffe used to bomb Belfast and had orders to ditch in Dublin harbor if they couldn't make it back. It was only a twenty minute flight. On any given night there were three hundred German airmen living here. They'd go out to the pubs at night. British flyers that were shot down used to stay here too and they'd go out to the pubs as well."

"How did that work out?" I asked, imagining Errol Flynn dropping a German pilot's boots over the enemy's airfield during a *Dawn Patrol.*

"They had lookouts. Somebody would run into the pub and yell, 'the British are coming' and they'd drink up and move to the next pub. The Brits would pick up where the Germans left off and nobody was the wiser. Eventually a German submarine would arrive to pick them up and the Brits quietly repatriated but that's the way the war was fought."

So that was the way the war was *really* fought. It made sense they'd never told us about that in the U.S. It would have made the hidden narrative behind World War II far too complicated to explain. Irish animosity toward London went all the way back to 1169 and they'd found a lot of like-minded allies on the way. A lot of people wanted British monopolies broken including a lot of American businessmen. But the story I wanted to tell was personal and now that I had returned twenty six years later with my wife, mother, two children and aunt, I realized just how personal this quest for the Grail was really going to be.

"Is this the way you remember it?" Liz asked as we made our way through the crowd to the rental car desk.

"No. It was two o'clock in the morning. The place was deserted and I was alone. Actually I never went into the terminal. The couple next to me offered me a ride to Howth where Dick Reed and his friends were staying and we just walked to their car."

"That was thoughtful."

"That was Irish. That's the way it was back then. We'll see what it's like now."

***

"You're an hour late and we had to let it go." The woman at the rental car desk said as we checked in.

The words hit like a brick. "The plane was late. We had to get our bags. We have two children and two seniors." Liz pleaded as the shock of losing our vehicle sank in.

"Your reservation was for 7:30. We held it for 15 minutes but I'm sorry there is nothing I can do."

I always found it amazing how unanticipated crises could emerge out of nowhere and threaten to destroy the most carefully laid travel plans. A broken lifter in the old 59' Chevy – a flat tire in the Ford. It had happened to me in Delhi on the way back from Afghanistan on my first trip in 1981. I was told by Pan Am that I would be charged thousands of dollars – I didn't have – to get all the equipment I'd brought with me, back to New York. That time I'd been saved by the clever Indian customs broker hired by CBS who suggested we strap all the different sized boxes together to get the pile down to an acceptable number of pieces.

"Mr. Paul," he said smiling. "We have a strapping machine at the office. I'll get it and be right back."

"You can do that?" I asked, totally stunned.

"Yes. We can do that." And he did and it worked.

The problem at hand was no less catastrophic. Prayer was not an option. So I popped the question. "What else have you got?"

The woman bit her lip then stared into her computer screen. "I have a Ford Cortina."

"We ordered a Toyota van. There are six of us."

The woman scoured the screen again.

"The only other van we have is in the shop. It won't be available until Wednesday."

"What's wrong with it?" I asked.

"It was scratched and has to be painted."

One look at our motley jet-lagged crew was enough for me to make the leap. "Is it drivable?"

"Oh, my yes. It's just the appearance." She said authoritatively.

"I don't care what it looks like. We'll take it." I said, breathing a sigh of relief.

Within minutes we were loading our bags onto the shuttle bus and on the way to the paint shop when the young driver posed a friendly question. "Who's the Fitzgerald?" He asked, scanning our motley crew.

"We are." My son Devon responded.

"Well so am I." He said, laughing.

Of all places meeting another Fitzgerald, "where are you from?" I asked.

"Oh it's a little village down past Limerick. I'm sure you never heard of it. It's called Abbeyfeale."

We hadn't been off the plane for an hour and the first ghost had already struck.

"That's my grandfather's village." I told him. "We're from the same place."

Same name, same village, same county, same country. We were probably related.

"How long are you here for?" He asked.

"Two weeks. We have a wedding up in Ardee. Then down to Abbeyfeale for the rest of the stay."

"Well whatever you do when you're in Ireland." He said smiling. "There's one place you must go. It's called New Grange – Brú na Bóinne in Irish. Angus's palace on the river Boyne. I'd take you there myself, but I've got to work. It's only a twenty minute drive from Ardee and it is the most amazing thing you will ever see anywhere."

***

"This is clearly not the same place I came to in 1971." I said to Liz as we bundled Alissa, Devon, Aunt Marge and my mother Theresa into the back seat of our blue Toyota Hiace van. "The last time I was here I had to get Dick Reed to drive me to Abbeyfeale. This time the little people from Abbeyfeale sent someone out to meet me at the airport."

"The funny thing is." Liz said, following up. "I've known you long enough to know you're not kidding. The place is already acting as if it knows you're here and what you've come for. Is that possible?"

"Of course it is." Alissa added as she tried to make herself comfortable in the stiff high-backed seats. "It's *The Secret Commonwealth* you told me about dad. Remember?"

"And what's the Secret Commonwealth?" Liz asked.

"*The Secret Commonwealth of Elves, Fauns and Fairies*" I said. "It's a famous study of the otherworld by a Scottish cleric and natural scientist named Robert Kirk written in 1691. It's an earlier version of Evans-Wentz's Fairy Faith in Celtic Countries but more first person."

"What do you mean by first person?"

"Kirk was kidnapped and brought to the other side by the unseelie court." Alissa said gleefully. "Some people think he never really died and that he can come and go as he pleases like an ambassador from the secret state."

"And we just got our own invitation from the secret state?" Liz asked with a curious grin.

"And he told us to go to New Grange." I added.

Liz smiled. "You are serious."

"You have to be serious for it to work." I said seriously. "It's the secret power of the commonwealth – the location, this location. Kirk wrote about it. It only works for the original inhabitants. I think there's a word for it."

"Autochthonous." Alissa said chiming in. "It's from the ancient Greek. The powers of the Secret Commonwealth reside only in the native inhabitants and their mythological figures. They can't be passed down to colonizers or their children."

"So you're being treated as a native inhabitant by the secret state. It must know your DNA." Liz added.

"And the location knows the sequence. It's been studied. I should say it used to be studied."

"Why not now?" Liz said, following up.

"It violates science's monopoly on reality. They don't want people doing something they can't control. But they'll secretly accept it. The mystical communications network of the Afghans – remember? There are all kinds of things that come under the umbrella. For Reverend Kirk it was the power of Second Sight."

"Second sight?" Liz asked.

"The ability to communicate with the dead – to see into the future" I answered.

"I can see why they wouldn't want that, it might come in handy." Liz said, chuckling.

I stared into the mirror at my mother and her sister plotting calmly in the back seat and wondered what would happen next.

"I'll see what I can do." I said.

Sunset at Newgrange

Chapter 33

I took the greeting at the airport as a sign. I was on track. I'd been getting signals all my life that I was being pointed in a direction. But what was I supposed to do about it at that moment? Driving up the M1 North to Ardee gave me time to adjust to the location. As a young man I'd driven from Paris to Istanbul and back, through big cities and small villages. But there was something personal about driving through Ireland.

"Did you catch the names of these places?" I asked Liz as we passed a sign for Swords. "They're all out of those books *Strongbow's Conquest* and *The Twilight Lords.* Viking settlements, Norman settlements, Flemish settlements, we're actually driving through the Irish Pale."

"What's the Pale?" Devon asked.

"The only land in Ireland the English King was able to control. By 1450 it had been reduced to the coastal area just south of Dublin to Dundalk up ahead."

"And who controlled the rest?"

"The Great Earls, The O'Neills, the O'Connors, the O'Briens and the Fitzgeralds."

"Our family *owned* Ireland?"

"A big piece of it."

"As big as the king's piece?

"Desmond alone was three times bigger and the king didn't like it at all, but there was nothing he could do about it."

"Until Queen Elizabeth came along." Liz said, chiming in. "There was a war – a big war against the Desmond Fitzgeralds." "And what happened?" Devon asked, growing wary.

"They lost everything." I said.

Devon slumped back in his seat and stared glumly out the window.

"Oh they were just farmers fighting over farmland anyway." My mother said, butting in. "There's nothing down south but farmland. The educated Irish were in the North where they had factories and made things. And that's where the Markeys came from."

And so my mother went on for another thirty miles with a story I'd heard a thousand times before. And so I drifted and wondered about these distant relatives of my mother we'd soon be meeting and especially about this place called New Grange. What was so important about it? And that was where my new understanding of Ireland really began.

***

Ardee was a medieval town of around thirty five hundred people on the banks of the river Dee fifty miles north of Dublin. All that was left of the old walled city was the 15th century castle in the center of town but that was all I needed to mark the way. Hollywood had done a disservice to the public with romanticized movies like Camelot, giving castles and chivalry and knighthoods a romantic glow they didn't deserve. Castles were built to ensure the nobility retained their wealth with force if necessary – not to entertain the childlike fantasies of the American masses. Medieval life was cold, cruel and backward. Literacy was confined to the clerical class and even the nobility weren't obligated to learn to read. As a peasant you did what you were told and aspired to nothing.

Ardee's castle was known as the largest medieval fortified tower house in Ireland. By American standards it looked like a moderately sized municipal building but *it was* a landmark and just a block from our appointed destination at Callaghan's butchers.

"It's so wonderful you could come all this way to visit. You must be Paul," said the lovely lady waiting for us at the front door of the shop. "Did you have any trouble with the roads?"

"No. Your directions were perfect and here we are," I said, introducing our passengers, one by one until my mother poked her head through the sliding door. "And this is Theresa."

Rosemary Callaghan had been corresponding with my mother over family history for years. By the time we pulled up in front of her storefront my mother had probably revealed more about us than we knew about ourselves. That was my mother's way. To her, life was a grand parade and she was a queen returning from a long absence. For her this was the homecoming she'd been dreaming about all her life and it was heartwarming to experience it with her in person.

Callaghan's butcher shop was a thriving local institution that been handed down from father to son for nearly a hundred years. Rosemary's husband Johnny and sons Peter and Andrew were the genus of sensible, hardworking and thoughtful men I thought had vanished with my father's generation and it was a pleasure to meet them. Johnny's Irish brogue was so thick as to not really be English at all. But if you bent your ear and listened hard, he had an uncanny way of making himself understandable and brilliantly funny.

Over the next six days we were made to feel at home in a very Irish way and when the opportunity presented itself, to tell Rosemary about our strange encounter at the Airport.

"So his name was Fitzgerald and he was actually from your grandfather's town?" She said, seriously wrinkling her forehead. "And you didn't know him?

"No. And he told us to go to New Grange. Do you know the place?"

"I've heard about it but never been. They say it's over five thousand years old."

"That makes it older than the pyramids." I said.

"I know they made a big fuss over it when they began the excavation back in the 1960s. That must be why." She said thinking to herself. "I'll call the bookshop next door. They have a lot of books like that and the owner's an expert on that sort of thing."

Within minutes Alissa was lording over our newly collected pile of books and perusing a copy of *Newgrange: Archeology, art and legend* written by the husband and wife team who'd done the restoration, Michael and Claire O'Kelly.

"Dad, we have to go there," she said sweeping through the pages as Rosemary and Peter packed up a lunch from their deli counter for us to take back to their house.

"It's a Neolithic passage grave." Alissa said reading from the book.

"What does that mean?" Liz asked.

"It means the New Stone Age. The Neolithic spanned from around 7000 B.C. to 2300 B.C. It's a tomb."

Alissa looked at me annoyed. "It says the Brú was obviously regarded by the various storytellers not merely as a burial place or mausoleum, but as an abode of some sort into which people could enter and emerge from at will."

"What's so special about that?" Devon asked.

"It means they're not mortal," Alissa snapped back as she read on, "that they are of a *supernatural* order and that the abode or house is not a conventional one."

"May I see that?" Liz asked.

"In mythological or supernatural contexts the Brú was associated with the Dagda, the Good God; his wife, Boann; and his son Oengus; all belonging to the Tuatha Dé, people said to have inhabited Ireland before the coming of the Celts and who thereafter retreated into the fairy mounds and forts of Ireland. They were not gods in the sense of deities to be revered, but were regarded as supernatural beings who could and did perform deeds beyond the power of mortals." "So the Bru is where the immortals live." Liz said, handing the book back to Alissa.

"I guess so." Alissa said. "But it says it also served as the burial place of the pagan kings of Tara.'"

"Wasn't that your dream with the German officer" Liz asked, "to be the Norman Hibernian King of Ireland?"

"Yea, but that was a long time after the Neolithic and the Fitzgeralds never got to be the kings of Ireland." I said. "They certainly tried though. What's that other book you came across?"

"It's a book written by Joseph Campbell called *The Masks of God.* The lady at the bookstore said that it had a lot about New Grange in it. 'By various schools of modern scholarship,'" she read, "'the Grail has been identified with the Dagda's caldron of plenty, the begging bowl of the Buddha in which four bowls, from four quarters were united, the Kaaba of the Great Mosque of Mecca, and the ultimate talismanic symbol of some sort of Gnostic-Manichean rite of spiritual initiation, practiced possibly by the Knights Templar."

"The Knights Templar" Liz repeated. "And what if the Gnostic-Manichean rites of initiation are the Mithraic initiation rituals?" She asked.

"Now that would be a connection. The Templars and their leader Jacques de Molay were burned at the stake as heretics." I said. "De Molay is an entry level youth group for Masonic initiation. I knew lots of De Molay growing up."

"And the 30th degree of Masonry is revenge for his murder and the Masonic day of revenge is November 22nd. Liz said.

"And there we are back where we started with JFK." I said, finishing off.

"So the Templars, JFK, Heinrich Himmler and the Masons and probably dozens of secret societies are all in competition for the Grail – 'the cauldron from which no company ever went unthankful,' whose contents both restored the dead and produced poetic inspiration," Liz read, quoting from Campbell's book.

"And we found the source of it right here in county Meath at a place called New Grange, thanks to another Fitzgerald from Abbeyfeale, a lady from Ardee and my mother, Theresa." I said. "God certainly does work in mysterious ways."

Dante Gabriel Rossetti, The Damsel of the Sanct Grael (1874).

Chapter 34

If the Dagda's bowl was the grail that restored the dead and produced poetic inspiration, then the legends were a lot older than anyone thought. The exclusively male Mithraic rituals of trial and self-discovery may have been brought to Wales by Roman legions in the first century. But the underlying mythology that spawned the rituals was much older. Versions of those rituals gained popularity with both men and women as they were mixed with Arthurian legends and spread through Europe following the Crusades. But the mythologies surrounding the Grail – the death and resurrection of sacred kings – had migrated to Ireland thousands of years before from the Near East and lived on in a passage tomb called Brú Oengusa on the banks of the river Boyne.

As Jesse Weston wrote back in 1920, the real story of the Grail was "not merely about mourning the untimely death" of a god but more so about that god's resurrection and the "restoration to life which is celebrated."

It all sounded so simple when Alissa first read it to me that day, sitting with a corned beef sandwich in Rosemary and Johnny's kitchen in Ardee. The Grail legend was about the sacrifice and death of the king in order to ensure the land was replenished. But resurrecting the king and restoring the "wasteland" to life (as T.S. Eliot referred to it) was a lot more complicated. As Alissa read on I realized that understanding the Ireland part of my own quest was just getting started.

"So the Dagda's caldron is the Grail which restores the dead and produces poetic inspiration." I said.

"And it inspired generations of poets and authors to immortalize King Arthur and his knights of the round table – Chrétien de Troyes, Wolfram von Eschenbach. That's easy enough to understand," Liz added. "But it doesn't end there." Alissa said, as she continued to finish the paragraph in the Campbell book. "'Such a caldron suggests derivation from a goddess; and the assignment to *a god* of the fatherhood of earlier goddesses also betrays the appropriation by the patriarchal deity of matriarchal themes – in a manner of the victories of Zeus, Apollo and Perseus over the Bronze Age goddesses and priestesses of the Aegean.'"

"Well there you are" I said. "We're getting down to the basic issue that defines civilization – the conflict between men and women."

Liz's back arched. "No, I think the basic issue between men and women stems from that which gave birth to it."

"You sound like Cotton Mather. And what might that be?" I asked.

"The son's struggle to establish his manhood apart from his mother; and his father's struggle to not see his son as competition for his wife's love."

"Hey mom that's really good." Alissa said smiling.

***

Liz had hit the nail on the head and Alissa confirmed it. I'd wanted to get back to Ireland since 1971. I knew there was something there and I wanted Liz to help me find it. I just never expected to go looking for it with my wife, mother, aunt and children in tow. As the leader of this caravan I'd planned to balance my family's expectations with my own despite being outnumbered. But since the landing at Dublin airport I considered myself to be in the hands of Aine and the people of the Sidhe, the Tuatha De Danann.

Despite being in the final planning stages of a huge family wedding, Rosemary had rolled out the red carpet and by the next day we were rolling with it.

"Peter and his fiancé are taking Alissa and Devon to Croke Park for an Irish football match." Rosemary told us the next morning. "What's your plan for Theresa and Marge?"

"I thought we'd venture down to Dublin for the day too." I said. "My mother wants to see the town again. There are places I remember that I'd like to take her to."

"It's a grand plan." Rosemary said.

Afghanistan had been an adventure fraught with danger at every step but leading my mother and aunt through Ireland posed problems I hadn't imagined. A third generation American, my mother's Ireland had been framed by the heroic stories of Irish patriots Parnell and De Valera, by James Joyce, the songs of John McCormack and the evils of the Satanic "Black and Tans." The Ireland of the late 1990s – ruled from Brussels to the beat of Bono and the Clash was a different planet and I could see by the look on her face – she didn't like it at all.

"She's not modern," I whispered to Liz as we ambled down Grafton Street ahead of them. "I always knew she lived in the past. But now I realize it wasn't even a past she knew. She's lost."

"Let's go into Bewley's." Liz said as we found ourselves within steps of the famous restaurant's front door. "Maybe it'll calm her down."

Bewley's was once described by an Irish poet as "the heart and hearth of Dublin," and if anything was going to bring my mother down to earth it was going to be a plate of heavily buttered toast and a cup of their famous coffee. In fact the last time I was there Bewley's was the only place in town whose coffee didn't taste like heated bog water. The place had been around since 1840 and been the center of Dublin's literary culture for over a century. Poetry readings in front of the fire – creaky floors, lace tablecloths and waitresses with white gloves; it reeked of Ireland's Ghost-writers.

"What is this place?" My mother asked, staring suspiciously around at the graceful century-old Victorian décor.

"It's a famous coffee shop, the most famous in Dublin." I said.

"Well I've never heard of it." She growled suspiciously.

"You always told me about Brendon Behan. You read the plays he wrote for the Abbey Theatre. Remember?" I said taking a deep breath. "You had them in your bookcase at home."

"Oh, yes," she said, struggling to recall.

"Well, this is where he used to come for a late breakfast after drinking all night."

For a moment my mother's apprehension lifted as she focused on the task at hand, but from that point on, it was easy. I'd given her something to connect with, if not terribly meaningful, at least something that once was. Our next stop at Christ Church Cathedral provided Theresa and Marge with a welcome breather as they caught up on their Irish history perched next to the Strongbow's life-sized effigy looming from the Cathedral floor.

It also provided us with a reminder of our mission to finish *The Voice* as we slipped next door to the museum and gazed at the display of Ireland's Viking past.

"I remember this from my last trip," I said to Liz as I marveled at the seven foot skeleton with sword in hand stretched out under a map of 9th century Scandinavian invasions. "It looks like they couldn't wait to get away from each other." I said staring up at the arrows. "Look at that. The Norwegians went West, the Danes went South and the Swedes went East into Russia and Ukraine."

"The Kyven Rus. Huh" Liz harrumphed. "So that's where the Russians come from – Sweden."

An afternoon exploring Dublin was not complete without a tour of Dublin Castle and after the short walk from Christ Church we found ourselves waiting in the courtyard for the next tour.

"What are we waiting for?" My mother asked, growing more intemperate by the minute.

"School's out," I said staring up ahead to the elderly guard in his dark blue uniform making a desperate attempt at crowd control. "They're lining up for the tours."

"I don't need a tour." She growled dismissively as she forged ahead. "I've been here before and they just let you walk right in."

Before anyone could react my mother had scooted behind the guard and was well on her way across the marble floor of the castle before the poor old guy caught sight of her.

"Ma'am Ma'am," he yelled as she reached the broad stairwell and started to climb – with him in hot pursuit. "You have to wait with the others."

Having been witness to my mother's queenly behavior all my life I had to admit that this public display of her mystical authority was a first. A magic spell had descended out of the mist the minute we'd landed and as she was led back to our little group, I decided the time had come to end our little sojourn to Dublin and beat a retreat back to Ardee.

***

I could hear the low grumbling from the back seat as my aunt consoled my mother, the way she'd been consoling her from the time they were children. As the youngest in the family Aunt Marge had sacrificed a career and marriage to care for her widowed mother and had been covering for my mother's erratic behavior ever since my grandmother died. But as we reached the outskirts of Ardee, I could tell the Grail quest was pushing her a notch too far as well. Marge had had it and I prayed the upcoming wedding would bring on an alchemical moment that would shake the mood and lift the load.

***

The wedding arrived and not a moment too soon. All the women in their beautiful hats and dresses – the men in their tuxedos and all "up market" as they say in the north. The ceremony brought back memories going back thirty years – weddings I'd sung at – the omnipresent influence of the Catholic Church over everything. Growing up Irish Catholic in Boston was belonging to a shared culture that had once been Irish but by the time I got there had become mostly American. The hardcore Townie populations of Charlestown and South Boston had long since left the docks and migrated to the suburbs. Worrying about Ireland wasn't something that crossed their minds.

Ardee's Irish culture was shared too but not in a way I suspected. In this small town North of Dublin the influence was distinctly British – not European – in the choice of music, their dress and in their way of thinking. And that was something I had not expected.

Devon and Alissa cut a rug on the dance floor while I sampled every offering of the seven varieties of potatoes that showed up at our table and they were all delicious. Marge and Theresa were the toast of the town as guests from America and were catered to like the queens they thought themselves to be.

And so I shifted to thinking about this place called New Grange and intended that tomorrow we would find an answer to all those things I didn't know I'd been looking for.

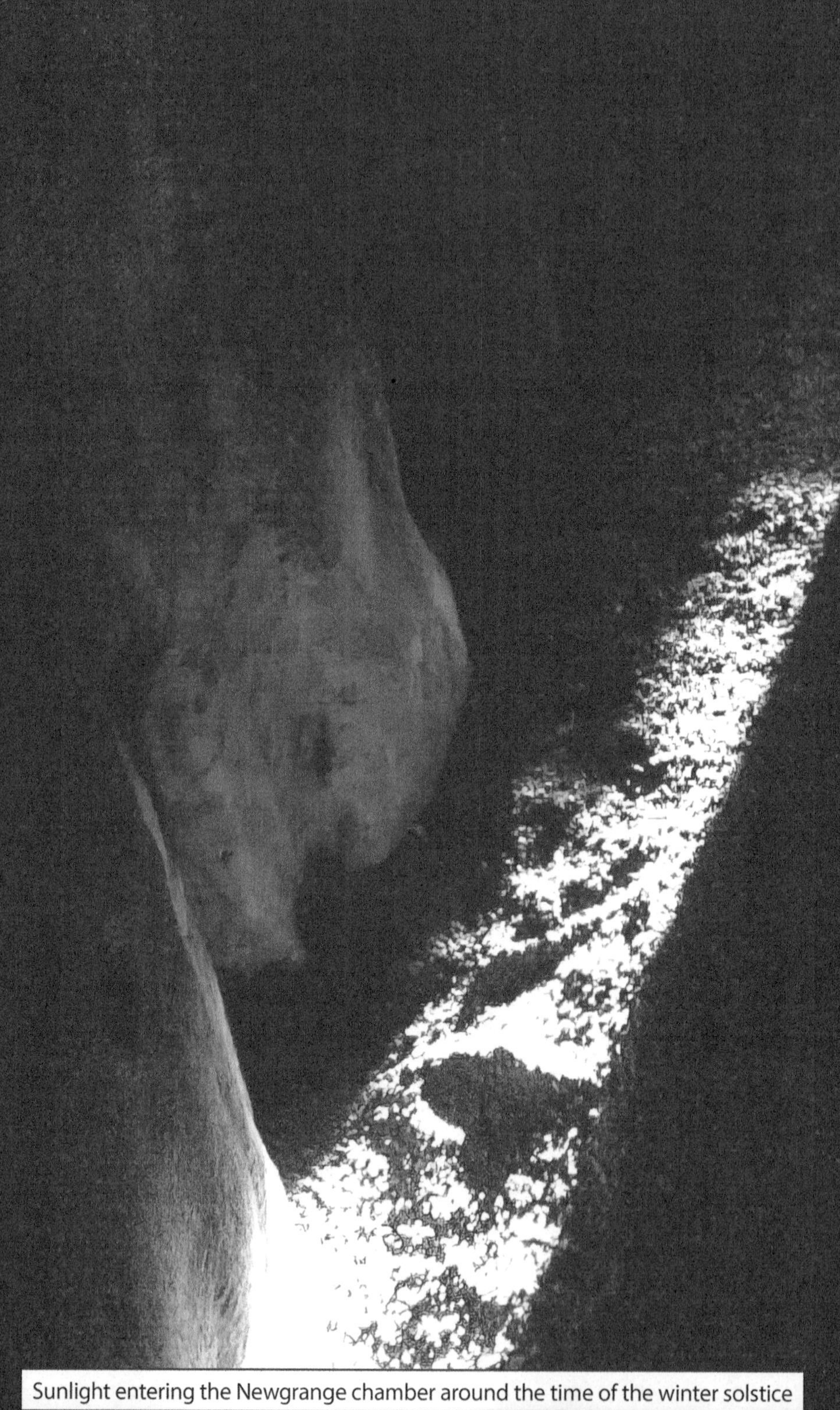

Sunlight entering the Newgrange chamber around the time of the winter solstice

Chapter 35

I had to shade my eyes from the glare of the quartz covered passage tomb – sitting on top of the hill overlooking the river Boyne like a huge glowing mothership.

"It looks like a giant time machine," I said to Liz as we waited for our tour guide to finish collecting tickets from the dozen or so other patrons.

"What makes you think that?" Liz asked, awed by the sight.

"The white quartz, clocks use quartz crystals for accuracy. Radios use crystals to broadcast on a certain frequency. Change the crystals – change the wave length."

"So you think whoever built this used it to travel back and forth through time?"

"Or dimensions, maybe both. The wave length determines the size of the dimension. Actually I think the length of a wave is a dimension – the distance between identical points in the adjacent cycle of a waveform."

"That's awfully technical." Liz said, astonished.

"I used to spend plane rides talking to Mark about these things. He taught at the MIT Media lab."

"I think our tour guide is ready." Liz said, as the young woman opened the gate and introduced herself.

"Hello everyone I'm Kelly, welcome to New Grange."

"So what exactly is a passage grave Kelly?" A fellow tourist asked as we began our climb up the pea-stone path to the monument.

"No one is completely sure," the young woman said. "The legends claim that Newgrange is a house where Angus, son of the Dagda, the sun god could come and talk to his dead friends."

"That's what grandma does when she goes looking for her relatives in the graveyard," Alissa said.

"And how old is it?" Another member of our group asked.

"Over five thousand years old. It was carbon dated to 3,200 BC based on some caulking material used to seal the roof. But then that may not have been part of the original construction.

"So it's older than the Pyramids" another man offered.

"At least, it was already ancient in the second century A.D. when wealthy Romans made pilgrimages to it from Britain. They left gold coins and jewelry to propitiate the gods."

"And who are the gods?" Liz asked.

"The magical people of the Sidhe, the Tuatha De Danann, the children of the Goddess Danu; they are said to have invaded Ireland around the same time that this was built."

"There seems to be a lot of these monuments in this area." I said chiming in."

"There are thousands of passage graves in Ireland and many more stone circles. But this is the largest and most important. It was originally built in the shape of an egg. The facade is covered in an eleven-foot wall of quartz crystal. On the shortest day of the year – the winter solstice – a seventeen-centimeter shaft of light penetrates the chamber inside for exactly seventeen minutes, focusing an almost laser-light into its deepest cavity."

Liz looked at me and whispered. "An eleven foot wall of quartz that houses an intense shaft of laser light for seventeen minutes. Room number 117 anyone?"

"Did anyone ever suggest it might be some kind of ancient technology?" A man asked.

"How do you mean?" The young women answered.

"Well there are so many things about its construction, its relationship to the winter solstice, even the location right next to a bend in the river."

"You mean its spiritual connection to the cosmos." Liz added.

"All of the passage tombs were coordinated with a celestial event. They may have functioned as a calendar. Some think perhaps an observatory. Masonic lore connects them to the Book of Enoch and the Great Flood – that Enoch was taken here and the Angel Uriel instructed him on the movement of the sun, the moon and the stars. It's been claimed Enoch received instruction here in astronomy and was able to warn his great-grandson Noah of the coming flood."

"So that's where British-Israelism comes in." I found myself muttering. "Through Masonry."

"Personally I think it's some kind of ancient telecommunications technology, built to receive and display the spirits of the dead. But that's not the official story of course." The woman said. "The legend does suggest that the mansion of Angus was more than just a burial mound or a mausoleum. It was said to be literally a 'house' where the dead could live and where the living could commune with the spirits of the Otherworld."

"Sounds like a hologram to me." Liz muttered quietly.

Let's go inside," Kelly said.

"This is like being born in reverse." Liz whispered as we hunched down and made our way through the narrow channel into the chamber.

"And there's the Dagda's bowl," I said as we reached the very back of the crypt.

Our guide pointed to the opening over the entrance at the front of the Brú. "And this is where the sun – coming through the light box like a laser – would be received on the winter solstice."

"And generate the endless plenty," I said, thinking about Joseph Campbell's description.

"Somehow I don't think this bowl is what people think of when they think of the Holy Grail." Liz said.

Kelly was quick to pick up. "The Dagda's bowl is not the cup of Jesus' blood and the Bru is not a burial chamber – although it once might have been used that way. The banks of the river are where the sun god came together with the river goddess Boann and created their son Angus and this is his home – the king of the Tuatha De Danann."

"That's the same mythology as Maurice Fitzgerald and Aine, isn't it? Alissa asked.

"Yes, exactly the same." Liz answered.

Kelly finished up. "Ireland was only Christianized in the fifth century. New Grange predates Christianity by at least four thousand years. To William Butler Yeats, Angus was a god of light – the supreme divinity that connected being with non-being. "

"I like that idea about the ancient technology." I said quietly. "It does sound like a hologram you're describing."

Kelly looked at me with a peculiar grin. "I've been here some nights when there are real hints of something going on. There are moments when you can almost see them dancing in the light of the solstice. And we might have been able to prove it if they hadn't torn the place down and reconstructed it with a concrete foundation underneath it."

"You mean this is a replica?" I asked.

"The stones are real and were put back in the same position. But I've heard from the old timers it's not the same."

"How not the same" Liz asked?

"They say that once you could actually engage the shining ones, hear their music and converse with them. Evans-Wentz came here at the beginning of this century. He talked to all the elders and discovered this story."

She said, revealing an old bound volume of *The Fairy Faith in Celtic Countries* from which she read.

> And even as he spoke, a light began to glow and to pervade the cave, and to obliterate the stone walls and the antique hieroglyphics engraven thereon, and to melt the earthen floor into itself like a fiery Sun suddenly uprisen within the world, and there was everywhere a wandering ecstasy in the sound: light and sound were one; light had a voice, and the music hung glittering in The air…

***

"It's no wonder they disassembled New Grange and put it back together so it didn't work," Liz said after we'd thanked our tour guide and headed back into the sunlight. "Didn't Joseph Campbell write that the Knights Templar were inspired by the Dagda's bowl to practice some sort of Gnostic-Manichean rite of spiritual initiation?"

"So now we know why Rome was so upset with what the Knights Templar were practicing" I countered. "The initiation taught you how to manifest in and out of a supernatural reality."

Liz smiled. "That kind of power could be a real problem. Of course you can't take those ancient stories seriously."

"No. But you can take seriously that the Fitzgeralds were engaging the very same rituals in Wales and Ireland as the Templars. Everybody was. Strongbow even funded some Templar monasteries. The Church banned the ancient rituals that connected you directly to the Otherworld – never approved of the Grail legends and made you reliant on the priesthood to talk to God."

"And that's why what you experienced in Afghanistan was so important." Liz said.

The connections are still real there. The Temple at Hadda you visited. The Mullahs you met. There is still a flesh and blood connection to the ancient past. It's not just an emulation. It's real.

***

On the way back to Ardee we paid a visit to nearby Tara, the seat of ancient Ireland's high kings and queens.

In the late 19th century, a fanatical group of British-Israelites had excavated the site attempting to prove Britain's connection to ancient Israel and the House of King David. Convinced the Ark of the Covenant was buried there, they found no Ark but did succeed in destroying four thousand years of ancient Irish history. Another blunder, or an intentional sabotage of the evidence? After seeing New Grange in all its shining holographic glory, Tara seemed more a looted graveyard than a magical court and we soon headed back to Ardee to bid our farewells.

To fulfill a promise, Rosemary had tracked down relatives that my mother had desperately wanted to connect with and we finished our last day touring the old farm her grandfather had left as a boy to come to America in the 1840's – and of course a nearby graveyard.

"Do you put any stock in the Old Faith?" I asked Rosemary after dinner as we sat in her living room.

"You mean the Faeries?" She said with a half-smile.

"My mother always said my grandfather Mike firmly believed in them and he was not a frivolous man."

Rosemary stared off into the distance with a glassy look in her eye. "I heard a noise one night. A crying sound and I went outside to see what it was but there was no one there. Later I went to bed and I heard it again, but I just went to sleep. The next day I heard an elderly man down the street had passed away in the night. Just around the time I'd heard the sound."

"So you do believe." I said.

"That's the way they say the Banshee comes. My mother's side of the family was Dowdalls. And the Dowdalls were known to have the gift."

"The gift" I asked?

"Of second sight, some families are known to possess it. They're more apt to see and hear things than someone else. They're very religious too, and very aware that things in this country are never quite what they seem.

P.Fitzgerald
LICENCED TO SELL BEER
WINE SPIRITS & TOBACCO
7 DAYS

Padraig Fitzgerald's Cellar Bar in Abbeyfeale.

The farm at Abbeyfeale.

View from the courtyard at the farm at Abbeyfeale.

Chapter 36

Looking at the map, the trip from Ardee to Abbeyfeale was a simple drive, two hundred miles. We'd have time to saunter along, stop for lunch and get there well before dinner. My fantasy! Ireland's main roads were not *main*. Americans had been spoiled by interstates. We had the Cold War and defense spending. Ireland had nothing but a tourist industry that relied on good weather. Still, it was beautiful, pastoral and very much *unlike* America. And so the slow-going gave us time to talk about what we were seeing and explore a countryside that couldn't have looked much different in 1169.

"This country is still steeped in the old religion, no matter what they say about the Catholic Church." Liz said scanning the books Alissa had found at the bookstore. "It says here that the tree at the bottom of Lough Gur where Maurice nearly drowned was a supernatural tree that brought the gods and humanity together and stands at the center of many European cosmologies."

"Cosmologies, 'As it is above, so is it below.' I can see that concept reflected in everything we've seen here. The landscape is a three dimensional map of the stars. The stone circles are galaxies and the stone monuments are the planets revolving around in it. Newgrange, with its quartz crystals keeping eternal time. Even the music, the Celtic reels that spiral round and round played on cosmic violins with strings winding from God's beard."

"It really is very much a Holographic Universe, isn't it" Liz said. "It's the Monad of form in which the Monad of spirit can live."

"Yea, the gods created the Universe as a hologram and sent us here to figure out what this thing called life was all about. So whatever *we* experience, whatever we feel becomes *their* reality."

Liz smiled. "I like that. It's not about them. It's about us."

"I noticed the tour guide brought up W.B. Yeats in reference to the god Angus." I said. "I get the feeling Yeats would have understood the metaphor of a hologram. It's like the Akashic record that Rudolph Steiner and

Edgar Casey spoke about. It contains a record of all the events that have ever occurred. All you have to do is figure out how to access it."

"That's why *A Vision* was so important. Yeats provided a system for accessing the unseen world. "Janet Yang suspected you'd used something to communicate with Oliver. That's why she asked you about it." Liz observed.

"Funny how it takes a complete stranger to explain to you what you've done. I think we're talking about rediscovering an ancient system that was practiced for thousands of years. We were taught to think we were crazy if we used it, but there's no doubt it's real. It surrounds us and interacts with us. We call it fate or the Daimon or destiny, but it's there with us all the time – like the hologram. It's an ocean and we're swimming in it." I said.

Liz saw the idea. "Maybe that's why all these families trace their roots to a water goddess like Boann or Aine who give birth to magical sons like Angus and Geroid Iarla."

"You're starting to think in metaphor like Yeats," I said.

"But there's a difference between Angus and Geroid Iarla isn't there?" Liz added. "Yeats reveled in the glory of Angus as a god. What did the tour guide say? 'Angus was a god of light – the supreme divinity that connected being with non-being.' He was an immortal and King of the Sidhe. But Geroid the Earl was a real man who wrote love poetry to Irish women – something he thought the other Norman lords needed to embrace – had a castle at Lough Gur – ten minutes from where JFK's great grandfather was born and forty minutes from where your grandfather was born in Abbeyfeale."

That made me wonder; "so does that mean that both the Dagda and Angus were men once too?" I asked.

"Maybe that's the way they became divine beings – they were immortalized by their own people who turned them into gods through myth."

"I like that," I said as I sighted a signpost up ahead with the word Uisnech written in Gaelic. "I think I saw that name in that *Mythic Ireland* book you were reading, the one by Michael Dames."

Liz picked up the book and fanned through the pages: "It says Uisnech, Co. Westmeath: synonymous with the hill of Mide, the mystical fifth province of Ireland. The hill represents the mystical center of Ireland and an invisible fifth province that unites the country into one.

"It's another metaphor." She said stopping to stare at the book.

"What's wrong?" I asked.

"Well it says that Mide presides over a dynamic pattern, where the entire island is affected by four 'provinces' of Time, with a capital T – Halloween (Samain), New Year (Imbolc) February 1, May Day (Beltaine), and Lughnasa the 1st of August. It says here: 'Mythic Ireland is centered on the story of a divine space-time cycle in which provinces of time continuously interact with provinces of space, thanks to a mythic narrative which draws them together as the visible life of the gods.' We arrived here on Lughnasa, the fourth province of time and converged with the mystical fifth province seven days later. We've been travelling into mythic time the whole trip." Liz said with a curious look.

"And you wonder what happened to the Fitzgeralds?" I said. "The same process is at work today as it was then."

The road was deserted as we approached the hill at Uisnech. I stopped the van on the soft shoulder and got out to survey the site. But as I passed through the unlocked gate and the cows grazing beyond I could feel myself at the center of an energy I hadn't felt since Afghanistan. Our trip to Ireland had given us access to mythic time, and our chance encounter with the mystical center of Ireland had crossed us over from the mundane into the sacred.

"What was it like?" Liz asked as I scraped the mud off my sneakers and got back into the van.

"It's beautiful up there. You can see for miles around, but there was a feeling." I said.

"A feeling of what?" Liz asked.

"That we just completed a milestone. I don't know why I feel that way but I think there's something waiting for us in Abbeyfeale. Someone has been expecting us to show up for a long time. And I think that moment has come."

As I fired up the High Ace and continued on our way, Liz continued reading from the *Mythic Ireland* book. "It's interesting you should say that you *felt* something about this place." She said. "Listen to this. 'Prior to the mechanization of thought in seventeenth – century England, those who had come for the conquest sooner or later entered into the body of Eriu's sacred word, name, and land, and in doing so, played out the role of the male gods. Like Geroid Iarla, they consummated the mythological marriage anew, sharing her bed, her food, and the grave of her outstretched form.'"

The countryside only became more beautiful and deeply Irish as we drew closer to the Southwest. Wherever we stopped we could feel the changes in the local manner, the sound and just the personality of the place that made it starkly different from Dublin and the Northeast. Old abandoned manor houses set off from the road dotted the countryside and I wondered what their barren walls would say if they could talk.

"It's almost like the tone has changed." Liz said as I pulled to a stop next to a circle of stones just off the roadway. "It really is different down here. I can hear it."

"You're in Desmond now. South Munster." I said spotting a handful of tourists investigating the Neolithic circle. "I sensed it when I was here that time in '71 but this time I can really feel it."

Up close I could see that the stone circle was much older than I'd thought from a distance. They almost looked like the ghosts of what they had once been and the other tourists seemed intent on finding out why.

"These megaliths are pretty worn." I said to a young woman who was photographing the stones and measuring the distance between them.

"Yes. I've been studying them in Europe and comparing their locations." She said in a thick German accent. "My mother has been doing it for all her life and believes they are markers for the ley lines."

"Ley lines, really?" I said.

"Yes. There were power lines under the earth used by an ancient people. You can find them with dowsing rods and also a tuning fork. They are weak but still give off energy. If you stretch out your hands over them you can feel it."

Our unexpected discovery was a terrific diversion and we were all soon walking from stone to stone, stretching out our hands and feeling the buzz.

"That was great." Devon said as we got back into the van and headed off for our last stop before Abbeyfeale. "I didn't know you could feel things like that."

"Well according to science you can't." I told him.

"But I felt it. We all did." Devon said.

"Western science dismisses anything that can't be duplicated in a laboratory. If they can't control it and make money doing, it's not real. And worse than that, they label you crazy for believing in it."

"Then I guess we all must be crazy." Devon muttered under his breath.

CHAPTER 37

As I negotiated the access road to Lough Gur I could see we were again in the presence of another stone circle only this one far larger than the one we had visited an hour before.

"You can see how these circles are clearly tied to some kind of ceremonial experience." I said as we walked the long path to the center of the deserted circle.

"It says here that it's roughly 150 feet in diameter. The sun comes up between those two megaliths over there on the summer solstice. It's like Stonehenge. There's your ceremony right there." Liz said.

"Estimated to be 4,100 years old; that makes New Grange a lot older."

Liz smiled. "But it shares the same mythology. Only this one is connected to the last Earl of Desmond and not Angus and the Dagda. His ghost rides his white charger with the silver shoes out of the lake every seven years."

"That's the hero who rises from the lake mythology. The black and white thing gets mixed up a lot. Maybe that's what happens at the end of time when the shoes are worn down to the thickness of a farthing and his phantom army comes alive again."

"That would be a sight to see." Liz said. "I can almost see them riding out in the moonlight."

"I wonder what they'll want to eat after being dead all those years underwater." I said, wondering.

"Look at the swan." Liz said as we started walking the perimeter of the lake. "Isn't the swan connected to Geroid Iarla too?"

"No. The swan is connected to Angus and the Bru. Angus was advised to turn himself into a swan to find his love who had transformed from a woman into a swan and then back again. Geroid Iarla transformed into a goose. But the bird mythologies are all connected. The German legends turned the prince from a goose into a swan, but they all involved the return of the dead hero for the final battle at the end of time."

"The end of time, that's something to think about. We'd better get going to Abbeyfeale before we run out of it." Liz said, frowning.

The road to Abbeyfeale looked just about the same as I remembered until we crested the top of the hill and encountered the Tesco Superstore.

"Does it look the same?" Liz asked as we headed down the hill on the N21.

"I don't remember that being here." I said grimacing at the garish SALE signs and sprawling parking lot. "It used to look like the land that time forgot. Now it looks like the land that time destroyed."

We made our way to the Bed and Breakfast recommended by Cousin Greta and her husband Willy and were soon checked in for our stay in Abbeyfeale. A quick call and we were set for a night's gathering at cousin Padraig's Cellar Bar and I soon picked up where I'd left off twenty six years before.

"How does it feel to be back?" Liz asked.

"Like I never left" I said. "I really like it here, except for the Tesco back there."

"Time will take care of that." Liz said knowingly.

Walking into the Cellar bar was like walking into the past – my past. And when I went downstairs to check out the billiard room I was reminded what that past sounded like.

"Let's swim to the moon uh huh. Let's climb through the tide."

I couldn't believe it. The first song I heard when I got to Abbeyfeale was not Irish. It was Jim Morrison singing like a goosey Geroid Iarla. Both Liz and I had long ago connected to his music but it wasn't until that moment that I'd understood the ancient mythos behind his poetry. He'd died in Paris that summer I was last here in 1971. They'd even found a screenplay from Oliver Stone in his apartment. Hearing him at that moment was like having him call out to say: "Welcome back to the land of the dead, Paul."

Back upstairs the party was in full swing with everyone engrossed in conversation.

"I'm surprised you didn't hear *Riders on the Storm* next." Liz said when I told her about it. "Apparently there was a huge storm that preceded us. Everybody wanted to know if we got caught in it. The sun came out just before we got here."

"This whole trip has been a storm." I said looking over at the corner where my mother was holding court. "It's a fitting metaphor."

It did all seem to fit together. We'd had been riding on the storm all the way from Dublin and hadn't seen a drop. The gods had been watching out for us and our mission to finish *The Voice*. I could only hope our luck would hold.

The rest of the evening was about family, Bill Clinton's visit and how Ireland was evolving on the American model. That didn't surprise me but my father's cousin Ned did; when he asked me out of nowhere what I thought of the Germans.

"Ever since Ireland joined the EU they've been showing up at the farm unannounced and I'm beginning to wonder about it." He said over a pint of Guinness. "The man from the Milk Control Board used to come down here once a month and dip the tanks and that was it. But the Germans keep showing up here all the time now and poking into things they have no business in."

Cousin Pat's son Padraig the businessman was concerned too, but on a more personal note. "And how exactly am I related to you?" He asked cocking his head to one side while squinting.

"My grandfather and your grandfather were brothers." I said as the curious look in his eye turned troubled.

"I'm related to everyone in this room." He said, expressing genuine shock. "But you're closer than any of them and I don't even know you."

And so it was with the Fitzgeralds of Abbeyfeale and it didn't come as a surprise. The feudal right of primogeniture was an honored rule with the Irish and the reason for suspicion amongst the natives. The child of a long forgotten eldest son returning to poke around like a German was bound to raise suspicions and I soon enlisted Greta to calm any fears about our sudden appearance on the scene.

"I'm not surprised there was no provision for the family after your grandfather's decision to pass the farm over to his brother." Greta told me the next day when I repeated the encounter. "It was just the way things were done back then and nobody questioned it. When someone went off to America or Australia it was considered to be final. You must remember. Things were terrible here. The English had taken everything of value. There was no reason to come back. They held your funeral for you before you left and never expected to see you again."

As a teacher, Greta took an interest in our historical work and the idea behind *The Voice* struck a chord.

"There's a museum in Tralee you should visit," she said gathering up some brochures she'd collected over the years. I don't know if it fits in with your book but it involves the history of the Fitzgeralds in this part of Ireland and it looks like it might be fun for your kids."

A ramble through time in nearby Tralee the capital of county Kerry was an unexpected surprise as well as a reminder that just being a Fitzgerald from this part of Ireland was a double edged sword.

> A stroll through the Medieval Experience reveals the streets of Tralee as they were in 1450 AD with all the sights, sounds and robust smells of a bustling community. See what people wore, what they ate, where they lived, and discover why the Fitzgeralds, the Earls of Desmond, who founded the town, also destroyed it.

"So the local legacy says the Fitzgeralds created a vibrant community and then destroyed it. How do you suppose that happened?" I asked Liz as our kids dressed up in medieval costumes and got into the swing of the 15th century.

"With a lot of help from their enemies," Liz said with a grin.

By the time we got back to Abbeyfeale the story had already advanced to another level as we soon discovered Greta didn't stand on ceremony.

"I called the Knight of Glin and told him you were writing a book about the Fitzgeralds, and he wants to meet you. He'll be calling any minute now." She said just as the phone rang.

"I'm on the road, but I'll be back at the castle in say half an hour." Desmond Fitzgerald said. "Why don't you come by then and we can talk."

Desmond John Villiers FitzGerald, Knight of Glin was an Irish author, antiquities expert and hereditary knight who'd inherited Glin Castle and the knighthood when he was a child. He'd spent much of his life attempting to restore the lost treasures of his family as well as the memory of the family lineage with his work as a genealogist. The chance to meet with him presented all kinds of opportunities, and Greta knew it.

"You take your car and we'll drive ahead and show you the way. It's not far." She said.

"And you'll come in with us." I said.

"No, no. This is your story and it should be done by you alone."

And so with a snap we were off. After a twenty minute drive we were sitting in an Irish castle on the banks of the Shannon River and waiting to get the proof of my thesis from a certified member of the Hiberno-Norman FitzGerald aristocracy – the Knight of Glin.

Chapter 38

We had waited no more than five minutes before erudite and polished Desmond Fitzgerald arrived and escorted us inside for a tour and a quick history of the estate.

"What were you thinking, joining a crazy family like ours?" He asked, staring Liz straight in the eye.

"I come from some pretty crazy stuff myself." Liz answered staring him back. "We are a perfect match."

Desmond paused a moment, then smiled and continued. "Come with me. I'll show you around. Glin castle isn't really a castle. It was built as a Georgian Manor House sometime in the 1780s by the 20th knight." He said walking us into the dining room. "That's his portrait on the wall.

"And how many have there been?" I asked.

"There were three hereditary knighthoods created early in the 14th century by the Earl of Desmond – the White Knight, the Green Knight and the Black Knight. I'm the 26th Black Knight and probably the last. I have no sons you see. The real castle is up the road at Askeaton – the Earl of Desmond's castle. It's a ruin now – blown to pieces in 1580 in the Desmond wars."

"Against the Elizabethans." I added.

Desmond smiled wistfully. "I often go there to watch the sunset and I wonder what might have been. During that time a ship came up the Estuary and a battle ensued here." He said pointing out toward the water. "The ship's captain captured one of the Knight's young sons, strapped him in front of a cannon and threatened to blow him up if he didn't surrender the castle. The Knight responded by telling him 'I've plenty more seed where he came from and a strong woman to bear the crop."

"And what happened?" Liz asked.

"He fired the cannon."

"Nothing like telling the truth." I said, wincing.

"There's a good book about the family by a man named Berleth, called *The Twilight Lords*. He really got it right."

"Yes. We have it." I said. "But he only deals with the ending. He doesn't lay out the beginning and what brought the Fitzgeralds here in the first place."

"And that's another story isn't it?" Desmond said with a wink.

And with that the Knight of Glin began a quick history of the family with some little known details I had yet to discover.

"The Fitzgeralds had a complicated relationship with the Normans and with Strongbow, the Earl of Pembroke, Richard de Clare." He said guiding us out to the garden. "The Fitzgeralds were soldiers, administrators and castle builders with family connections in Europe. Strongbow's lineage went back to Rollo, the same as Duke William of Normandy."

"William the Conqueror. So that put Strongbow somewhere in the line of royal descent." I said.

"And a real challenge to Henry II who became king through his mother Matilda, the daughter of William's son King Henry I. You see the families were all intertwined. Nesta was the mother of the Fitzgeralds, but she'd also had a son by Henry who was raised by her husband Gerald."

"So the sons of Gerald were half-brothers to Matilda's half-brother." I said.

"Whose second marriage was to Geoffrey of Anjou. Who fathered Henry II. "

"And thus the Angevins."

"As Henry I's designated heir, Matilda was to be crowned Queen of England but the Anglo-Norman barons wouldn't have it."

"And Strongbow was an Anglo-Norman baron." Liz said, getting the drift of the story.

"Strongbow supported Matilda's cousin Stephen of Blois to the bitter end. A civil war known as the Anarchy ensued which her eldest son eventually won and was crowned king as Henry II in 1154." Desmond said.

"And then came the invasion of Ireland in 1169." Liz said, finishing off.

"Henry II wasn't pleased. The Fitzgeralds were intermarried with the Norman De Clares as well as the Welsh nobility and Strongbow had sided with Stephen against his mother. The De Clares were getting independent financial backing from England's wealthiest banker, Aaron the Jew of Lincoln. And at that moment they were building a military-industrial complex of 10,000 people on the border with England to produce weapons and armor. That village was nearly a third the size of London at the time. The Anglo-Normans already controlled Wales. Having an independent state in Ireland ruled by them threatened the entire Angevin empire."

"And so began the grudge against the Fitzgeralds." Liz said.

Desmond looked distant. "And then four hundred years later the sky fell in. Raleigh, Sidney, and Edmund Spencer – even Christopher Marlowe signed on to Francis Walsingham's service as secret agents for the Puritan cause and for total war. Holinshed wrote an account of it at the time, but the edition was so filled with horrors against the Irish it was called in by the authorities and destroyed. There really wasn't much left for them to do but convert or flee. My family chose to convert to the Church of England to save the castle and the property." Desmond said. "I assume yours didn't?"

Desmond had struck a chord. "No. They stuck it out. Like JFK's people. In fact my grandfather once got together with Honey Fitz in Boston and compared notes. It turned out they were pretty closely related."

Desmond's ears perked up. "Jean Kennedy Smith is down here all the time looking for relatives." He said. "The family used to farm over in Bruff near Lough Gur."

"Mine farmed in Abbeyfeale. They still do." I said, handing over the folder that my uncle Harold had put together. "I've brought along a family genealogy. I don't how much of their land was confiscated but they seem to have gained a good deal of it back."

"The Descendants of William Fitzgerald, Sr. 1806 -1904." Desmond read out loud, turning to the first page before falling silent for a long moment. "It says here that in 1850/52 William was leasing 59 acres of land including a house and an office from Viscount Guillamore in Dromtrasna South. Viscount Guillamore?" He repeated with great surprise. "That's O'Grady. Standish O'Grady. His title was Viscount Guillamore, but I never knew he owned land in Abbeyfeale."

"It also says that by 1901 William was the landholder." I added.

"William eventually owned 500 acres in Meenahala, Limerick, Ireland. He had three farms: one he gave to his son, William, and a second, to his son David and kept one for himself which he gave to his daughter Bridget." Desmond said, slowly dropping the genealogy onto a bench by the side of the house as if he'd been hit by a bolt of lightning. "O'Grady would always work with only one family to farm his estates. That was his custom. There might be a half dozen sons in one family and he'd send three of them to one place and three to another. JFK's great grandfather farmed Guillamore's estates in Bruff. Your people farmed his estates in Abbeyfeale. That proves it." He said now looking me in the eye. "You're clearly one of those Fitzgeralds."

The surprise visit to the Knight of Glin's castle had been the highlight of the trip and as we circled back for the short drive back to Abbeyfeale, I felt a relief that our Grail adventure was coming to a successful conclusion.

"So we've done it. And thanks to Greta we now know why you've been having those dreams with the Black Knight." Liz said as we drove through the village of Askeaton and took in the ruined castle as the sun set on the Shannon Estuary. "What it must have been like to live here in the 15th century. I can see it." Liz said.

"The whole thing seems like a dream, but I wonder if people could really appreciate how much of the experience we've had is real." I said. "So many synchronicities and chance encounters. Alissa and her dream with my father and the eight hundred year old man in the funny suit who turned out to actually be connected to Afghanistan. Dreaming about being asked to join with the black knights and then finding out I'm already connected to a real one? Meeting Desmond Fitzgerald explains a lot, but it raises more questions. There is a power here we don't understand. We keep bumping into it – moving into and out of it but at least now we know it's not our imagination. It's real. Now we just have to make it work for *The Voice*."

***

"And did he offer you anything to drink?" Greta asked when we saw her later that evening.

"He did." I said.

"A mixed drink?"

"He did."

"And what did you have?"

"Sparkling water."

"And what brand was it? Ballygowen?'

"Nash water." I said.

"Oh my lord. He *would* be serving you Nash water. It's so like *them*." She said.

"Like them." I thought. Those Fitzgeralds, the ones with the capital G. I had learned after our brief stay that there were strict rules to living in Irish society – especially when it came to the gentry like Desmond Fitzgerald. I was grateful that Greta had taken the time and the interest to act as instructor.

What the rules had to do with drinking the correct sparkling water I couldn't imagine. We'd been drinking Ballygowen since we'd arrived in

Ireland. But when I learned that Ballygowen water was famous for being drawn from the same holy well once used by the Knights Templar I found myself scratching my head. We'd been drinking the Knights Templar's holy water from the start of our visit. They'd had us under their spell from the outset and I didn't even know it.

Paul at Dublin Castle, 1997.

Chapter 39

We spent our last day in Abbeyfeale visiting the family farm at Meenahalla and then the nearby beach at Ballybunion in the shadow of another famously ruined 13th century Fitzgerald Castle. Four hundred years after the last Earl of Desmond's head was piked on London Bridge, his ghost could still be heard whispering over the waves *I will rise again.* And even after our return home the memory of our encounter lingered.

"I found this book on Irish castles this weekend," a close friend said only a few days after we'd got back. "Glin Castle is in here and I thought you'd want to have it."

Liz took the heavy book and turned the pages. "It explains here about the creation of the knights and especially the Black Knight of Glin but they can't seem to understand the hereditary part. 'The nature of the hereditary Knightly titles borne by several branches of the Desmond Geraldines cannot be explained by the usages of the feudal system. That the honor of knighthood should be inheritable is contrary to all the principles of chivalry.' It says."

I laughed. "Principles of chivalry? Who wrote this? Emily Post? Obviously they don't understand that being a Fitzgerald means defying convention. How do they think they wound up in such trouble with Queen Elizabeth?" I said.

Liz laughed and then continued. "It gives the impression they were not very much liked in the neighborhood either after they converted to the Church of England and the village remained Catholic. Listen to this. 'John Fraunces Fitz-Gerald was born in 1791. He was nicknamed the 'Knight of the women' by the local people. In an election broadsheet of 1830 he was lampooned as follows: This hoary old sinner, this profligate rare, Who gloats oe'r the ruin of virtuous and fair, In gambling and drinking and wenching delights, And in these doth he spent both his days and his nights, Yet, this is the man who's heard to declare 'Gainst O'Grady he'll vote if the priests interfere, But the priests and O'Grady do not care a pin, For the beggarly, profligate, Knight of the Glin.'"

"Wow. O'Grady? That must refer to the Viscount Guillamore. Maybe that explains the look on Desmond's face when he saw the name in Harold's genealogy. It's personal with him," I said reading on. "'His vices have made, and still make him, so poor That Bailiff or Creditor's ne'er from the door, But deep tho' in debt, yet he's deeper in sin, That lecherous, treacherous Knight of the Glin.'"

"No wonder Greta made that remark about *them*. The Knights of Glin have a reputation with the locals and it's not a very good one." Liz added.

Later that week I looked up Standish O'Grady and discovered that the title of Lord Guillamore had spanned nine different O'Gradys from 1766 to 1955 with the family highly esteemed in service to the British Empire, to Ireland and to their community.

"The first Viscount served as Attorney General for Ireland and Lord Chief Baron of the Exchequer." I told Liz. "His son, the second Viscount fought against Napoleon at Waterloo with the 7th Hussars and was made aide-de-camp to Queen Victoria in 1842. His cousin, Standish James O'Grady was an influential Irish author and historian who'd championed the Celtic Revival, Irish independence and heavily influenced the works of W.B. Yeats."

"No wonder O'Grady liked your family. You were of those Fitzgeralds who'd embraced the Irish and never gave up on them, unlike the Knights of Glin." Liz said.

"The O'Grady's were obviously a force to be reckoned with." I added. "My great grandfather's relationship to the Viscount must have hit a sore spot so deep, Desmond couldn't even respond to it."

"Right before we left, the woman who ran the B&B we'd stayed at told me that I could have been born in Abbeyfeale," I said to Liz. "She shook her head and said America hasn't changed you one bit. You're just like them."

"It doesn't surprise me she'd feel that way." Liz said. "Desmond may be carrying the title but you carry the voice and people know it. He may be the last official Black Knight. But you're the real one."

We had travelled through the fifth province of Mide in getting to Abbeyfeale and found the reality behind the meaning of *The Voice*. The Fitzgeralds had rediscovered the mystical beauty of a lost world when they came to Ireland in 1169 and had been defeated four hundred years later trying to preserve it. The author Richard Berleth believed that they had been fighting for a hopeless cause. He'd dubbed the Fitzgeralds the Twilight Lords because they had occupied a realm between reality and legend that had by the 16th century already disappeared into the mists of time.

But as we began our final stretch to finish *The Voice* it was becoming clear to both Liz and I that far from being at the end, the Twilight realm might actually be undergoing a resurrection.

Desmond Fitzgerald was going to be the last Knight of Glin and thereby the last real Black Knight. Was the dream of a Celtic Norman-Hibernian kingdom coming to an end with his passing? Or had the knighthood already fulfilled its deeper mission by removing the final bricks of the black Pyramid as in my dream; allowing for the Saošyant's return and the final battle between good and evil to begin.

The dreams had been telling us for years that some kind of threshold was being crossed. We had used W.B. Yeats' system to explore the realm of the Daimon and allowed the *Spiritus Mundi* of universal memory to do its work. The rough beast, after twenty centuries of stony sleep was now slouching towards Bethlehem. Our meeting at Glin Castle had informed us that the conditions had been met. Its hour had come round at last and the birth was soon to come.

***

I awoke from a dream and realized I had seen my grandfather Mike. I'd never dreamed of him before and he was my direct connection to Abbeyfeale. In the dream I had been setting up a gathering in a small hotel. The woman behind the front desk had been helping me to register guests when I saw him come in and tell her he had arrived for the meeting. She asked him to take a seat on the couch which he did after taking off his hat and coat. I was surprised that he had come at all given that I had long since lost touch with relations in Abbeyfeale. But then he had died in 1959 when I was only eight years old and I hadn't known him very well to begin with. So this was important to me and I went into the waiting room and sat down next to him to reintroduce myself.

Liz was on it like a psychic. "It must have been that post card from the Hofbräuhaus in Munich he sent to your father back in 1954. You said you read it just the other day. I mean he actually licked the stamp and touched it. His DNA must be all over it."

"So what do you think he came for?" I asked.

"To congratulate you for completing the quest and for accepting that hard Irish life your father couldn't complete. Your father wasn't able to go back to finish the story of your family. So you picked it up where he left off and your grandfather showed up to let you know it worked. They told you in Abbeyfeale that you had remained true to what they were no matter that you weren't raised there. It's clear Paul – the mystical communication network is real. You went back to the origin of your family line and you fulfilled your destiny by using it." Liz said emphatically.

"Then we have broken on through to the other side just like Jim Morrison said. We have lived the myth and brought it home." I realized.

"Myths are the stories that make humans immortal. W.B. Yeats admitted wrestling with it in his plays, remember? The plays externalized his internal quest." Liz said. "It's all in that play you read at school – *On Baile's Strand.* The one your teacher told you you needed to read. It explains the soldier's dilemma. Knowing when to stop the fighting and seek peace, knowing when enough is enough. When Cuchulain realizes he has been tricked into killing his own son out of loyalty to King Conchubar he goes mad and has no choice but to take himself out."

"And so my father took himself out. It's what happens when you've fought the war for too long. I could see it in Oliver Stone" I said. "I've seen it in all the veterans, no matter what war they fought in. They hit a wall they can't go past. And they either go mad or take themselves out."

"But you went past it." Liz said. "You transformed it and Oliver couldn't understand you any more than your father could. The war has deep psychological roots and the violence marks them. They can't go back to being the person they were before it happened. They can't go back because they've reached the end of what it is to be human and they realize there is more to being a human than what they fought for. War is facing the abyss. Crossing over into the abyss gives you the chance to transform." Liz said.

"Into what? A god or a human being?" I asked.

"Why not both. I think the gods are looking to us for answers. War dates back to the beginning of human consciousness and our relationship to the divine. That's why Yeats *A Vision* is so important. That whole idea of him getting answers about himself from watching his own plays? That's mystical." Liz said.

"I think maybe there's something more to tie this all together." I said reaching for the Berleth book again. "Remember what I read about the Russian mystics and their restoring the Garden of Eden? Berleth attributes the same beliefs about restoring Eden to Edmund Spencer. But for him the garden is Ireland not the Pamirs. But the key idea is time. It takes time to restore what once was. Listen to what he says about Spencer.

> Time is central to his vision, for through time and its record – history – man interprets his experience and discerns the divine intention.

> First, a lesson could be learned from Ireland's state – past and present; and second that lesson spoke eloquently to all men in all places.

"That sounds like an ideal and not a reality to me." Liz said.

"Spencer fell in love with Ireland too, but in a way she could never love him back." I said.

"Maybe that's the problem with divine intention." I added. "You're never going to know what God wants."

"So let's try to figure this out." Liz said. "The Manichean war of light against dark was condemned by the Church as heretical and your father got a hint of it in France at Carcassonne. Your mother said he was compelled to be in that war. You weren't compelled that way and she understood that about you. Maybe his message was deeper. He brought it home but didn't know how to explain it to you and then he died. He signaled you through Alissa and Alexander Gardner that he's with you. He wants the resurrection to begin and the garden restored. It wasn't possible in his lifetime but it is possible now." Liz said, smiling.

"You know I started thinking about all this when my godfather Ray Custer died. I got the feeling that he'd waited all his life for that moment and when it finally came he didn't like it. That feeling I got with him surrounded by all those monks, walling him off from his family. You remember what he said when he visited us that day."

"He said he'd made a mistake by ordering his life God, the company and his family. 'I should have ordered it God, my family and the company.' Liz said."

"Well I'm glad to realize now that my father didn't make the mistake that Ray made and my grandfather Mike has stepped in to let me know that when it comes to your family, they've got to be first and whatever else comes, God will understand."

The British Occultist, Alchemist and Medium spiritist Sir Edward Kelley with John Dee. Portrait by unknown engraver titled: Edward Kelly a Magician, raising the ghost of a person lately deceased, in the Church Yard of Walton, Lancaster. Published in London, 1590.

Epilogue

We had found our way to the other side of the mirror, been to Newgrange and met the Black Knight in person – and all because of serendipity. We had experienced a direct link from our dreams to the real world which strongly suggested the existence of a hidden influence on reality. There was a place beyond the senses we'd never been told about and another dimension to history in which my own family had been directly involved. But if it hadn't been for coincidence and making ourselves aware of some subtle clues to its existence we would never have been the wiser.

Our background research into the family indicated there was something more about the Elizabethan war against the Geraldines than just grabbing land and depriving a rival family of political influence. We discovered that the Fitzgeralds had come to Ireland in 1169 guided by dreams and visions. The twelfth century was a time when reawakened pagan mystery religions were gaining influence over the courts of Europe and swamping the church with heresies. The new Norman leadership of Britain needed myths to promote their legitimacy and latched on to local legends and Grail sagas to rally popular imagination to their cause. Religion and politics had been entwined from the start as were family rivalries. The Fitzgeralds played an important role in the struggle between the Papacy and the Holy Roman Empire and had found their way into the medieval European power-structure. Following the Reformation they had remained Catholic and loyal to Rome while Elizabeth I had become a protestant monarch and at the same time, head of the Church of England making her authority both spiritual and temporal.

Unbeknownst to most historians or at least discounted by them, some of her more zealous supporters had latched on to the mission of making her the center of a mystical empire more powerful than the Popes'. Further research revealed that Courtiers Edmund Spenser, John Dee and a circle of others had taken the idea steps further by applying the principles of Renaissance Neoplatonism in an effort to bring forth a prophesied utopia.

A study by Frances Yates titled *The Occult Philosophy in the Elizabethan Age* revealed that a deeper "Hermetic-Cabalist core" had inspired Spencer and provided answers to historical enigmas never before dreamed of by literary historians. "Alastair Fowler has argued for intricate numerological patterns in *The Faerie Queene*, and for an astral or planetary pattern in its themes." She wrote in 1979. "Angus Fletcher has drawn attention to the Hermetic–Egyptian setting of Britomart's vision in the Temple of Isis."

Ficino, Pico, Reuchlin, Giorgi and Agrippa are all analyzed in Yates' book as is the influence of "Cabalist-Neopythagorism, with its emphasis on number ... leading to a world-wide reforming movement, with Queen Elizabeth I in the leading role." According to Yates, the Renaissance had revived more than just interest in the ancient writings of Plato, the study of astronomy and alchemy. It had revived the ancient magical practices needed to make it all work. The Elizabethan circle had restored a belief in the power of what they called "white magic" and they had brought it to Ireland and used it against the Geraldines.

So what did it all mean to us that something more than just a political rivalry had been stoked against the Fitzgerald family? And why had we been the ones to rediscover a secret that had lain dormant since the death of the last Earl of Desmond and the foundation of the British Empire in 1583?

By the late 1990s we assumed that Afghanistan was over as a focus of our work. The 1996 takeover of Kabul by the Pakistani-created Taliban had moved Afghanistan off the front pages. The mainstream news media had no interest in delving into what the Taliban or Al Qaeda were up to especially when it came to the rights of Afghanistan's women. The supposed concern for the Afghan people that had powered Washington's human rights campaign against the Soviet occupation had disappeared once the Soviets withdrew. The Clinton administration's ship of state was now steaming toward a full Taliban recognition but life on the Lido deck for Washington's mandarin culture was slowing down.

By 1998 the U.S. supported narrative behind the expansion of "political Islam" was showing holes. Bombings of U.S. embassies in Tanzania and Kenya and the deaths of over 200 people made it hard to ignore the blowback from what the U.S. had done by advancing terrorism into Central Asia.

Things were happening. That same year, Zbigniew Brzezinski's boast that he'd intentionally lured the Soviets to their doom in Afghanistan threatened the carefully crafted victimhood narrative created by America's defense intellectuals and their media cheerleaders. The whole Reagan evil-empire campaign had hinged on the Soviet threat to world peace. Had it all been a fraud? Yes. Brzezinski's boast vindicated everything that we had set out to prove in going to Afghanistan. Liz had even dreamed that he'd been sending a positive message five years earlier when working on the screenplay for Oliver Stone. Now we had it.

That same year we chanced upon meeting Sima Wali, President of an NGO named Refugee Women in Development. Sima was the first Afghan refugee to arrive in the United States following the Marxist coup of 1978 and had been personally hosted by former U.S. Ambassador to Afghanistan, Theodore Eliot.

As a cousin to the 1920s Afghan King Amanullah Khan, Sima came with the authority of the Afghan royal family and after asking us why the Afghan problem had gotten worse instead of better following the Soviet withdrawal we found ourselves being drawn back into the story.

Despite our efforts to separate from the Afghan debacle, Sima's challenge renewed our belief that something had to be done and we were soon assisting her by writing articles and speeches which she delivered to the most prestigious audiences. But despite Sima's importance it soon became obvious that mainstream media had no interest in the issue of Afghanistan whatsoever and so began a new and unexpected chapter in the saga.

At the time the Clinton administration was being pressured by the oil industry to recognize the Taliban in order to pave the way for a pipeline to Europe through Afghanistan from the Middle East. Nobody was talking about how bad the Taliban were for the Afghan people with the exception of Ellie Smeal's Feminist Majority and the Hollywood entertainment media. According to the *Washington Post* the impact of the Feminist's effort against "the Taliban's 'war on women' has become the latest cause celebre in Hollywood. Tibet is out. Afghanistan is in."

Organized by Sima, a meeting in Washington in 1999 brought us together into a strange alignment of Feminist die hards and a couple of right wing Republicans which culminated for us that year in a Hollywood bash at the Director's guild.

According to the *Washington Post,* while the event "was a must-attend happening, gathering perhaps the largest number of celebrities for a single cause since the 'We Are the World' campaign 14 years ago. Some 70 household names – everyone from Vince Gill to Marlo Thomas to Lionel Richie to Paula Abdul to Christine Lahti – were on the guest list. Richie sang an anthem he donated, 'Love, Oh Love,' and Naomi Judd and Gill also performed. Alfre Woodard, Gillian Anderson and Lily Tomlin were among the speakers."

But despite the powerhouse presentation and the newly acquired media attention, the only outcome that succeeded was the failure of the Taliban to gain recognition by the Clinton administration and had no effect whatsoever on the crisis for Afghan women and the nature of Afghanistan as a terrorist base.

Everyone knew that Afghanistan was a ticking time bomb and as we continued to help Sima spread her vision of what needed to be done through the years that followed, the phone didn't ring until September 11, 2001 and the world was changed for everyone, forever.

PRAISE FOR *Valediction: Three Nights of Desmond*

"Few outsiders have been engaged with Afghanistan for as long as Gould and Fitzgerald, and few have learned more about the hidden side of America's long misadventure there. *The Valediction* is a wild ride through the underside of the American war and propaganda machines. It does not tell the story of the Afghan War that appeared in our news media, but something very different and immensely valuable: the real story."

—**Stephen Kinzer**, author of *Overthrow: America's Century of Regime Change from Hawaii to Iraq, Poisoner in Chief: Sidney Gottlieb and the CIA Search for Mind Control* and *The Brothers: John Foster Dulles, Allen Dulles, and Their Secret World*

"Weaving ancient family history and contemporary world politics, Fitzgerald and Gould offer a riveting tale of intrigue that shines a light on the murky but orchestrated events precipitating the December 1979 Soviet intervention in Afghanistan. The book's fast-paced narrative and cast of (mostly rogue) characters is complemented by sober assessments of American imperial hubris and media self-censorship. The book is bound to resonate with a wide array of readers."

—**Valentine M. Moghadam**, Professor of Sociology and International Affairs, Northeastern University

"Time to leave behind the old world view and discover what lies beyond the veil. Paul Fitzgerald and his beloved wife, Elizabeth Gould, have an epic story to tell, deeply personal, and yet very political, historical, and mythological, as well, spanning many empires, cultures, to the very roots of our ancestors. There are more multifaceted truths in this novel than can be found on the evening news. However, that is a major point in Paul's story; he was a journalist, one of the rare few, whose findings contradicted the 'official narrative' the narrative used to justify invasions, war, the conquest other people's lands. This is a heroic tale and should inspire all of us to seek our own truths and challenge those narratives which threaten all of us."

—**Carol Brouillet**, organizer, activist, Founder of the Northern California 9/11 Truth Alliance

"Going back to Afghanistan right now is a long, long journey. Although I've never been there in person, I feel like I've been there through your minds."

—**Oliver Stone** expressed these thoughts to the authors about their work

"As media pundits and government officials continue to struggle over how Afghanistan could have unraveled so quickly as the Taliban took control over the country, Fitzgerald and Gould dig deep into the period when Afghanistan was under the control of the Soviets (1979 -1989), providing crucial answers to the present situation. In their compelling narrative, they unravel the mystery of why U.S. Ambassador to Afghanistan, Adolph Dubs, was assassinated in 1979, leading to the Soviet invasion of Afghanistan nine months later. The most significant outcome – the ultimate defeat of the Soviets and the subsequent U.S. invasion of Afghanistan in 2001 –is a disturbing commentary on the U.S.'s long range intensions in Afghanistan, and why the Americans were doomed to fail in the 'Graveyard of Empires.'"

—**Charlotte Dennett**, a former Middle East reporter, investigative journalist, and attorney is co-author of *Thy Will Be Done: The Conquest of the Amazon: Nelson Rockefeller and Evangelism in the Age of Oil* and author of *The Crash of Flight 3804*

"In our presently beleaguered era, caught as we are at the final stages of an empire, the region of Afghanistan has become the center of world attention once more.

"This is a region which is shaped by greater forces of history than most realize. On the one hand, it is a historic bridge between civilizations east and west as a node on the ancient silk road (a role it might hopefully regain today). On the other hand it has earned its title as "The Graveyard of Empires" for any imperial force wishing to dominate this center-piece of the World Island.

"In *The Valediction: Three Nights of Desmond* (Book 1), Paul and Liz have painted an earth-shaking picture of the strategic dynamics shaping not only Afghanistan, but also the dynamics shaping the takeover of the US foreign policy establishment over the dead body of JFK and the launching of the Vietnam war.

"Having been in the unique position as the sole American journalists permitted into Afghanistan in 1981 and again in 1983, Paul and Liz ran directly into powerful forces shaping the levers of power and mass perception from the highest echelons of media, finance and intelligence agencies then centered around the CIA and Trilateral Commission of Zbigniew Brzezinski and David Rockefeller.

"In mapping out their personal experiences, Paul and Liz have reconstructed not only their own process of discovery in an autobiographical format that reads like a detective story, but have also shed light onto the complex forces operating above nation states which maneuvered to assassinate an American Ambassador in Kabul, pull the Soviet Union in an unwinnable quagmire, amplify the international drug trade and grow the monster of Islamic terrorism which plagued humanity for the next 40 years... all while maintaining a veneer of "liberal democracy" for public consumption.

"How Paul and Liz were able to render these creatures of the shadows stretching to the highest echelons of the European old nobility and associated secret societies intelligible for readers of any level of awareness is admirable.

"This book is a must for anyone wishing to understand not only what has so misshapen US foreign policy, artificially lit the middle east on fire or what possible solutions to this unwinnable dark age agenda that is still shaping much of our lives."

—**Matthew Ehret**, Editor-in-Chief of *The Canadian Patriot Review* and Author of *The Clash of the Two Americas*

"*The Valediction* is a real-life thriller – a mix of mystery, mysticism, and geopolitics – that shines a bright light on the darkest and most tragic secrets about America's role in Afghanistan and the extent to which the deep state will go to hide them. Paul rides along with – and encounters – some of the most pivotal figures in the history of the Cold War – including a few who seem ripped right from the pages of a Ludlum novel. But *Valediction* is much more than a harrowing adventure, for the shocking details of one truth-seeking journalist's struggle against the most powerful interests in Washington is bound to shatter any reader's illusions about the objectives of U.S. foreign policy."

—**Michael Hughes**, journalist, foreign policy analyst, State Department Correspondent and senior editor for an international news agency

"It is impossible to stop reading *The Valediction*! The motives of those who really rule this world will forever remain inscrutable to those who remain cloistered in the left/right paradigm offered for what passes as education. *The Valediction* offers a chance to take a peek behind the veil. This is a very exclusive club. You must be born into it. But I must warn you, to paraphrase Jim Morrison paraphrasing William Blake, *Realms of Bliss, realms of light, some are born to happiness. Some are born to endless night...* "

—**Jack Heart**, journalist specializing in the esoteric behind geopolitics, and author of *Those Who Would Arouse Leviathan: Memoirs of An Awakening God.*

"Outstanding! Gould and Fitzgerald meticulously document generations of catastrophic US policies towards Afghanistan and the Middle East recklessly supporting, funding and arming to the hilt the most barbaric extremist Islamist terrorist groups that killed scores of thousands decent mainstream Muslims in their wild and ferocious grasps for power. Reading this book is like being face-slapped by reality."

—**Martin Sieff**, Senior Fellow, American University in Moscow, Former Senior Foreign Correspondent, *Washington Times*, Former Managing Editor, *International Affairs*, and *United Press Internationa*

Praise for Previous books

Invisible History: Afghanistan's Untold Story (2009); Crossing Zero The AfPak War at the Turning Point of American Empire (2011); The Voice (2001)

"Readers with a serious interest in U.S. foreign policy or military strategy will find it helpful.... Bob Woodward's recent *Obama's War* focuses on the administration's AfPak deliberations, but this book provides a wider perspective

—**Marcia L. Sprules**, Council on Foreign Relations, *Library Journal*

"Journalists Fitzgerald and Gould do yeoman's labor in clearing the fog and laying bare American failures in Afghanistan in this deeply researched, cogently argued and enormously important book. "

—***Publishers Weekly*** (starred review)

"A probing history of the country and a critical evaluation of American involvement in recent decades.... A fresh perspective on a little-understood nation."

—***Kirkus***

"*The Voice* takes its audience on a quest for the real Holy Grail, entwining scientific mythology with geopolitical intrigue in an esoteric thrill-ride Dan Brown couldn't dream up..."

— **Michael Hughes**, Huffpost Books

"Paul Fitzgerald and Elizabeth Gould have seen the importance of the 'Great Game' in Afghanistan since the early 1980s. They have been most courageous in their commitment to telling the truth—and have paid a steep price for it."

—**Oliver Stone**

"Fitzgerald and Gould have consistently raised the difficult questions and inconvenient truths about western engagement in Afghanistan. While many analysts and observers have attempted to wish a reality on a grim and tragic situation in Afghanistan, Fitzgerald and Gould have systematically dug through the archives and historical record with integrity and foresight to reveal a series of misguided strategies and approaches that have contributed to what has become a tragic quagmire in Afghanistan."
--**Professor Thomas Johnson**, Director, Program for Culture and Conflict Studies, Naval Postgraduate School, Monterey California

"A ferocious, iron-clad argument about the institutional failure of American foreign policy in Afghanistan and Pakistan."
— **Daniel Ellsberg**

"*Crossing Zero* is much more than a devastating indictment of the folly of U.S. military intervention in Afghanistan. Paul Fitzgerald and Elizabeth Gould demonstrate that the U.S. debacle in Afghanistan is the predictable climax of U.S. imperial overreach on a global scale. Like their earlier work documenting the origins of U.S. involvement in Afghanistan during the Cold War, *Crossing Zero* deserves the attention of all serious students of U.S. foreign policy."
—**Selig S. Harrison**, Co-author with Diego Cordovez of *Out of Afghanistan: The Inside Story of the Soviet Withdrawal*

"An extraordinary contribution to understanding war and geo-politics in Afghanistan that will shock most Americans by its revelations of official American government complicity in using, shielding, sponsoring and supporting terrorism. A devastating indictment on the behind-the-scenes shenanigans by some of America's most respected statesmen"
—**Daniel Estulin**, author of *The True Story of the Bilderberg Club*

"Americans are now beginning to grasp the scope of the mess their leaders made while pursuing misguided military adventures into regions of Central Asia we once called 'remote.' How this happened--and what the US can do to extricate itself from its entanglements in Pakistan and Afghanistan – is the story of *Crossing Zero.* Based on decades of study and research, this book draws lines and connects dots in ways few others do."
—**Stephen Kinzer**, author of *All the Shah's Men* and *Reset: Iran, Turkey and America's Future*

"In this penetrating inquiry, based on careful study of an intricate web of political, cultural, and historical factors that lie in the immediate background, and enriched by unique direct observation at crucial moments, Fitzgerald and Gould tell 'the real story of how they came to be there and what we can expect next.' Invocation of Armageddon is no mere literary device."

—Noam Chomsky

"A serious, sobering study ... illuminates a critical point of view rarely discussed by our media ... results of this willful ignorance have been disastrous to our national well-being."

—Oliver Stone

ABOUT THE AUTHORS

Paul Fitzgerald and Elizabeth Gould, a husband and wife team, began working together in 1979 co-producing a documentary for Paul's TV talk show. Called, *The Arms Race and the Economy, A Delicate Balance,* they found themselves in the midst of a controversy that was to boil over a few months later with the Soviet invasion of Afghanistan. Their acquisition of the first visas to enter Afghanistan granted to an American TV crew in 1981 brought them into the middle of the most heated Cold War controversy since Vietnam. But the pictures and the people inside Soviet occupied Afghanistan told a very different story from the one being broadcast to Americans.

Following their exclusive news story for the *CBS Evening News,* they produced a documentary, *Afghanistan Between Three Worlds,* for PBS and returned to Kabul in 1983 for *ABC Nightline* with Harvard Negotiation Project director, Roger Fisher. They were told that the Soviets wanted to negotiate their way out. Peace in Afghanistan was more than a possibility, it was a desired option. But the story that President Carter called, "the greatest threat to peace since the second World War" had already been written by America's policy makers and America's pundits were not about to change the script.

As the first American journalists to get deeply inside the story they not only got a view of an unseen Afghan life, but a revelatory look at how the U.S. defined itself against the rest of the world under the veil of superpower confrontation. Once the Soviets had crossed the border into Afghanistan, the fate of both nations was sealed. But as Paul and Liz pursued the reasons behind the wall of propaganda that shielded the truth, they found themselves drawn into a story that was growing into mythic dimensions. Big things were brewing in Afghanistan. Old empires were being undone and new ones, hatched. America had launched a Crusade and the ten year war against the Soviet Union was only the first chapter.

It was at the time of the first World Trade Center bombing in 1993 when Paul and Liz were working on the film version of their experience under contract to Oliver Stone, that they began to piece together the mythic implications of the story. During the research for the screenplay many of the documents preceding the Afghan crisis were declassified. Over the next decade they trailed a labyrinth of clues only to find a profound likeness in Washington's official policy towards Afghanistan – in the ancient Zoroastrian war of the light against the dark – whose origins began in the region now known as Afghanistan. It is a likeness that has grown visible as America's entanglement in Afghanistan threatens to backfire once again.

Afghanistan's civil war followed America's Cold War while Washington walked away. A new strain of religious holy warrior called the Taliban arose but at the time few in America cared to look. As the horrors of the Taliban regime began to grab headlines in 1998 Paul and Liz started collaborating with Afghan human rights expert Sima Wali. Along with Wali, they contributed to the *Women for Afghan Women: Shattering Myths and Claiming the Future* book project published in 2002 by Palgrave Macmillan. In 2002 they filmed Wali's first return to Kabul since her exile in 1978. The film they produced about Wali's journey home, *The Woman in Exile Returns,* gives audiences the chance to discover the message of one of Afghanistan's most articulate voices.

In the years since, much has happened to bring Paul and Liz's story into focus. Their efforts at combining personal diplomacy with activist journalism are a model for restoring a necessary dialogue to American democracy. Their book, *Invisible History: Afghanistan's Untold Story,* published by City Lights (2009), lays bare why it was inevitable that the Soviet Union and the U.S. should end up in Afghanistan and what that means to the future. Their book, *Crossing Zero The AfPak War at the Turning Point of American Empire,* published by City Lights (2011), lays out the contradictions of America's AfPak strategy. It clarifies the complex web of interests and individuals surrounding the war and focuses on the importance of the line of demarcation between Afghanistan and Pakistan called the Durand line. Their novel *The Voice,* published in 2001, is the esoteric side of their Afghan experience. Theirs novelized memoir, *The Valediction Three Nights of Desmond* was published by TrineDay (2021).